SEMANTIC WEB AND BEYOND
Computing for Human Experience

Series Editors:

Ramesh Jain
University of California, Irvine
http://ngs.ics.uci.edu/

Amit Sheth
University of Georgia
http://lsdis.cs.uga.edu/~amit

As computing becomes ubiquitous and pervasive, computing is increasingly becoming an extension of human, modifying or enhancing human experience. Today's car reacts to human perception of danger with a series of computers participating in how to handle the vehicle for human command and environmental conditions. Proliferating sensors help with observations, decision making as well as sensory modifications. The emergent semantic web will lead to machine understanding of data and help exploit heterogeneous, multi-source digital media. Emerging applications in situation monitoring and entertainment applications are resulting in development of experiential environments.

SEMANTIC WEB AND BEYOND
Computing for Human Experience
addresses the following goals:

➢ brings together forward looking research and technology that will shape our world more intimately than ever before as computing becomes an extension of human experience;
➢ covers all aspects of computing that is very closely tied to human perception, understanding and experience;
➢ brings together computing that deal with semantics, perception and experience;
➢ serves as the platform for exchange of both practical technologies and far reaching research.

Additional information about this series can be obtained from
http://www.springer.com   ISSN: 1559-7474

The Semantic Web
Real-World Applications from Industry

edited by

Jorge Cardoso
University of Madeira
Funchal, Portugal

Martin Hepp
University of Innsbruck
Innsbruck, Austria

Miltiadis D. Lytras
University of Patras
Patras, Greece

 Springer

Jorge Cardoso
Universidade da Madeira
Department de Matematica e Engenharias
9000-390 FUNCHAL
PORTUGAL
jcardoso@uma.pt

Martin Hepp
Universität Innsbruck
Digital Enterprise Research Institute
Technikerstr. 21a
6020 INNSBRUCK
AUSTRIA
mhepp@computer.org
http://www.heppnetz.de

Miltiadis D. Lytras
University of Patras
Research Academic Computer Tech. Inst.
Computer Engineering & Informatics Dept.
PATRAS
GREECE
lytras@ceid.upatras.gr

The Semantic Web: Real-World Applications from Industry
Edited by Jorge Cardoso, Martin Hepp and Miltiadis Lytras

ISBN-13: 978-0-387-48530-0   e-ISBN-13: 978-0-387-48531-7

Library of Congress Control Number: 2007934284

Printed on acid-free paper.

9 8 7 6 5 4 3 2 1

springer.com

Dedication

"To simple minds and simple thinkers..."

Jorge Cardoso

"To my academic mentor, Prof. Rainer Thome, who has kept on reminding me that the proof of the pudding is in the eating"

Martin Hepp

"To whom makes me dream"

Miltiadis D. Lytras

Contents

Contributing Authors

Subodh Agrawal
Athens Heart Center, Athens, GA, USA

Jürgen Angele
Ontoprise GmbH, Karlsruhe, Germany

José Arancón
ArcelorMittal, Avilés, Spain

Sinuhé Arroyo
University of Alcalá de Henares, Alcalá de Henares, Spain

Richard Benjamins
iSOCO, Madrid, Spain

Diego Berruela
CTIC Foundation, Gijón, Spain

Mercedes Blázquez
iSOCO, Madrid, Spain

Antonio Campos
CTIC Foundation, Gijón, Spain

Jorge Cardoso
University of Madeira, Funchal, Portugal

Pablo Castells
Universidad Autónoma de Madrid, Madrid, Spain

Iván Cantador
Universidad Autónoma de Madrid, Madrid, Spain

Kei-Hoi Cheung
Yale University School of Medicine, New Haven, USA

Jesús Contreras
iSOCO, Madrid, Spain

Mike Davis
U.S. Department of Veterans Affairs, Washington, DC, USA

Nicolás de Abajo
ArcelorMittal, Avilés, Spain

Donald Doherty
Brainstage Research, Pittsburgh, PA, USA

Christian Drumm
SAP Research, Karlsruhe, Germany

María Jesús Fernández
City Government of Zaragoza, Zaragoza, Spain

Kelly Gallagher
Athens Heart Center, Athens, GA, USA

Elena Garcia-Barriocanal
University of Alcalá de Henares, Alcalá de Henares, Spain

Michael Gesmann
Software AG, Darmstadt, Germany

Jose Manuel Gómez-Pérez
iSOCO, Madrid, Spain

Joanna Guss
EADS France, Suresnes, France

Martin Hepp
University of Innsbruck, Innsbruck, Austria

Ivan Herman
World Wide Web Consortium (W3C), Amsterdam, Netherlands

Raymond Hookway
Hewlett Packard, Marlborough, MA, USA

Vipul Kashyap
Partners Healthcare System, Welleley, MA, USA

Rubén Lara
Tecnología, Información y Finanzas (TIF), Madrid, Spain

Jonathan Lathem
University of Georgia, Athens, GA, USA

Jens Lemcke
SAP Research, Karlsruhe, Germany

François-Marie Lesaffre
ArcelorMittal, Fos, France

Joanne Luciano
Harvard Medical School, Boston, MA, USA

Miltiadis D. Lytras
University of Patras, Patras, Greece

M. Scott Marshall
University of Amsterdam, Amsterdam, The Netherlands

John A. Miller
University of Georgia, Athens, GA, USA

Anne Monceaux
EADS-Innovation Works, Toulouse, France

Ambjörn Naeve
Royal Institute of Technology (KTH), Stockholm, Sweden, and
University of Uppsala, Uppsala, Sweden

Daniel Oberle
SAP Research, Karlsruhe, Germany

Nicole Oldham
Athens Heart Center, Athens, GA, USA

Richard Scott Patterson
Knowledge Integrity Inc., Silver Springs, MD, USA

Luis Polo
CTIC Foundation, Gijón, Spain

Amit P. Sheth
Wright State University, Dayton, OH, USA

Miguel-Angel Sicilia
University of Alcalá de Henares, Alcalá de Henares, Spain

Diego Patón
iSOCO, Madrid, Spain

Luis Rodrigo
iSOCO, Madrid, Spain

Matthias Samwald
Medical University of Vienna, Vienna, Austria

Susie Stephens
Oracle, Burlington, MA, USA

Harry Wingate
Athens Heart Center, Athens, GA, USA

Prem Yadav
Athens Heart Center, Athens, GA, USA

Foreword

The first half-century of Computer Science, marked by amazing advances as well as massive growth in automation and information, dramatically improved the world of business, and subsequently, enabled by the World Wide Web, the quality of everyday life through worldwide access to information and services. Now, we are now entering a new era, Computer Science 2.0. While Computer Science 1.0 focused on technology and was characterized by precise solutions to business and other problems, it came to be characterized by information overload and complexity. The amazing power of conventional computing is reaching its limits in its ability to scale, both conceptually and in terms of volume and performance. Computer Science 2.0 is the first fundamental shift in the brief half-century history of computing. Computer Science 2.0 will be vastly more facile, useful, and powerful. It will focus on problem solving and the imprecision of our everyday lives.

Computer Science 2.0 is blooming at all levels of computing from core technologies like virtual networks, storage, and computing, to the new service-oriented computational model, and to the very nature of problem solving. Computer Science 2.0 will raise the level of abstraction so that financial managers will solve financial problems using the concepts and tools of the financial world, as opposed to the computing tools of Computer Science 1.0, such as Excel and SQL. Semantic technologies will enable a higher level of abstraction and thus dramatic improvements in problem solving, management of complexity, dealing with imprecision, and productivity. While, Computer Science 2.0 will take a decade or two to mature, this book provides an early glimpse into semantic technologies, one of Computer Science 2.0's core enabling technologies, and how they solve real enterprise class problems.

Semantic technologies have a rich history addressing complex and arcane topics such as knowledge representation and reasoning, but have been opaque to most computer scientists. In its 40 year history several successful spin-offs, such as rule-based systems, have been adopted into conventional IT after being dramatically simplified compared to their laboratory predecessors. Even in their simplified form, expert systems solved enterprise class problems. They are no longer considered part of semantic technologies but of information technology where they continue to provide significant value as integral parts of information systems, transparent to all users. This is an example of the phrase "A little semantics goes a long way[1]" in conventional applications. We are now opening the door to the next generation of semantic technologies.

In 2007 the door is opening to semantic technologies to meet the genuine industrial and societal needs to deal more intelligently with the unimaginably vast amount of information resources exposed to the world by the Web soon to be accelerated by another emerging Computer Science 2.0 technology, Service-Oriented Computing. The door is being opened by software industry leaders such as IBM, BEA, Oracle, Microsoft, SAP, and others that are providing initial support for semantic technologies in some of their most significant product lines, e.g., Service-Oriented Architectures, to achieve the promise of service-orientation though the semantic Web Services, and the promise of the Web through the semantic Web.

This book offers a glimpse into the opening door of semantic technologies by means of concrete examples of semantic applications in real production environments. Large enterprises, such as Oracle, Vodaphone, Adobe, and Nokia have been operating successful semantic Web-based applications since 2004. In mid 2007, more than 40 significant production semantic technology-based applications were reported at major conferences[2] from enterprises such as AGFA, British Telecom, Boeing, Chevron, and Eli Lilly. This book presents eleven concrete, enterprise class applications that are enabled by semantic technologies across five major industry sectors.

This book describes how enterprises can benefit from the semantic Web and reviews some of the related challenges. It offers a rich collection of semantic web applications in major industry segments. The case studies provide detailed illustrations of how semantic technologies are being applied and the value they produce. More importantly they offer a glimpse into the semantic enterprise – how enterprises can benefit from semantic

---

[1] Prof James A. Hendler, senior constellation professor of the Tetherless World Research Constellation, Rensselaer Polytechnic Institute
[2] Semantic Technology Conference 2007 (http://www.semantic-conference.com/), 1st European Semantic Technologies Conference (http://www.estc2007.com/)

technologies and Computer Science 2.0. Hence, the book offers a glimpse of the next generation of information systems.

Semantic technologies will be a pillar of Computer Science 2.0 and will enable the semantic Web and semantic Web Services. This book provides an excellent introduction to Computer Science 2.0 through the lens of semantic technologies as applied to real applications of the semantic Web and semantic Web Services. These are all hot terms and ideas. Once the hype has past, and it will, they will become core technologies and will be called simply information technology.

Michael L. Brodie
Chief Scientist
Verizon Communications
Cambridge, MA, USA
June 10, 2007

Preface

Part I presents two chapters that cover semantic enterprises. **Chapter 1** was written by the editors and presents their views on the future of the Semantic Web for enterprises. We begin by explaining the original idea of the Semantic Web and its main objectives. We also make clear what the importance of ontologies is. The reader will understand why the world requires new approaches for information systems development. While Semantic Web technologies can be used in various domains, we have decided to focus on their usefulness for enterprises. In this context, we explain and express the emergent need for a new kind of systems, ontology management systems. Finally, we enumerate the contributions of this manuscript. **Chapter 2** provides an overview of some of the business and technology challenges that companies are facing today, and describes how a number of these difficulties could be overcome with the use of Semantic Web technology. In order for Semantic Web technologies to be adopted within an enterprise setting, there must be mature tools that support the scalability, availability, and reliability requirements of such companies. To assess this, the chapter summarizes the state of the art in software tools and technologies, including both open-source and commercial products.

Part II is also composed of two chapters and describes the use of Semantic Web technologies in the financial domain and for municipal services. **Chapter 3** recognizes that data, information and knowledge management are key activities for finance. The volume, complexity and value of economic and financial information make finance a strategic area for research and innovation on information modeling, exchange and integration and, consequently, there is an increasing interest in evaluating what semantic technologies can contribute to this domain. **Chapter 4** describes an intelligent search engine for online access to municipal services. Currently, most public administrations provide citizens with online access to their services. In fact, as of 2006, Spanish citizens have the possibility to perform 80 % of the city government services from their homes. However, there is still a big gap between the language used by public administrations and the way citizens refer to these services, which makes it difficult to match citizen requests. The use of semantic technology in this scenario allows bridging this gap.

Part III illustrates two domains that have adopted with a significant success Semantic Web technologies: Healthcare and Life Sciences. **Chapter 5** presents an application of ontology-based data integration for biomedical research. In this chapter, the authors explore the area of translational medicine that aims to improve communication between the basic and clinical sciences so that more diagnostic and therapeutic insights may be derived. Translation research goes from bench to bedside, where the effectiveness of results from preclinical research are explored with patients, and from bedside to bench, where information obtained from patients can be used to refine our understanding of the biological principles underpinning the heterogeneity of human disease and polymorphism(s). **Chapter 6** focuses on active semantic electronic medical records. The healthcare industry is rapidly advancing towards the widespread use of electronic medical records systems to manage the increasingly large amount of patient data and reduce medical errors. In addition to patient data there is a large amount of data describing procedures, treatments, diagnoses, drugs, insurance plans, coverage, formularies and the relationships between these data sets. Active Semantic Electronic Medical Record (ASEMR) application discussed here uses Semantic Web technologies to reduce medical errors, improve physician efficiency with accurate completion of patient charts, improve patient safety and satisfaction in medical practice, and improve billing due to more accurate coding. This results in practice efficiency and growth by enabling physicians to see more patients with improved care.

Part IV illustrates the use of Semantic Web technologies in education. **Chapter 7** presents a Semantic Web-based approach for targeting learning resources in competency-based organizations. This chapter addresses a concrete case study in which competencies inside an aeronautical organization have been modelled through ontologies, and Semantic Web technologies have used to devise the technical solution for delivering the competency gap analysis facilities and the subsequent match of the appropriate learning resources. This case study may serve as a reference for other organizations that aim at using the competency paradigm for the planning of organizational learning. **Chapter 8** explains how to develop a Course Management System (CMS) using Semantic Web technologies. While semantic Web technologies have reached a certain level of maturity, the industry is still skeptical about its potential and applicability. Many vendors seem to be adopting a "wait-and-see" approach while emerging standards and solutions become more fully developed. The industry and its main players are waiting to see how real-world applications can benefit from the use of semantic Web technologies. The success of the Semantic Web vision is dependant on the development of practical and useful semantic Web-based applications. To demonstrate the applicability and the benefits of using semantic Web technologies, the authors have developed a real-world application, a semantic CMS (S-CMS), entirely based on the semantic Web that uses the latest technologies of this field such as OWL, RQL, RDQL, SPARQL, and SWRL.

Part V targets business and customer management. **Chapter 9** presents a case study on the integration of customer information using Semantic Web technologies. For the integration of data that resides in autonomous data sources Software AG uses ontologies. While data sources themselves normally represent more or less static data structures, the semantics of these data structures and their usage resides in application programs. However, it is essential to understand and model the semantics of these data sources when trying to integrate the data coming from disparate data sources. To bridge the gap between the pure structure information in single sources and the needed semantically enriched description of an integrated view we use semantic technology in terms of ontologies. **Chapter 10** explains how to support business process management with Semantic Web technologies. The authors show how existing Semantic Web service composition approaches can be applied to automate the design of Collaborative Business Processes (CBP). Furthermore, the authors show how message mappings between different message formats can be (semi-)automatically created based on a domain ontology. Although modeling efforts have to be invested, it is argued that semantic technologies are very helpful to counter current drawbacks. On the one hand, they allow saving efforts for the design of collaborative business processes and, on the other hand, the semi-automatic creation of mappings significantly reduces the required development efforts.

Part VI covers enterprise management and security. **Chapter 11** describes an ontology-based knowledge management system developed for the steel industry. Big companies have to face both internal and external challenges in order to deal with complex logistics, business processes and human resources management. The Semantic Web technology appears as a suitable candidate to address these problems and to provide innovative solutions in an open environment of decentralized resources. In this context, this chapter presents the experiences of Arcelor Mittal, the leader steel making company. In particular, the advantages of ontologies as knowledge representation artifacts are identified, driven by a handful of use cases within the company, such as knowledge capitalization tools, an unified data description layer and supply chain management. **Chapter 12** explains how to bring semantic security to Semantic Web services. Semantic Web services begin to emerge as the next evolution of the Service Oriented Architecture. It has become clear that authorization is going to be one of the biggest challenges. A step toward resolving this problem is Semantic Authorization which provides an efficient means for a client to discover whether it may have permissions to access resources available through Semantic Web services.

PART I – SEMANTIC ENTERPRISES

Chapter 1

THE FUTURE OF THE SEMANTIC WEB FOR ENTERPRISES

Jorge Cardoso[1], Miltiadis Lytras[2] and Martin Hepp[3]
[1]*Department of Mathematics and Engineering, University of Madeira, Funchal, Portugal – jcardoso@uma.pt*
[2]*University of Patras, Computer Engineering and Informatics Department, Greece – mdl@aueb.gr*
[3]*Semantics in Business Information Systems Research Group, DERI, University of Innsbruck, Austria – mhepp@computer.org*

1. THE EARLY SEMANTIC WEB

The original idea of the Semantic Web was to bring machine-readable descriptions to the data and documents already on the Web, in order to improve search and data usage. The Web was, and in most cases still is, a vast set of static and dynamically generated Web pages linked together. Pages are written in HTML (Hyper Text Markup Language), a language that is useful for publishing information intended only for human consumption. Humans can read Web pages and understand them, but the inherent meaning is not available in a way that allows interpretation by computers.

The Semantic Web aims at defining ways to allow Web information to be used by computers not only for display purposes, but also for interoperability and integration between systems and applications. One way to enable machine-to-machine exchange and automated processing is to provide the information in such a way that computers can understand it. To give meaning to Web information, new standards and languages are being investigated and developed. Well-known examples include the Resource Description Framework (RDF) (RDF 2002) and the Web Ontology Language (OWL) (OWL 2004). The descriptive information made available by these languages allows characterizing individually and precisely the type of resources in the Web and the relationships between resources.

Today, the Semantic Web is not only about increasing the expressiveness of Web information to enable the automatic or semiautomatic processing of Web resources and Web pages. Academia and industry have realized that the Semantic Web can facilitate the integration and interoperability of intra- and inter-business processes and systems, as well as enable the creation of global infrastructures for sharing documents and data, make searching and reusing information easier.

Figure 1-1 illustrates the various tasks for which semantic technologies can be used. We can see that semantics can help not only system (semantic machine interface), but also human integration and interoperability (human machine interface). In both cases, semantic functions can be used to discover, acquire and create semantic metadata and provision, present, communicate, and act using semantics.

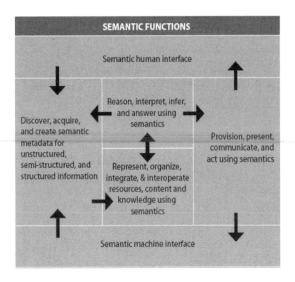

Figure 1-1. Semantic functions for inter-enterprises[3]

---

[3] Source: TopQuandrant

2. ONTOLOGIES: THE CORNERSTONE OF THE SEMANTIC WEB

The Semantic Web relies on the theoretical research done in the context of ontologies as a formal support for communication between agents and for the exchange of knowledge representations. Ontology-based human communication aims at reducing and eliminating terminological and conceptual confusion by defining a shared understanding, that is, a unifying framework enabling communication and cooperation amongst people in reaching better inter-enterprise organization. Presently, one of the most important roles an ontology plays in communication is that it provides unambiguous definitions for terms used in a software system, but they can also support communication, coordination, and cooperation between human actors.

The use of ontologies for improving communication has already been shown to work in practice. Interesting examples of successful ontologies include the Disease Ontology[4] (a hierarchical and controlled vocabulary for human disease representation), the FAO[5] (Food and Agriculture Organization of the United Nations) – which is committed to help information dissemination by providing consistent access to information for the community of people and organizations – and the Open EDI ontology[6] which defines the ontology for data management and interchange between enterprises. Other well-known and successful ready-to-use ontologies that have been developed include: CYC upper ontology[7], LinkBase[8], Towntology project, DAML ontology library[9], Ontolingua[10], OWL ontology library[11], Kactus library[12], and eClassOWL[13].

The most referred-to definition for ontology is given by Gruber (Gruber 1993), describing an ontology as an explicit specification of conceptualization. Explicit means that it cannot be implicitly assumed and should be processable by machines. This definition has been criticized by Guarino (Guarino 1998). After examining many possible interpretations of ontology, Guarino concluded that an ontology describes a hierarchy of

---

[4] http://diseaseontology.sourceforge.net
[5] http://www.fao.org/agris/aos/
[6] http://www.jtc1sc32.org/, known as ISO/IEC JTC 1/SC 32
[7] http://www.opencyc.org/
[8] http://www.landcglobal.com/pages/linkbase.php
[9] http://www.daml.org/ontologies/
[10] http://www.ksl.stanford.edu/software/ontolingua/
[11] http://protege.stanford.edu/plugins/owl/owl-library/index.html
[12] http://web.swi.psy.uva.nl/projects/NewKACTUS/library/library.html
[13] http://www.heppnetz.de/eclassowl/

concepts related by subsumption relationships; in more sophisticated cases, suitable axioms are added in order to express other relationships between concepts and to constrain their intended interpretation.

The effort of the Semantic Web community to apply semantic techniques in open, and distributed and heterogeneous Web environments are beginning to pay off. Not only is the number of developed ontologies increasing dramatically but also the way that ontologies are published and used has changed. We see a shift away from the first generation Semantic Web applications towards a new generation of applications, designed to exploit large amounts of heterogeneous semantic markups.

3.   CHALLENGES FOR A NEW SEMANTIC WORLD

As with every technological evolution, the Semantic Web and ontologies need to promote their unique value proposition for specific target groups in order to achieve adoption. A common pitfall made in the studies of the Semantic Web is the limited focus on "technological perspectives" or, in the other extreme, the difficulty to communicate the underlying capacity of semantics and ontologies to meet critical real world challenges. An interesting starting point for analysis, which also justifies the contribution of this edition, relates with some of the characteristics of our world and society.

3.1   Characteristics of a new world

We live in a world where information and knowledge are considered to be key enablers of business and economic performance and critical pillars of sustainable development. At the global level, the following are some of the characteristics of the new world context:

- **Globalization**: Creation and consumption of knowledge and information are made in the global context. From this perspective, the elimination of local boundaries and the exploitation of synergies and capacities beyond boundaries require advanced adoption mechanisms that permit realization of opportunities, deep understanding of threats and strategic fit to human and social networks towards new levels of performance.
- **Networking**: In our era, business and economic activities, as well as competition, require new models of business networking. Within this context, advanced documentation of skills, competencies, business models and context based collaboration define new demands for advanced business and social networking at a global level.

- **Shared models**: A global consensus towards peace, development, prosperity and a better world needs to be based on shared conceptual models that define the average common understanding of human societies for the "issues" that matters at a global scale. And while this can be perceived either as a "too optimistic" scenario, or as a wisgfull wishful thinking case, in the global information landscape shared models are required for interoperability, exploitation of synergies and definition of new milestones for collective intelligence.

- **Collective intelligence**: The increased capacities of networking as a result of globalization and widespread adoption of shared models has resulted in the development of a global trend to apply collective intelligence filters or collaborative filtering in the context of the global information world. Such development challenges many traditional models of business performance, marketing and profitability.

- **Open paradigm:** This is a key new characteristic of our world. Open paradigm relates with several complementary movements, like the ones of open source software, open content, open access, open knowledge, open research, and open culture. The underlying idea has an amazing capacity to support new business models and several applications in the short and long term horizon.

3.2   Challenges for Semantic Web applications

The previous list of characteristics of the modern world provides the "playground" for Semantic Web based applications. Globalization, networking, shared models, collective intelligence, and open paradigms are only a few of the silver bullets for the exploitation of Semantic Web technologies. We summarize a selective list of challenges for Semantic Web applications in close relevance to the previous discussion:

- **Definition of new modes for human, knowledge and business networking beyond local boundaries**: Traditional business and knowledge networking emphasized on a narrow perspective for the ultimate objective of networking. Semantic Web through ontologies and social networks anchors networking to well-defined conceptual models that match information sources and human services. By providing an infrastructure of shared semantics and ontologies where reasoning and trust are "process and service oriented", we have a great opportunity at the business level.

- **Globalizing information and definition of new contexts for value exploitation**: The provision of local information assets at a global level and the design of new contexts for exploitation are for the Semantic

Web two of the key value propositions. The design of multiple reference levels to the same set of information and knowledge delivers a new level for dynamic, and personalized systems.

- **Delivering and integrating quality to information**: One of the main obstacles of the current Web relates with a very limited performance on the quality assessment of content. It seems that we suffer from an enormous explosion of content diffusion and a very poor performance on capacities to explore qualitative information. And while information quality is a very subjective concept, businesses and people as customers, citizens, patients, learners, professionals, etc. require systems and infrastructures that deliver assessment models of information quality.

- **Integration of isolated information assets**: In any context, personal, organizational or global integration of isolated information is a key challenge. The "value" related with integration is always related with the inquiry. In simple words integration has always a very concrete "gap" component. Individuals, organizations, society requires integration for addressing specific performance gaps that relate with limited capacity to build more meaningful services.

- **Support of business value and co-located/distributed business models**: It is obvious that the Semantic Web evolution requires the adoption from industry. This critical milestone implies that Semantic Web technologies can integrated to business models of modern organizations and businesses. As always, such requirement challenges the strategic fit of technologies to business perspectives. From a business strategy point of view, there is a crucial demand to "translate" the key aspects of Semantic Web technologies to business terminology. Semantics, ontologies, resource description frameworks, etc, means nothing to business people that have an absolute different way to interpret business requirements.

- **Promotion of a critical shift in human understanding and interacting with digital world**: The Semantic Web needs to respond to human great demand to explore new modes of interactivity with the digital world, and it is obvious that people prefer to behave with similar conscious and intelligent mechanisms. The sooner the Semantic Web will prove its capacity to provide these intelligent mechanisms, the greater its adoption and support at global level.

4. THE IMPORTANCE OF SEMANTICS FOR ORGANIZATIONS

Today, integration is a top priority for many European and worldwide enterprises. The European community alone is investing, through the Seventh Framework Program, more that €200 million on research involving inter-enterprise interoperability and semantics. Most organizations have already realized that the use of Semantic Web technologies is a promising candidate solution to support cross-organizational cooperation for SME (Small and Medium-sized Enterprises) that operate in dynamically changing work environments. Semantic Web technologies are more and more considered as a key technology to resolve the problems of interoperability and integration within the heterogeneous world of ubiquitously interconnected systems with respect to the nature of components, standards, data formats, protocols, etc. Moreover, we also believe that Semantic Web technologies can facilitate, not only the discovery of heterogeneous components and data integration, but also the communication between individuals.

Semantic inter-enterprise interoperability is the key for the implementation of the idea of a knowledge-based economy where networks of enterprises (and SME in particular) can gain advantages from the peculiarities of the productive European fabric (many small companies, highly specialized, closely connected with each other, highly flexible thanks to the diffusion of knowledge and very skilled people in the whole fabric). The world-class competitiveness of enterprises strongly depends, in the future, on their ability to rapidly set-up, and maintain, virtual, networked enterprise structures. Novel technologies for interoperability within and between enterprises need to emerge to radically solve a problem that has not been sufficiently addressed by the research community before. In fact, managing the semantics of business-to-business interaction may be the most challenging task in integrated e-business value chains, and there is more and more evidence that Semantic Web technology has the potential to actually mitigate such problems.

4.1 Ontology Management Systems

In the previous section, we saw that ontologies are the latest technological innovation that can enable inter-enterprises to establish dynamic working networks. Therefore, to provide a holistic management, there is the need to support the entire lifecycle of inter-enterprise ontologies, including ontology creation, storage, search, query, reuse, maintenance, and integration (Li, Thompson et al. 2003).

Modern organizations are realizing that shared ontologies and understanding is fundamental to create the next generation of networked inter- and intra-enterprises (Wache, Voegele et al. 2001). Shared understanding is a basis for communication, coordination, and collaboration between people and interoperability between systems (Vernadat 1993). It should be clear to the reader that interoperability is not only a concern for software applications and hardware platforms but also for human resource enterprise (i.e., employees, managers, and individuals in general).

In the near future, an increasing range of inter-enterprise applications will be requiring an Ontology Management System (OMS) that helps externalize ontological information for a variety of purposes in a declarative way. Such management systems provide ontology with independence to applications and people in a similar way that database management systems provide data with independence. The primary objective of an OMS is to provide a full and efficient control over management activities for ontological information by externalizing them from application programs. One of the pragmatic challenges for ontology management system research is how to create the missing technology pieces, and to engineer them with existing results from prior research work to provide for a holistic management system (Harrison and Chan 2005).

An OMS needs to address a wide range of problems: ontology models, ontology base design, query languages, programming interfaces, query processing and optimization, federation of knowledge sources, caching and indexing, transaction support, distributed system support, and security support, to name a few (Lee and Goodwin 2005). An ontology management system provides a mechanism to deal with ontological information at an appropriate level of abstraction. By using programming interfaces and query languages the ontology management system provides application programs, can manipulate and query ontologies without the need to know their details or reimplement the semantics of standard ontology languages.

4.2   Challenge

Networked enterprises made available a wealth of information to many people worldwide: blogs, wikis, web sites, collaborative and social networks, etc. This has unleashed numerous resources and possibilities. Since the volume of information that is being generated and made available is overwhelming, current software systems are not prepared to deal with this. Nowadays, enterprises have been unprepared for environments where so much information is being generated every year. Since business success often depends on decision makers having timely access to the right information and knowledge (Vernadat 1993), the need arises for systems that are able to provide this knowledge. It is our firm belief that, given the growing role of the internet on human and business activity and the sheer growth in the volume of available information, there will be a growing demand for infrastructures such as OMS.

The challenge for inter-enterprises is that there is simply too much content being generated for a human to follow. Let us illustrate this challenge expressed by one of our partners located in Spain, Arcelor Mittal, the world's number one steel company, with 330,000 employees in more than 60 countries. Arcelor Mittal produces flat steel products of high quality, according to the customer's expectations many different technical demands have to be fulfilled: innovative and adequate product, research process definition, excellent plant technology, suitable plant maintenance, good quality raw materials, suitable automation systems, proper set points for control systems, etc.

Arcelor Mittal employees, with different profiles have gathered much information/knowledge during many years developing new products, designing and carrying on processes to manufacture those products, investigating cause and effect relationships regarding quality defects and process disturbances. All this knowledge is continuously being formalized in different formats and applications, which in many cases contribute to extract new knowledge. Unfortunately, all this information is very often limited to a small circle of persons or to an individual. As a consequence, many times people reinvent known relationships because of poor exchange of information inside the company or because experienced people left the company. The knowledge acquired and put in operation by these individuals in their everyday tasks, should be extended and contrasted with that of other group of individuals or enterprise entities who are operating in a different context.

Search and taxonomies are not the answer!!!

Search is not the answer, because people and work groups do not know that they need to search. Additionally, relying exclusively on existing "top-down" taxonomies is not the answer. If a taxonomy already exists then projects must also already exist, and if projects exist then there are existing procedures that enable people to know about them and contribute to them. We are interested in discovering and mining emerging ideas, new projects and thoughts within the organization, and how to bring together the team that can make them happen. This means that we are interested in "the ontology of tomorrow", which is something that has not been formally built yet.

5.   THE CONTRIBUTION OF THIS EDITION

While dealing with this edition we had to face two critical challenges: on the one hand, we had to give answers to "thirsty" people for practical issues, delivering a manuscript about the state-of-the-art for various domains and, on the other hand, we also had to give a glance of our perception for the required efforts towards the adoption of the Semantic Web technologies to real world contexts. We decided to organize the contents of the book in six general pillars that represent six excellent domains for the Semantic Web technologies exploitation. The following list provides a summary of the main sections:

- Semantic Enterprises
- Finance and Government
- Healthcare and Life Sciences
- Education
- Business and Customer Management
- Enterprise Management and Security

The twelve chapters of this edition contribute in three directions:

- **Highlight the full range of business and technological issues that must be addressed in every real world application of Semantic Web technologies**. The variety of contexts discussed in the book (e.g. finance, health, government, and education domains) gives the reader the opportunity to see the "forest" of Semantic Web adoption. In fact, the reader is able to realize underlying methodological approaches, key business issues, decisions related to the selection of technologies and tools, change management approaches, return on investment, alignment with overall IT strategy and many more issues.
- **Provide a comprehensive discussion of the required integration of Semantic Web and business strategy.** The presented applications, systems, projects, cases, and implementations help the reader to realize the "business" perspective of the Semantic Web, ontological engineering, semantics exploitation, semantic Web Services, semantic search engines, semantic interoperability and integration, enterprise application integration, enterprise information systems, and semantic portals. The topics discussed in this edition are challenging the reader to realize that any successful implementation of technology and applications within organizations requires business champions, anchors to business strategy and the justification of the return on investment.

- **Set a context for critical thinking.** In the 12 chapters of the book, the reader is challenged to explore his/her knowledge in relevance to practical issues faced in real world applications. In a way, this edition goes beyond the academic flavor of most scholar publications. The editing strategy we followed and the excellent quality of the contributors delivered a manuscript in which every chapter enables the reader to build incrementally a Semantic Web awareness and expertise with great potential.

6.   NEXT MILESTONES

We are very happy, since after many months of preparation this edition is finally published. We are really looking forward for your comments, ideas and suggestions for improving the next versions. For the time being, we are planning a new reference edition for the role of the semantic Web towards the realization of close-to-market business strategies.

7.   QUESTIONS FOR DISCUSSION

Beginner:
1. Contrast the "Syntactic" Web with the Semantic Web.
2. What are the main functions of semantic for organizations?

Intermediate:
1. What are the main characteristics of the new world with respect to the Semantic Web?
2. Do you consider that technology is already mature to answer to the challenges of the Semantic Web?

Advanced:
1. Describe briefly the main challenges for Semantic Web applications.
2. What is an ontology management system?
3. Why are search and taxonomies not the only solution for the current requirements of enterprises?

Practical exercises:
1. Browsing the Web, describe the various ontologies listed in section 2?
2. How many concepts and properties each ontology has?
3. Are these ontologies generic or domain specific?

8.   SUGGESTED ADDITIONAL READING

The suggested readings enumerated in this section are publications from the editors of this manuscript.

- Cardoso, J. *"Semantic Web Services: Theory, Tools and Applications"*, IGI Global, Hard cover:978-1-59904-045-5, e-Book:978-1-59904-047-9, 2007. This book provides a good introduction to the use of Semantic Web technologies in the context of Web Services.
- Cardoso, J., Sheth, A., *"Semantic Web Services, Processes and Applications"*, 2006, Springer, Hardcover, ISBN: 0-38730239-5, 2006. This book also explain how semantic can be applied to Web Services.
- Sheth, A. and Lytras, M., *"Semantic Web-based Information Systems: State-of-the-art Applications"*, 2006, IGI Global, ISBN: 1599044277. This provides an interesting overview of the latest applications that were developed using Semantic Web technologies.
- Lytras, M. and Naeve, A., *"Ubiquitous and Pervasive Knowledge and Learning Management: Semantics, Social Networking and New Media to Their Full Potential"*, 2007, IGI Global, ISBN: 1599044838. Another book that described the use of semantics, but in the context of social networks and digital media.
- Hepp, M., De Leenheer, P., de Moor, A. and Sure, Y., *"Ontology Management: Semantic Web, Semantic Web Services, and Business Applications"*, 2007, Springer, ISBN: 038769899X. This book has not yet been published. It described the use of Semantic Web technologies to deploy Web Services and business applications.

9.   ACKNOWLEDGMENTS

This work was partially funded by FCT, POCTI-219, and FEDER.

10.   REFERENCES

Gruber, T. R. (1993). "A translation approach to portable ontologies." Knowledge Acquisition 5(2): 199-220.

Guarino, N. (1998). Formal Ontology and Information Systems. Proceedings of FOIS'98 Trento, Itália, Amsterdan, IOS Press. pp. 3-15.

Harrison, R. and C. W. Chan (2005). Distributed ontology management system. Canadian Conference on Electrical and Computer Engineering pp. 661- 664.

Lee, J. and R. Goodwin (2005). Ontology management for large-scale e-commerce applications. International Workshop on Data Engineering Issues in E-Commerce, Tokyo, Japan. pp. 7- 15.

Li, Y., S. Thompson, Z. Tan, N. Giles and H. Gharib (2003). Beyond Ontology Construction; Ontology Services as Online Knowledge Sharing Communities. The SemanticWeb - ISWC 2003. Berlin/Heidelberg, Springer. 2870/2003.

OWL. (2004). "OWL Web Ontology Language Reference, W3C Recommendation." Retrieved 22 June, 2007, from http://www.w3.org/TR/owl-features/.

RDF. (2002). "Resource Description Framework (RDF)." Retrieved 9 May 2007, from http://www.w3.org/RDF/.

Vernadat, F. (1993). CIMOSA: Enterprise Modelling and Enterprise Integration Using a Process-Based Approach. JSPE/IFIP TC5/WG5.3 Workshop on the Design of Information Infrastructure Systems for Manufacturing, Tokyo, Japan. pp. 65-79.

Wache, H., T. Voegele, V. U., S. H., G. Schuster, H. Neumann and S. Huebner (2001). Ontology-based integration of information - a survey of existing approaches. IJCAI workshop on Ontologies and Information Sharing, Seattle, WA. USA. pp. 108–117.

Chapter 2

THE ENTERPRISE SEMANTIC WEB
Technologies and Applications for the Real World

Susie Stephens[14]
Oracle, 10 Van de Graaff Drive, Burlington, MA 01803, USA – susie.stephens@gmail.com

1.   INTRODUCTION

In recent years, much progress has been made in developing ideas and tools to enable the growth of the Semantic Web. The core standard recommendations have reached a level of maturity that allows them to be widely adopted. A range of open-source and commercial software tools is now available. Commercial organizations are also increasingly using Semantic Web technology. However, the Semantic Web still has some distance to go before it reaches a point of widespread adoption.

There are many benefits that would be attained with the extensive adoption of the Semantic Web vision. For example, it would become easier for individuals to find information of interest on the Web and perform computation on that data. Yet, it is expected that many of the initial implementations of Semantic Web technologies will occur within commercial enterprises, and that these will pave the way for the creation of more general applications that operate on the Semantic Web. Consequently, it is very important that state of the art Semantic Web tools are able to meet the scalability, availability, and reliability requirements of commercial organizations.

This chapter reviews some of the business and technology challenges that companies are facing today, and describes how a number of these difficulties could be overcome with the use of Semantic Web tools and technologies. An

[14] Currently at Lilly Corporate Center Indianapolis, Indiana 46285, USA.

overview is then given on the state of the art of these tools and technologies. Use cases are provided that describe real world implementations and areas in which there would be significant benefit in the deployment of Semantic Web technology based solutions. Further, the chapter highlights why it is expected that mainstream adoption of the Semantic Web will initially occur within an enterprise setting.

2. BUSINESS AND TECHNOLOGY DRIVERS OF THE SEMANTIC WEB

Commercial organizations are always under pressure to perform financially. They need to ensure that they meet shareholder expectations while operating under increasingly stringent regulatory controls. Modern companies need to ensure that they can respond rapidly to changing business conditions, as the world continues to move at an ever-quickening pace. Companies are beginning to recognize that information technology can provide a strategic advantage in responding to key business drivers.

Companies today have a growing interest in being able to integrate all data related to the core components that drive their success. Consolidating information about key concepts – such as employees, customers, competitors, operations, and products – enables them to make decisions based on a comprehensive understanding of their business environment. Achieving this vision, however, is no easy task.

Organizations need to integrate not only structured data, but also the increasing volume of unstructured data that they collect and generate. Such unstructured data can take the form of text documents, emails, and presentations. As this unstructured data includes valuable, and sometimes hard-won knowledge, it is especially critical that these resources can be accessed and effectively used across the organization.

Many industries are moving toward more collaborative business models. For example, in the life sciences industry, it is common for companies to outsource various components of their pipeline from drug discovery to clinical evaluation. It is necessary for companies to have flexible data architectures so they can integrate data from collaborators with internally generated data. This becomes a real challenge when companies have many partners and have to manage many interrelated projects.

Increasingly, companies conduct business in many countries around the globe. Ensuring that their operations meet the legal requirements of each country is a complex and dynamic challenge. In addition to archiving information related to those operations, companies may have to record the context in which information was collected or generated to demonstrate that they have met all compliance requirements.

Integrating data across departments also comes with many challenges. It is common for different departments within companies to use their own specialized vocabularies and to use data about the same business elements, but described at different levels of granularity.

While it is theoretically possible for companies to build comprehensive relational models of their data, this approach is somewhat inflexible. For example, it does not enable data to be easily shared with partners during collaborations. The complexity of such a data representation and the difficulties involved in reliably managing any changes to the model would not leave companies well positioned to rapidly adapt to business change. As business conditions continue to evolve quickly, it is imperative that organizations build enough flexibility into their architecture to ensure that it enables, rather than hinders, their ability to respond rapidly to change.

Increasingly, companies are recognizing that their data is their most important asset and that they must be able to control its use. Consequently, they do not want it locked into software that uses proprietary schemas or Application Programming Interfaces (APIs). They want to be able to access the data and use it in ways they did not plan for when their information systems were initially designed. They also need to be able to integrate their own data with data that was created completely independently.

Semantic Web technologies and design principles provide a framework that should make it possible for enterprises to continue to achieve their business goals in the face of change and an increasing dependence on effective use of business data.

3.   THE ENTERPRISE SEMANTIC WEB

Resource Description Framework (RDF) is one of the core Semantic Web recommendations from the W3C (Manola, Miller, et al. 2004). RDF represents data using subject-predicate-object triples (also known as 'statements'). This triple representation connects data in a flexible piece-by-piece and link-by-link fashion that forms a directed labeled graph. This is a very simple, flexible, robust, and expressive model for representing data. As RDF does not have a rigid data structure, it provides a strong framework for seamlessly incorporating new, even unexpected, data with heterogeneous structure. Further, a graph structure simplifies the modeling of data, as it tends to more closely mirror the real world than other data representations that are commonly used.

The components of each RDF statement are identified using Uniform Resource Identifiers (URIs). It is the use of URIs that gives the Semantic Web a fundamental benefit over other technologies. As URIs can be made globally unique, each occurrence of the same identifier means the same thing. The use of URIs enables people and software to know precisely what it is that is being referred to. When a fact is exerted against a URI, there is no possibility of any ambiguity. As there is no ambiguity, it becomes possible to aggregate all data that refers to a given resource. Further, it becomes simpler to integrate data sources that were created independently, as it is not necessary for the data to contain the same values. This makes it simpler for organizations to selectively reuse data.

The approach taken to identify entities using the Semantic Web is very different from the way relational databases identify entities. In a database, all of the identifiers are local. For example, there may be information within a database that refers to the concept of a "purchase order." However, without understanding the schema of the database or seeing the database application, it would not be possible to know if these were purchases that the user of the database wishes to make or whether these are orders from customers. It, therefore, would not be possible to automate the integration of such data with purchase order data from other sources. With the current pace of acquisitions, it would be helpful for commercial enterprises to be able to take advantage of well-defined global identifiers to streamline integration of such business data.

The above description of the benefits of using URIs for integrating information assumes that URIs are being shared and reused. However, this need not be the case, as anyone can generate a URI to describe a concept. If multiple URIs are discovered to represent the same concept, it is possible to use constructs within Web Ontology Language (OWL), such as sameAs or inverseFunctional, to enable such URIs to be used interchangeably. As RDF provides a common framework that is grounded in the Web it allows mappings between data sources to be shared, thus enabling the network effect for data integration.

It is simpler if the same URI is always used to describe the same concept. Within a single company it should be relatively easy to maximize coordination in the assignment of URIs, and this is one of the reasons why the Semantic Web approach is expected to flourish within the enterprise at a relatively early stage.

OWL is another core standard recommendation from W3C for the Semantic Web (McGuinness and van Harmelen 2004). OWL is a more expressive language than RDF. It provides more ways to define terms as classes and instances, and allows users to define relationships between them, which is useful for modeling real-world objects. The data expressed in OWL can be queried, checked for consistency, and have new relationships inferred based on the complex definitions it allows. A further important standard is SPARQL, which is the query language for RDF and OWL. SPARQL contains capabilities for querying by triple patterns, disjunctions, conjunctives, and optional patterns. As a data access language, it is suitable for local and remote use (Prud'hommeaux and Seaborne 2005).

4.   SOFTWARE FOR THE SEMANTIC WEB

For companies to fully benefit from the Semantic Web approach, new software tools need to be introduced at various layers of an application stack. Databases, middleware, and applications must be enhanced in order be able to work with RDF, OWL and SPARQL. As application stacks become Semantic Web enabled, they form a flexible information bus to which new components can be added.

As the Semantic Web continues to mature, there is an increasing range of data repositories available that are able to store RDF and OWL. The earliest implementations of RDF repositories, or triple stores as they are also known, were primarily open source. The technology providers adopted varying architectural approaches. For example, 3store (http://threestore.sourceforge.net/) employs an in-memory representation, while Sesame (http://sourceforge.net/projects/sesame/) and Kowari (http://kowari.org) use a disk-based solution. More recently a number of commercial triple stores have become available. These include RDF Gateway from Intellidimension (http://www.intellidimension.com/), Virtuoso from OpenLink (http://virtuoso.openlinksw.com), Profium Metadata Server from Profium (http://www.profium.com/index.php?id=485), and the Oracle Database from Oracle (http://www.oracle.com/technology/tech/semantic_technologies). An interesting trend is that solutions from both Oracle and OpenLink enable RDF/OWL to be stored in a triple store alongside relational and XML data. This type of hybrid solution enables a single query to span multiple different data representations.

Although the ability to store data in RDF and OWL is very important, it is expected that much data will remain in relational and XML data formats. Consequently, tools have been developed that allow data in these formats to be made available as RDF. The most commonly used approach for mapping between relational representations and RDF is D2RQ (http://sites.wiwiss.fu-berlin.de/suhl/bizer/D2RQ/), which treats non-RDF relational databases as virtual RDF graphs. Other toolkits for mapping relational data to RDF include SquirrelRDF (http://jena.sourceforge.net/SquirrelRDF/) and DartGrid (http://ccnt.zju.edu.cn/projects/dartgrid/dgv3.html). Alternative approaches for including relational data within the Semantic Web include FeDeRate (http://www.w3.org/2003/01/21-RDF-RDB-access/) that provides mappings between RDF queries and SQL queries, and SPASQL (http://www.w3.org/2005/05/22-SPARQL-MySQL/XTech.html) which eliminates the query-rewriting phase by modifying mySQL to allow parsing SPARQL directly within the relational database server.

It is also important to be able to map XML documents and XHTML pages into RDF. W3C will soon have a candidate recommendation, Gleaning Resource Descriptions from Dialects of Languages (GRDDL) (http://www.w3.org/2004/01/rdxh/spec), that enables XML documents to designate how they can be translated into RDF, typically by indicating the location of an XML Stylesheet Translations (XSLT). Work is also underway to develop mapping tools from other data representations to RDF (http://esw.w3.org/topic/ConverterToRdf). The ability to map data into RDF from relational, XML, and other data formats, combined with the data integration capabilities of RDF, makes it exceptionally well positioned as a common language for data representation and query.

If a company has been able to consistently assign URIs across all of their data sources, then integrating data is straightforward with RDF. However, if different departments initially assigned different URIs to the same entity, then OWL constructs can be used to relate equivalent URIs. Several vendors provide middleware designed for such ontology-based data integration. These include OntoBroker (http://www.ontoprise.de/content/e1171/e1231/), TopBraid Suite (http://www.topquadrant.com/tq_topbraid_suite.htm), Protégé (http://protege.stanford.edu/), and Cogito Data Integration Broker (http://www.cogitoinc.com/databroker.html).

A number of organizations have developed toolkits for building Semantic Web applications. The most commonly used is the Jena framework for Java-based Semantic Web applications (http://jena.sourceforge.net/). It provides a programmatic environment for reading, writing, and querying RDF and OWL. A rule-based inference engine is provided, as well as standard mechanisms for using other reasoning engines such as Pellet (http://pellet.owldl.com/) or FaCT++ (http://owl.man.ac.uk/factplusplus/). Sesame is another frequently used Java-based Semantic Web application toolkit that provides support for both query and inference (http://www.openrdf.org/about.jsp). A further commonly used application is the Haystack Semantic Web Browser that is based on the Eclipse platform (http://haystack.csail.mit.edu/staging/eclipse-download.html). There are also many programming environments that are available for developing Semantic Web applications in a range of languages (http://esw.w3.org/topic/SemanticWebTools).

5. USE CASES

This section of the chapter describes some use cases of Semantic Web technologies within an enterprise setting. The first three examples are hypothetical, but describe how the Semantic Web could play an important role within a services industry, manufacturing, and government. The next use case describes the deployment of Semantic Web technologies within a life sciences company. The final use case highlights the use of the Semantic Web for content search within a technology company. The use cases section is completed with a brief description of some other application areas where it is expected that there will be significant benefit in the adoption of Semantic Web technologies.

5.1 Enhancing effectiveness of recruitment services

One of the main strengths of the Semantic Web is its ability to integrate disparate data. This use case describes how the technology can be of benefit to recruitment services.

Typically, when a company is looking to hire a person with a particular skill set, they will start a search by engaging the recruiting agencies with which the company works. Each recruiting agency will then perform a search of their proprietary database to identify the best possible candidates for the position. Once the candidates have been identified, the company that is hiring has to compile and manage a list of all appropriate candidates from all of the recruiting agencies.

It would be more efficient if the company that was hiring was able to perform a single query across all of the recruiter databases, thereby retrieving information about all candidates in a consistent format. This would save time in describing the job opening to each agency and minimize potential miscommunications between the company and the recruiting agency. It would also allow the hiring company to directly identify the candidates they believe would be the best match for the role, rather than having to engage in a back-and-forth dialogue about candidates with the recruiting agency. Further, it would become possible to identify internal and external candidates using the same query.

This use case describes how it would be possible to uniformly access all of the recruiter's databases using Semantic Web technologies. Importantly, for the hiring company, this approach would enable querying across different recruiter databases depending on which agencies are currently under contract.

In order to enable querying across multiple recruiter databases, the hiring company would encourage all of its recruitment agencies to make a subset of their data available in RDF, using a common vocabulary and exposing this data by publishing a SPARQL endpoint. It likely that the hiring company would specifically request that it wants to be able to identify job titles, employers, location, qualifications, and willingness to relocate. Figure 2-1 shows a subset of such a schema.

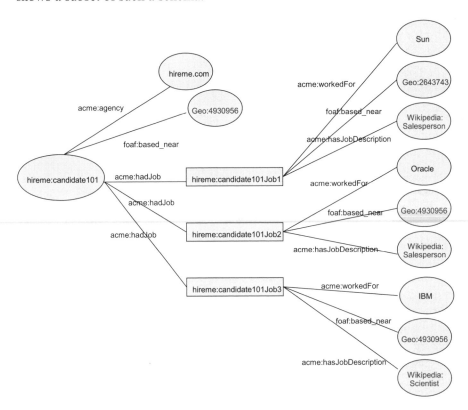

Figure 2-1. The diagram highlights the schema used to represent information about an individual job candidate. The name of the hiring agency that the candidate is working with is shown, along with the location of the agency. Information regarding all three of the candidate's past positions is also shown

Recruitment agencies have two options for making their data available as RDF. They could convert some of their existing relational data into RDF and then store it in a triple store such as Sesame. Alternatively, they could map the relational data to RDF using a technology such as D2RQ. Recruitment agencies would typically use the mapping approach, because this would only require them to map the data once; whereas if they choose to convert their data to RDF, they would need to keep updating the RDF store as their database changed.

The hiring company would likely specify that, in order to query across the data, they would like the agencies to use widely shared URIs. For example, they may require agencies to use the Wikipedia list of occupations (http://en.wikipedia.org/wiki/Occupationlist) to describe the roles candidates have held, and Geonames (http://www.geonames.org/) to describe the geographical location of the positions.

It is likely that a recruiting agency will not store all of its data in the representation required by the hiring company. For example, a U.S.-centric recruiting agency may only store zip codes for location, while the hiring company may require Geoname URIs to be used. In this case, the recruiting agency would need a method to convert a zip code to a Geoname. A Web Service such as GetInfoByZip (http://www.webservicex.net/uszip.asmx) could be used to convert the zip code into an address, and then a Web Service provided by Geonames could be used to convert the addresses into a Geoname URI (http://www.geonames.org/export/geonames-search.html).

The recruiting agency would also need to create some URIs. For example, they would need to create a URI for the agency itself, which would have properties that include telephone number, address, and contact person. The agency could be a foaf:organization (http://xmlns.com/foaf/0.1/#term_Organization), and the contact could be a foaf:Person. They would also need to create a URI for each candidate, which could also be a foaf:Person.

Once all of the agencies have made their data available in RDF via a SPARQL endpoint, it would become straightforward for the hiring company to query for candidates of interest across all agencies. It would also be fairly straightforward for the hiring company to add a new recruitment agency to their list of partners.

Going forward there are many reasons why the hiring company may decide to extend its Semantic Web infrastructure to include OWL. The hiring company may decide there are too many terms that describe similar skill sets, so choose to simplify its queries by using an ontology of occupations. For example, it would be useful if there were a class that described candidates with legal skills, thus avoiding the need to search for candidates with job titles that include lawyer, chief council, solicitor, and legal representative. OWL would also be useful for more advanced querying in which, for example, searches are performed for candidates who have worked at two Fortune 500 companies. OWL would be needed for such a query, as RDF does not provide support for cardinality constraints. Further, ontologies could be used to extend search capability so that they include geographical regions as well as towns.

5.2   Enhancing agile manufacturing

Food manufacturers operate in an environment in which there is severe cost pressure. It is one of the few industries in which purchase decisions are made based on price differences of a few pennies. These cost pressures have resulted in manufacturers shifting from an approach in which equipment is dedicated to the production of a single product, to one in which equipment can be used for multiple products. There has also been a trend toward the reuse of ingredients across different products and greater variety in size of packaging. The shift to equipment that can be used for many purposes puts pressure on manufactures to produce the right product, in the right quantity, and at the right time. This requires a better understanding of consumer demand, the ability to rapidly source ingredients from suppliers, and the need to switch products runs with minimal downtime.

Food manufacturing is also an industry that is facing increasing pressures to be agile. The industry needs to be able to recognize the latest food craze, and to modify the ingredients in products and labeling accordingly. It is also an industry that needs to respond to regulatory agencies such as the U.S. Food and Drug Administration regarding the labeling of products that claim to have health benefits (http://www.cfsan.fda.gov/~dms/lab-ssa.html). Further, the industry must respond to increasing regulations regarding the use of ingredients that are common allergens (http://www.cfsan.fda.gov/~dms/alrgqa.html).

In order to effectively manage these business drivers, companies use a number of enterprise applications. One of the key applications has been manufacturing resource planning software that is designed to handle sales order management, inventory control, accounts receivable and payable, purchasing, payroll, and other front-office functions. Another critical application is the manufacturing execution system. This software analyzes performance and allows dynamic decision making about production floor activities, including process control, work in process, throughput, downtime, changeover time, scrap, and other functions and parameters. Scheduling software is commonly used to identify any potential bottlenecks or critical disruptions in production by taking into account factors such as changeover time, ingredient or package continuity, and parameter changes.

Traditionally within organizations, enterprise resource planning applications have been implemented to support business processes. These applications have evolved over recent years from large monolithic systems, to a more agile Web Services-based approach. However, even with the new approach, it is frequently difficult to integrate such disparate applications, as they often support different underlying data models.

The Semantic Web provides the ability to represent concepts within an ontology. Architecturally, the ontology is used at the interface between the application and the database. With this approach, databases focus on the persistent storage and indexing of data. The application code could be dedicated to implementing the business logic, which it does using terms defined by the ontology, thus creating a unified data model across multiple databases.

The benefits of such an approach include the fact that ontologies name and organize the key concepts within the organization, which have a tendency to change relatively slowly. Software engineering is, therefore, more robust against change when ontologies are employed. Having the concept definitions, constraints, and relationships in the ontology makes it easier for data to be reused by applications for which it was not originally intended. It is also easier for people who understand the business to help work on developing ontologies than it is for them to create database schemas. Further, it is relatively simple to extend the capabilities of an ontology by adding to its constituent relationships, or by linking to a different ontology altogether.

There already exist a number of food ontologies that a company could use (http://www.schemaweb.info/schema/SchemaDetails.aspx?id=61). If a company used an ontology to define all of its ingredients, as well as defining all of its products in terms of those ingredients, it would make it possible to re-classify products as necessary. Recently there have been regulations imposed within the United States that require finer-grained labeling of products that contain common allergens, such as nuts. By adding new definitions of product classes based on ingredients named in these regulations, automated classification would make it easier to identify which products require such labeling. Similarly, in order to support marketing, classes could be defined that capture the balance of ingredients that meet government regulations for when health claims may be made, or which satisfy the latest popular weight loss diets. As regulations or fads change, these definitions could be modified or augmented. Ontology reasoning services could then identify existing products that can be marketed in new ways.

By taking advantage of Semantic Web technologies it would be much simpler for companies to incorporate new data that is deemed relevant. For example, a company may decide that the weather is a strong predictor of the popularity of certain types of food. With a Semantic Web approach it could be easier to incorporate this new data source into decision-making.

5.3   Identification of patterns and insights in data

Semantic Web technologies can be used to find patterns and insights across data that originates from many sources. This approach has much applicability to projects relating to national security as facts and correlations of interest would frequently only be observed when disparate information is brought together.

Within government agencies much information is captured in the form of reports. Text mining approaches could be pursued to extract core information from these documents. With natural language processing the extracted data is commonly in the form of a triple. It is straightforward to take the extracted triples, convert them into RDF, and store them in an RDF repository. The latest release of the Oracle Database could be used as the triple store as it provides support for RDF (Murray 2005).

Once the data has been loaded into the system it forms a directed labeled graph. Users can then query the data using Oracle's SQL extensions for RDF, which makes it simple for a user to query for all information that relates to a particular individual or place. It also becomes possible for a user to follow a chain of links within the data. Importantly for this use case, it further enables a user to find pairs of individuals who know each other, where their combined activities may lead someone to suspect that suspicious activities were being undertaken.

The Oracle Database also provides support for a range of graph analytics, and network constraints (Stephens, Rung, et al. 2004). This functionality is available to RDF data through a Java API. Users can either build in-house applications that work against the API, or use applications that are already integrated such as Cytoscape (Shannon, Markiel et al. 2003) or Tom Sawyer (http://www.tomsawyer.com). Graph visualization and analysis tools are well suited to represent networks of individuals. Such applications would allow users to identify who knows who, recognize sets of individuals that form groups, and find the well-connected individuals who form key hubs both within and between groups.

This use case has focused on analyzing information that was originally contained within government reports. However, it would also be possible to incorporate data that is in other representations into the analysis. One approach would be to convert existing relational or XML data into RDF, and to then load it into the triple store for incorporation into the analysis. The other approach would be to use the power of SQL to perform queries that span relational, XML and RDF data.

In the next release of the Oracle Database support will also be provided for OWL. There will be native, forward-chaining based inference for an expressive subset of OWL Description Logic (basic constructs, property characteristics, class comparisons, individual comparisons, and class expressions). This would allow users to performed more advanced inferencing over data within the Oracle Database. The next release will also include new SQL semantic operators to enhance the query of relational data using ontologies.

5.4   Integration of heterogeneous scientific data

Many pharmaceutical companies are interested in the data integration capabilities promised by the Semantic Web (http://www.w3.org/2004/10/swls-workshop-report.html). This is because drug discovery and development is a very expensive and time-consuming process. To get a drug from bench to market averages 5,000 screened compounds, 15 years and nearly $1 billion (Wolfson 2006). Companies want to minimize costly late-stage attrition by identifying and eliminating drugs that do not have desirable safety profiles or sufficient efficacy as early on as possible (Lesko and Woodcock 2004). It is also important for companies to be aware of competitive offerings or patents that may reduce the market potential of drug candidates. In order to be able to make such decisions, companies need to have an integrated view of their data (Stephens, Morales et al. 2006).

The integration of data, however, has proven to be far from straightforward. Data commonly originates in different departments in which varying terminologies are used. Further, the data itself is very heterogeneous in nature, and consists of data types that include chemical structures, biological sequences, images, biological pathways, and scientific papers. Many companies have attempted to create data warehouses that contain all of this data, but many have found this approach lacking the flexibility required within a scientific discipline. Consequently, companies are exploring alternative approaches to data integration.

A number of pharmaceutical companies are now exploring the use of Semantic Web technologies as a framework for integrating heterogeneous data. Most early projects are focused on integrating data within drug discovery, although ultimately companies are striving to provide a unified view of data from the laboratory bench to clinical observations (Payne, Johnson et al. 2005).

Semantic Web implementations in pharmaceutical companies have involved the development of tools that provide insight into the key entities encountered within drug discovery (Wolfson 2006). These entities typically include genes, proteins, compounds, samples, diseases, projects, and companies. When a user interrogates a particular instance of an entity it becomes possible to view all other information that relates to the object. Frequently the results of such queries display a set of entities as a graph in order to assist the user in visualizing and navigating among the relationships between the entities. This approach enables scientists to discover information as they navigate through available knowledge, rather than necessarily having to have a specific query in mind at the outset. When ontologies are used in combination with such a tool, it enhances the user's ability to retrieve all information of interest even if specialist terminology was originally used to record the data. When querying, it can also help by recognizing identical terms used in different contexts. For example, an ontology would have different concepts for GSK the company versus GSK the protein. Upon querying for GSK, the tool would recognize the ambiguity, and could offer the user a choice of browsing by company or by protein.

There are a number of areas in which the pharmaceutical industry is interested in further exploring the use of the Semantic Web. One additional area of interest is in identifying whether a common biological pathway relates two separately occurring observations, for example, a change in brain pathology and a change in body temperature. This could occur by integrating an ontology that relate clinical conditions to symptoms, and another ontology that relates clinical conditions to possibly modulated pathways. Another area of interest is in the use of ontologies with images. For example, the annotation of medical images by terms in a well-designed anatomy ontology, such as the Foundational Model of Anatomy ontology (http://sig.biostr.washington.edu/projects/fm/), would make possible the retrieval of all relevant images. Moreover, it would be very interesting if image sections could be overlaid with terms from an ontology that effectively defined a coordinate system. This would allow biological mashups in which, for example, a gene expression pattern could be identified as having originated from cells within a certain part of an image.

5.5   Optimizing enterprise search and navigation

Content search is an area in which several companies are using Semantic Web technologies. Leading commercial vendors in this space include Siderean   Software   (http://www.siderean.com/)   and   Endeca (http://endeca.com/). The following use case describes how Semantic Web technologies have been harnessed to improve search within a large corporate enterprise.

The Oracle Technology Network (OTN), part of the Oracle.com Web site, is the main source of technical information for the Oracle developer community. The Web site provides access to product documentation, notifications of product releases, software download, blogs, podcasts, and a discussion forum. The richness, complexity and dynamism of this information have made it challenging for traditional search and navigation techniques to provide effective access to and discovery of information of interest. Oracle has worked with Siderean Software to apply Semantic Web technologies to the Web site to help to address this problem. The Web site is available at: http://otnsemanticweb.oracle.com

The solution is based on the integration of Siderean's Seamark Navigator and Oracle Secure Enterprise Search. This combination of technologies enhances information access by aggregating multiple sources of content and providing it via a single portal. The application enables a common approach for searching and browsing over the rich multi-media data. Such unified access to information is valuable in helping users to identify all information of interest with a single request. Users also have the ability to personalize their environment by selecting the feed items they want to incorporate and the layout of the information. In addition, many of the information types support data visualizations, including tag clouds, contributor clouds, and timelines. These visualizations have been designed to help guide the user by suggesting ways to find the precise information that they are looking for. Figures 2-2 and 2-3 show screen snapshots of the capabilities on the enhanced OTN Web site.

To keep the Web site up to date, every hour the application pulls content of interest to the Oracle developer community from multiple RSS feeds. Although each item in an RSS feed contains some metadata that describes it, often it is not sufficiently detailed or organized. The Seamark Metadata Assembly Platform enhances this metadata by using a combination of pattern-matching techniques to identify the subject matter of an item. Once the subject matter has been determined by Seamark, terms from an Oracle proprietary taxonomy are used to record the concepts and entities to which the item refers. At this point, XSLT is used to convert the XML based RSS syntax into RDF. This approach provides the annotation required to support the rich discovery experience based on dynamic navigation of entities and their relationships. For example, since terms are taken from an ontology, parent terms are more general than their children. Consequently, sets of search results whose metadata include different child terms can be grouped together and labeled using the parent concept. This makes it possible for a user to understand more results at once, and it makes it easier for them to narrow those results to a precise topic of interest.

The search interface also provides the ability to create customized RSS feeds based on user-defined queries. As terms for the concepts and entities in metadata are standardized, feeds constructed using this technology tend to be more targeted, with fewer inappropriately included items. Since the same method of associating metadata is applied to all media types, these feeds can deliver relevant content from diverse media platforms.

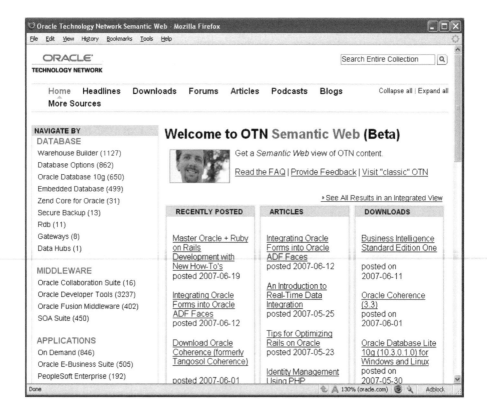

Figure 2-2. Oracle OTN Web site

The Figure 2-2 provides a screen snapshot of the Oracle OTN Web site. Dashboard portlets have been selected by a user to enable simultaneous navigation over multiple repositories. The panel on the left contains facets that are available for navigation, and highlights the number of items available for each link.

Integration and deployment of the solution was very fast and straightforward as both Seamark and Secure Enterprise Search are available as Web Services. The system was designed such that at query time Seamark calls the Secure Enterprise Search API, and then displays the results in the Seamark Relational Navigator framework. The total integration and deployment time for the OTN solution was about eight weeks. Expected future enhancements include support for additional data types, more personalization options, and more innovative visualizations.

Figure 2-3. Oracle OTN Web site – Blogs

In Figure 2-3 shows the Oracle OTN Web site. It now supports a range of visualization capabilities alongside the Semantic Web search and navigation functionality. The screen snapshot shows the results of a search for blogs that mention Java, and that were written between May 29, 2007 and June 14, 2007. The tag cloud shows that Jean-Pierre Dijcks and Tim Dexter have written many of the blogs that meet these requirements. The bar chart depicts the number of blogs that were written on each day over the selected time period. A list of the search results is shown towards the bottom of the page. It is now possible to view blogs according to multiple dimensions that include author, time, and topic.

This search solution was implemented by an enterprise wanting to enhance search and navigation for their customers. In the process of reaching this goal, Semantic Web technologies were used. As a byproduct, the data is now available in RDF, and can be queried through a SPARQL interface. This is, therefore, a good example of how Semantic Web technologies employed to achieve enterprise goals can pave the way for creation of more general applications on the Semantic Web.

An interesting extension to this capability would be to broaden the search and navigation to include business applications. To achieve this objective, it would be necessary to extend the ontology to include all of the entities represented within the business applications. For example, transactions within an inventory tracking system could be provided as RSS feeds with metadata recording the items being added to or removed from the inventory. If the inventory feeds were added to the ones monitored by the portal, it would enable the existing search and navigation facilities to explore inventory as well. This approach would become increasingly interesting as data is incorporated from additional business applications.

5.6   Additional applications of the Semantic Web

The previous section highlight in detail some use cases of the Semantic Web. There are, however, several other application areas in which Semantic Web technologies are expected to provide significant benefits. A brief overview is provided of three such areas:

- **Compliance and Regulation**. There is a growing and increasingly complex set of regulatory requirements to which companies must adhere, including Sarbanes-Oxley, Health Insurance Portability and Accountability Act (HIPAA), and Basel II. The regulatory organizations typically define their policies independently, yet companies must apply all of them to their data. If Semantic Web technologies were used to model the policies related to the regulations, it would make it simpler for enterprises and legislators to merge policies and, thereby, keep abreast of the ramifications of complex interacting policies. In addition, many regulations require organizations to be able to trace and verify data movements and relationships. These requirements are also well suited to the capabilities of the Semantic Web.

- **Event Driven Architecture.** Semantic Web technologies could also aid our ability to more rapidly perceive, process, analyze and act in response to changes in data. These capabilities would be especially valuable when responding rapidly to an emergency, when unexpected relationships between data may need to be explored. For example, if there was a flood, it may be necessary to examine data according to terrain elevation. Another likely use of event driven architectures would be with sensor information. Monitoring signals from Radio Frequency Identification (RFID) tags that include URIs could greatly enhance the effectiveness of condition monitoring, maintenance planning, and the documentation of the technical status of systems and components on offshore platforms or ships, based on using networked devices for remote access during maintenance planning or for *in situ* access during inspection.
- **Service Oriented Architecture Metadata.** The Semantic Web will likely play an important role within Service Oriented Architectures (SOA). The ability of the Semantic Web to assign metadata will help with true dynamic service discovery, invocation, and composition. The Semantic Web could, therefore, improve the inherent flexibility of a SOA infrastructure.

6. CONCLUSIONS

This chapter reviews some of the business and technology challenges that companies are facing today, and describes how a number of these difficulties could be overcome with the use of Semantic Web technologies. However, in order for Semantic Web technologies to be adopted within an enterprise setting, there must be tools that are available that support the scalability, availability, and reliability requirements of such companies. To assess this, the chapter summarizes the state of the art in software tools and technologies, including both open-source and commercial products. A number of use cases are provided that describe real-world implementations and examples of situations in which there would be significant benefit to implementing Semantic Web technology-based solutions. Importantly, the chapter describes why it is likely that mainstream deployment of the Semantic Web will occur first within an enterprise setting and how that can then pave the way for the creation of more general applications of the Semantic Web.

7.   QUESTIONS FOR DISCUSSION

Beginner:
1. How could a company generate URIs from existing unique identifiers?
2. What would you use as the namespace for your company?

Intermediate:
1. How could a food company make use of recipe collections on the Web to propose new products?
2. What are some of the limitations of Wikipedia's list of occupations? How would you address some of these limitations?

Advanced:
1. What other business applications do you think would benefit most from the adoption of Semantic Web technologies?
2. What biological or business mashups would you envision to be of value?

Practical exercises:
1. How would you write a SPARQL query to identify the recruitment agency that represents hireme:candidate10021?
2. What facets would you select for navigating the Oracle OTN Web site?

8.   SUGGESTED ADDITIONAL READING

- Davies, J., Studer, R., and Warren, P. *Semantic Web Technologies: Trends and Research in Ontology-based Systems.* Chichester, UK; John Wiley & Sons, 2006. A thorough overview of the Semantic Web and interesting use cases.
- Antoniou, G. and van Harmelen, F. *A Semantic Web Primer.* Cambridge, MA; MIT Press, 2004. This book provides a good introduction to the Semantic Web.

9.   ACKNOWLEDGEMENTS

I would like to acknowledge Alan Ruttenberg for his contribution to the development of the use cases, and for proof reading the manuscript. I would like to express thanks to Ivan Herman for his feedback. I would also like to thank Brian Anderson for his input to the enterprise search use case.

10. REFERENCES

Lesko, L.J., J. Woodcock (2004). Translation of Pharmacogenomics and Pharmacogenetics: a regulatory perspective. Nature Reviews Drug Discovery. **3**: 763-769.

Manola, F., E. Miller, et al. (2004) RDF Primer. W3C Recommendation 10 February 2004. http://www.w3.org/TR/rdf-primer/

McGuinness, D. L. and F. van Harmelen (2004) OWL Web Ontology Language Overview. W3C Recommendation 10 February 2004. http://www.w3.org/TR/owl-features/

Murray, C. (2005) Oracle Spatial. Resource Description Framework (RDF) 10g Release 2 (10.2). http://download-west.oracle.com/otndocs/tech/semantic_web/pdf/rdfrm.pdf

Payne, P. R. O., S. B. Johnson, et al. (2005) Breaking the Translational Barriers: the value of integrating biomedical informatics and translational research. Journal of Investigative Medicine. 53(4): 192-200.

Prud'hommeaux, E., A. Seaborne (2005) SPARQL Query Language for RDF. W3C Working Draft 21 July 2005. http://www.w3.org/TR/rdf-sparql-query

Shannon, P., A. Markiel, et al. (2003) Cytoscape: a software environment for integrated models of biomolecular interaction networks. Genome Research 13: 2498-2504.

Stephens, S., J. Rung, et al. (2004) Graph Data Representation in Oracle Database 10g: Case studies in Life Sciences. IEEE Data Engineering Bulletin 27: 61-67.

Stephens S.M., A. Morales, et al. (2006) Application of Semantic Web Technology to Drug Safety Determination. IEEE Intelligent Systems. 21: 82-86

Wolfson, W. (2006) Oracle OpenWorld 2006: Pharma Stuck on Semantic Web. Bio-IT World. http://www.bio-itworld.com/issues/2006/nov/oracle-openworld/

PART II – FINANCE AND GOVERNMENT

Chapter 3

SEMANTIC WEB TECHNOLOGIES FOR THE FINANCIAL DOMAIN

Rubén Lara[1], Iván Cantador[2] and Pablo Castells[2]
[1]*Tecnología, Información y Finanzas (TIF), Madrid, Spain – rlara@afi.es*
[2]*Escuela Politécnica Superior, Universidad Autónoma de Madrid, Madrid, Spain – ivan.cantador@uam.es, pablo.castells@uam.es*

1. INTRODUCTION

Data, information and knowledge management are key activities in modern economies, consuming a considerable amount of the efforts and resources in organisations and businesses (Alexiev 2005). Information management involves, in most cases, the integration of data from disparate and heterogeneous channels, including information from third parties. An optimal handling of information assets is especially critical in the financial field, a conceptually rich domain where information is complex, huge in volume, and a highly valuable business product by itself, and where the exchange and integration of information for its posterior analysis is a key task for financial analysts. The volume, complexity and value of economic and financial information make finance a strategic area for research and innovation on information modelling, exchange and integration. For this reason, there is interest in evaluating what the emerging semantic-based knowledge technologies can achieve in this context, and what is needed for them to be adopted by businesses in this area.

Along these lines, we have worked on two applications of Semantic Web technologies to the financial domain, namely: a) the management of economic and financial information (Castells et al. 2004), and b) the building of explicit information models for the exchange of information in the investment funds market, comparing the use of XBRL and the use of semantic languages such as OWL (Lara et al. 2006). These two applications, and our experiences and lessons learnt, are presented in this chapter, along with a general analysis of the possible uptake of Semantic Web technologies in finance, the potential benefits of such uptake, and the requisites for it to happen. The goal of the chapter is thus to illustrate and analyse the possibilities for exploiting Semantic Web technologies in the financial domain, the achieved and expected benefits therein, the problems and obstacles to be overcome, and an analysis and reflection on the potential of Semantic Web technologies for finance in the future.

2.   SEMANTIC TECHNOLOGIES FOR ECONOMIC AND FINANCIAL INFORMATION MANAGEMENT

2.1   Description of the domain

A huge amount of valuable economic and financial information is produced world-wide every day, but its interpretation and processing is a hard and time-consuming task, as a major part of the information generated is mainly textual and, therefore, the possibilities for automated management are quite limited, whereby a considerable amount of human involvement in the loop is needed. Moreover, the manual management of information resources is error-prone and time consuming (Ding and Fensel 2001), searches are often imprecise or yield an excessive number of candidate matches through which users need to clear their way in order to find the sought information. In order to overcome these problems, efficient filtering, search, and browsing mechanisms are needed by information consumers to access the relevant contents for their needs or business, and find their way through in an effective way. On the information provision side, efficient production, management and delivery technologies are needed as well.

Semantic Web technologies are foreseen as a possible solution to such problems by providing an explicit and formal representation of the semantics underlying information sources and by exploiting such formal semantics (Berners-Lee et al. 2001). Ontologies have been proposed as a backbone technology for the Semantic Web and, more generally, for the management of formalised knowledge in the context of distributed systems (Gruber 1993). They enrich content with machine-processable semantics, which can be communicated and processed by software programs. The main principle in this vision is to make information understandable for computers, thus enabling new, more powerful information processing and management capabilities, and reducing the involved costs.

As an experience towards this vision, we have developed an ontology-based platform for managing economic and financial data. TIF, a Spanish provider of information technology solutions for the financial domain, was involved in this research. One of the core business activities of the corporation TIF is part of[15] is the creation, management and delivery of added-value economic and financial contents, such as market research, market analysis, or investment recommendations. Thus, the purpose of the research presented herein is to evaluate the improvements the application of semantic technologies can bring to current information management and delivery practices in such areas.

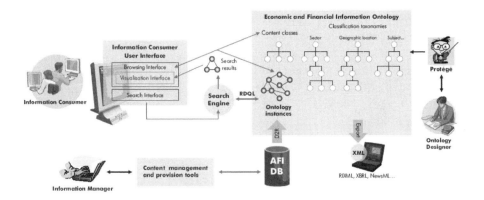

Figure 3-1. Platform architecture

The main components of the developed platform are shown in Figure 3-1:

- A domain ontology that formally models the economic and financial information produced, managed, and delivered to customers by TIF.
- Import (from corporate databases) and export (to different formats) facilities.
- Content management and provision tools.
- A visualisation component for information consumers and managers.
- A search engine.

Each of these components is described in the sections that follow.

---

[15] www.grupoanalistas.com

2.2   An ontology for content management in the economic and financial domain

The information generated by providers and consumed by requesters always refers to some particular context. However, the common situation is that this information does not refer to any explicit model of such domain, or it only refers to an ad-hoc model. Furthermore, if a model is available, it is in most cases purely syntactic, which limits the automatic processing of information that would conform to such model, in particular, reusing data in another context or transforming it according to another model.

Before the project we describe in this section was accomplished, TIF made use of a partially explicit, syntactic domain model to create, manage and deliver economic and financial information and data. In particular, a custom content management system was used to, based on this model, create, manage and deliver, through different channels (e.g. Web sites, XML syndication), contents to customers with different profiles such as banks and financial institutions, SMEs which use the information for decision making and foreign trade activity, and distributors who publish the information in printed and digital specialised media.

In this context, the first task we faced in the project was the design of an explicit and formal model for economy and finance, i.e., the creation of an ontology for the economic and financial domain covering the business needs of the company.

2.2.1 Ontology definition

The creation of the ontology started with a study existing domain models which could be reused. However, no suitable ontologies for our target domain were found, and the use of taxonomies such as the Global Industry Classification Standard (GICS)[16] for the classification of industry sectors was discarded as it did not meet the requirements of TIF. Thus the domain ontology was essentially defined from scratch. The design procedure was incremental, interacting with domain experts in order to produce refined versions of the ontology. Two main steps were followed in the creation process:

1. A first version of the ontology was created based on the existent, semi-explicit domain model and on the corporate databases scheme.

---

[16] www.mscibarra.com/products/gics/

2. We interacted with domain experts in order to refine the ontology, adding missing concepts, relations and properties, and to evaluate to what extent the target domain was covered by the defined ontology.

The interaction with domain experts was the most crucial step for a successful design of the ontology, as they contributed with numerous and valuable improvements to the first version of the ontology. The first step was motivated by the need to make the current model fully explicit, so that a starting point for the interaction with domain experts was available.

2.2.2 Root ontology classes

The interaction with our financial and technical staff led us to consider four distinct kinds of concepts (classes) in the ontology:

1. *Contents.* They reflect different types of documents and contents created by domain experts, such as reports, analysis, studies, recommendations, etc. All economic and financial contents generated by TIF are modelled as an instance of a content class.
2. *Classification categories.* These categories serve to classify the contents generated according to topics, sectors, etc.
3. *Entities.* They represent contents which are not economic and financial contents themselves, but which are referred to in the economic and financial contents generated by financial experts. Examples of these concepts are companies, banks, organisations, people, information sources, events, etc.
4. *Enumerated types.* They provide sets of values (controlled vocabularies) for certain properties. These concepts have a fixed set of instances.

From our experience in ontology engineering for information systems, the consideration of these four kinds of concepts is an interesting and recurrent distinction that arises in many, if not most, information management systems in diverse domains. In fact, a similar approach can be found in information exchange standards like RIXML[17] and other standards in the controlled vocabulary community (Fast et al. 2002). However, this distinction is sometimes not a sharp line.

The resulting ontology provides explicit connections between contents, categories, and other concepts, which were only semi-explicit in the current content management system. These relations are now well characterised, and can be further described in as much detail as needed and allowed by the

---

[17] Research Information Exchange Language, http://www.rixml.org.

Semantic Web technology employed. As it will be later described, the defined ontology is exploited in our platform to support more expressive and precise search capabilities, and for the automation of the generation of user interfaces (query input forms, content presentation views, and content provision forms).

2.2.3 Ontology language

For the description of the ontology, RDF(S) was used (Brickley and Guha 2004). The reasons for this choice were:

1. RDF(S) was a World Wide Web Consortium (W3C)[18] recommendation, which was a guarantee of its maturity and stability. OWL (Bechhofer et al. 2004) was also considered, but at the time the ontology was defined this language was still in the process of becoming a W3C recommendation.
2. RDF(S) had the widest tool support at the time the ontology was created. This reduced the risks in the development and the time required to implement our platform.
3. The expressivity of RDF/RDFS was considered enough for a first evaluation of the benefits of an ontology-based platform for content management. The transitive closure of *subPropertyOf* and *subClassOf* relations in RDF(S), domain and range entailments, and the implications of *subPropertyOf* and *subClassOf* have been the inference mechanisms exploited by the developed platform.

The OWL ontology language and its foreseen extensions can be considered in the future for the evolution of the platform. In fact, OWL has been used in other developments we have later undertaken, as will be described in the section 3.

For the definition of the ontology, Protégé[19] was used, as it offers a complete and well-tested set of capabilities for ontology modelling.

---

[18] http://www.w3.org
[19] http://protege.stanford.edu

2.3   Semantic content description and exploitation

2.3.1 Integration of legacy content

Once an ontology is available that captures and formalises the domain in which the company produces and manages information, new contents can be created in the form of instances of concepts of the ontology from the outset. This way, newly created contents conform to a well-defined, formal, and agreed upon model, greatly facilitating the automated processing of contents by semantic-aware software programs, as we will describe later in this section. However this solves only a part of the problem, since huge volumes of information are already stored in corporate databases, based on conventional (relational) information models. In order for these legacy assets to benefit from the ontology-enabled semantic-based search, visualisation, and generation capabilities which will be described in this section, new ontological descriptions of the old contents need to be added to the management system.

We used the open source tool D2R[20] for this purpose. D2R can extract information from relational databases supporting JDBC or ODBC and, using an XML mapping file, generate RDF instances. An XML mapping file has to be created for each concept in the ontology. This mapping defines how the results of an SQL query over corporate databases are mapped to attributes of an instance of a particular concept in the ontology. We have defined such mappings, based on which the available contents stored in corporate databases have been translated into domain ontology instances. These instances have been in turn stored in corporate databases for persistency. In particular, Jena[21] has been used to retrieve RDF instances of the ontology from the files generated using D2R and to store them in a database back-end.

Our platform aims at improving current content management systems, but without interfering with existing production systems. This means that all the information (both old and new) should remain available in the old database model for its use by production systems. Therefore, two versions of the produced contents are maintained, one conforming to the old scheme, and one described in terms of the domain ontology. In order to reuse the already defined mappings for the annotation of existing contents, newly generated contents are first stored in the old model; afterwards, the mappings defined are used by D2R to annotate these contents, and the resulting RDF instances are stored in the database back-end.

---

[20] http://sites.wiwiss.fu-berlin.de/suhl/bizer/d2rmap/D2Rmap.htm
[21] http://jena.sourceforge.net/

2.3.2 Ontology-based search

Our platform provides a search module which can be used by customers, content providers, content managers and administrators to query for contents in terms of the defined ontology. In this way, users can go beyond keyword-based search, full-text search, and structured search based on a semi-explicit, syntactic model. In particular, our search module supports full structured search in terms of any dimension of the ontology, and allows setting different levels of detail for expressing the search query (different partial views of the ontology) depending on the user profile.

Furthermore, the inference capabilities enabled by RDF(S) are used to obtain search results. In particular, the transitive closure of *subPropertyOf* and *subClassOf* relations in RDF(S), domain and range entailments, and the implications of *subPropertyOf* and *subClassOf* are exploited to obtain contents that match a user query.

In our system, the user interacts with an HTML search form where he can select concepts in the ontology (content classes), and provide search values for properties of the selected concept. Thus, the user can formulate his needs in terms of concepts, properties, and relations among concepts as defined by the ontology.

Search forms are automatically generated from the definition of ontology concepts. In particular, we have defined a search form generation mechanism which provides a default procedure to generate forms adapted to the structure and the types of properties of concepts in the ontology. In the default procedure, the properties of content classes have a Boolean *searchable* metaproperty, used by ontology designers to control whether the generated search forms should include an input control where search values for this property can be provided. If a property of a class is searchable, the search form generation procedure selects different HTML/JavaScript controls depending on the type of the searchable property.

Furthermore, it is usually necessary to create a custom search form following particular design and brand image considerations. This is achieved in our system by creating form templates for each content class, where all aspects of the design can be defined in as much detail as desired. Our template definition language is based on JSP, where custom tags have been defined to reference properties of concepts in the ontology and to include other ontology graph traversal expressions. The language also includes primitives to easily specify HTML or JavaScript input components, and facilities to define global layout constructs. Wherever details are not explicitly indicated in the template, the system tries to provide appropriate default solutions. An example of the search form generated for a particular concept in the ontology can be seen in Figure 3-2.

It is generally more adequate to provide customers with fairly simple and easy to use search interfaces (Green et al. 1990), whereas experts and content managers, who have better knowledge of the domain, can benefit from more complex and powerful search facilities. This is supported in our platform by creating different templates for different user profiles and usage modes, thus enabling the creation of as large and varied an array of power levels and modalities as needed in a highly modular and extensible way (see (Hearst 1999) for an overview of user interface approaches for searching).

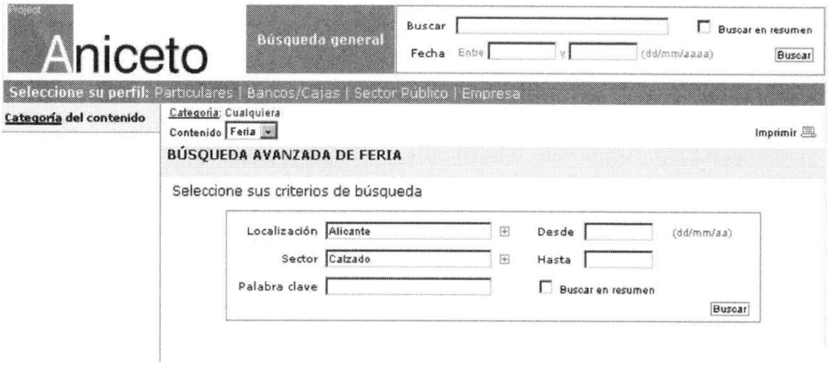

Figure 3-2. Search

The possibilities to use the model defined by the ontology to formulate search queries go beyond specifying property values for content concepts. The search module allows the user to combine direct search, using content classes and properties, with navigation through the classification categories defined by the ontology. This approach follows the classic combination of searching and browsing in systems like Yahoo! and others (Hearst et al. 2002). In particular, users can restrict their search queries to selected classification categories. Furthermore, search results indicate the categories returned contents belong to, which allows the user to narrow or widen his search query to particular categories, or to browse the contents in the same category as returned contents.

The search module converts the information query conveyed by the user into an RDQL (Seaborne 2004) query, which is executed against the ontology and the knowledge base, yielding the set of RDF instances which match the query. These instances are presented to the user, who can view their detailed description. The visualisation of ontology instances is controlled by a visualisation module which is described next.

2.3.3 Ontology-based information visualization

Our platform includes a specialised module for the presentation of ontology instances (contents), i.e., for the visualisation of information units and for the navigation across units. This module is based on our early work on the Pegasus tool (Castells and Macías 2001).

The visualisation module dynamically generates Web pages from the description of ontology instances. How contents are visualised depends on the definition of the concepts they are instance of, which includes the definition of their properties and relations. Instead of hard-wiring this treatment in visualisation code, our platform allows defining the presentation of ontology concepts declaratively, using one or several visualisation models per concept.

The presentation model defined for each concept establishes the parts of an instance that have to be shown, in what order, and under what appearance. This model is defined with a fairly simple language which permits referencing and traversing the parts of the ontology the instance refers to. The presentation engine dynamically selects the appropriate view of the content depending on the concept the content is an instance of. The visualisation module also takes care of presenting on the same page other instances related to the content currently presented, or of generating hyperlinks to them in order to navigate across ontology relations.

The presentation language is based on JSP, with a library of custom tags which includes a) ontology access expressions, b) HTML / JavaScript primitives to display ontology constructs, and c) layout constructs. The presentation language also offers the possibility to express conditions on user profiles, the access device, the state of the application, or the characteristics of the information to be presented. These conditions can determine the choice of one or other presentation model for an instance, or at a more detailed level, establish the aspect of small parts of the presentation, the inclusion or not of certain information fragments, the generation of hyperlinks, or the selection of user interface components (lists, tables, trees, etc.).

Three presentation models have been defined: extended view, to show instances with maximum level of detail on a single page; summary view, to show lists of instances e.g. search results; and minimum view, to be used for example as the text of the link to an instance. Figure 3-3 shows an example of an extended view of an instance of the Fundamental Analysis concept.

User profiles have been defined, referring to the domain ontology created, to express preferences on specific categories or content classes. The user profiles defined include: a) professional profiles, and b) subscription profiles. The subscription profile defines access permissions to different parts of the ontology; when instances are visualised, only parts to which the user has been granted access will be shown. The professional profile defines a scale of interests for different categories and types of contents, which determines the order (priority) and amount of information that is presented to the user, depending on the typology and relevant subject areas for his profile.

Figure 3-3. Extended view of an instance of the "Fundamental Analysis" concept

2.3.4 Content managers

Precision in locating the right contents, and ease of navigation through them, are essential for authors who create, classify, maintain, or link contents. To this end, the content management system used at TIF has been adapted to incorporate the creation and management of contents in terms of the domain ontology defined, making use of the search and visualisation modules developed.

For the creation and edition of different types of contents, appropriate Web forms are automatically generated based on the definition of the content class in the domain ontology. These forms are dynamically generated in the same way search forms were: there is a default generation mechanism which takes into account the definition of the concept and the type of its properties to generate appropriate input controls, and custom forms can be defined for each content class. The main difference between content creation forms and search forms is that search forms will usually correspond to a partial view of the content class as defined by the searchable meta-property, i.e., not all class attributes are interesting for searching contents but, usually, all properties of a content have to be provided when the content is created. Similarly, the set of instance properties presented to end users is typically a superset of the properties which appear in a search form for this instance class, and a subset of all fields required by a content creation form.

2.4   Experience and results

The development of the platform presented in this section and its application to the management of economic and financial contents at TIF gave raise to an initial knowledge base of 180,831 instances and 2,705,827 statements. With this knowledge base, we have been able to evaluate the benefits achieved by adapting our content management system to make use of an explicit and formal domain model, exploiting some of the features of semantic technologies. In particular, the following improvements are achieved:

1. Definition of a completely explicit information model: the building of a completely explicit model has necessarily driven to a review of the existing model. Furthermore, both old and new systems and applications have now a clear and shared information model to follow, which can considerably ease information integration and sharing among internal applications. In general, the existence of an ontology serves as reference for communication (both among persons and computers) and helps to improve data quality based on a shared conceptualisation of the domain.
2. Improved search capabilities: by describing economic and financial contents in terms of a well-defined and formal domain model, we can:
   a) Automatically generate user interfaces for search from the concept definitions provided by the ontology.
   b) Apply standard inference mechanisms to obtain richer search results.
   c) Easily interleave structured search and browsing.

d) Declaratively and based on explicit models adapt search results to different user profiles and, in general, to the context of the search.

4. Improved visualisation: contents can be dynamically and following general procedures visualised according to the definition of concepts in the domain ontology. Furthermore, different visualisation modes can be dynamically selected based on declarative descriptions of user profiles.

5. Improved management of information: by exploiting the search and visualisation capabilities resulting from the use of a domain ontology, more efficient management of information can be achieved. Furthermore, the existence of a clear information model, evaluated by domain experts, helps manage contents better; contents are created, linked and maintained following an agreed and explicit model.

However, some problems have been encountered for the development of the platform, as well as some limitations:

1. Maintenance of the model: the maintenance and evolution of the model is a critical task and can become a bottleneck if it is not properly monitored.

2. Scope of the model: while the domain model has been defined to cover the contents created by TIF and by the group of companies it is part of, it is insufficient for the general exchange of information with other parties, as other parties might use a different (most likely syntactic and semi-explicit) model. Therefore, mediation mechanisms or the joint definition of an ontology by major actors in the market is required for easing the exchange of information between parties. Otherwise, the model defined can be exploited internally but its benefits are reduced when used for the exchange of information.

3. Creation of ontologies from scratch: the creation of an appropriate and *shared* domain model is a fundamental task for achieving the benefits semantic technologies can offer. However, we have detected a lack of existing models or, at least, of existing semantic models in the financial domain. This makes the definition of new models necessary, and reaching an agreement with other parties for the use of a shared model more difficult.

The ontology defined has served to generate and manage contents created by TIF. However, it does not cover the reception of information from other parties, its processing, and its possible delivery. In the next section, we discuss the definition of a model for the reception, integration, processing and delivery of information in the Spanish investment funds market. We focus on building a model to be used for the exchange of information across organisational boundaries and on the comparison of the XBRL language

(Engel et al. 2005), which is being widely adopted and promoted in the financial domain, to a semantic language such as OWL.

3.   SEMANTIC TECHNOLOGIES FOR INVESTMENT FUNDS MARKET

3.1   Description of the domain

The analysis of the investment funds market requires the availability of harmonised information on the considered funds, including both last-minute and historical data, which is usually generated and provisioned by different parties and in heterogeneous formats. Furthermore, added-value information such as risk-profitability ratios of commercialised funds is demanded by different customer profiles. For example, final investors demand this kind of information for supporting their investment decisions, so funds managers do in order to compare the evolution of their funds with respect to the general market behaviour.

Current mechanisms for the exchange of information among the different actors in the investment funds market (investment firms, management firms, stock markets, analysts, investors, market supervisors) are not based on uniform and explicit information models, hampering an agile exchange and requiring important efforts to process and integrate such information. Furthermore, a situation where the exchange and processing of information is time-consuming and error-prone leads to a reduction of market transparency.

In this context, the gathering and integration of information from disparate, heterogeneous sources becomes a key task that can be considerably eased by the availability of explicit and shared information models. Moreover, the analysis process leads to the generation of analytic, added-value information, the consumption of which by other parties can also benefit from the existence of agreed information models.

TIF, in conjunction with AFINet Global[22], is the leading provider of analytical information of investment funds in the Spanish market. For providing this service, TIF continuously receives and aggregates information from the national stock markets, from firms managing investment funds, and from the national market supervisor (the CNMV)[23], covering all the investment funds currently commercialised in Spain and counting with a 10-

---

[22] http://www.grupoanalistas.com
[23] http://www.cnmv.es

years historical base (over 6000 investment funds at the time of writing). The information received includes all the descriptive aspects of a fund when it starts to be commercialised (entity commercialising the fund, investment policy, commissions, etc.), changes on any of these aspects, and the Net Asset Value (NAV) of the fund at different points in time.

The different parties from which TIF receives and aggregates information currently use heterogeneous information models and formats. This makes the reception, validation, and aggregation of the information a difficult task, and requires ad-hoc validation procedures and a rather costly maintenance, as providers sometimes introduce changes on their information models and formats. In this setting, when heterogeneous information about a certain fund or group of funds is received, it has to be validated first (sometimes it has not been properly validated in origin) and transformed so that it follows a uniform information model. After that, the analytical indicators associated to these funds are (re)calculated and published via different channels, currently including XML syndication and direct access via a number of information portals[24].

The part of the investment funds information life-cycle relevant for TIF is depicted in Figure 3-4. Descriptive information about investment funds commercialised in the Spanish market is provided by the CNMV, and periodical information such as the NAV of a fund is provided by the national stock markets (Madrid, Barcelona, Bilbao and Valencia) and by the firms managing the funds. This information is validated, converted and aggregated, leading to the creation of an aggregated and consistent information base that is ready for analysis. The analysis process leads to analytical, added-value information which is consumed by agents such as management firms, sellers, or directly by investors.

A gain in efficiency in the life cycle of Figure 3-4 can be achieved if the validation and conversion process, instead of dealing with heterogeneous information, would receive information according to a shared model so that ad-hoc processing can be avoided and maintenance needs are reduced. Furthermore, if the analytical, added-value information produced also follows an agreed model, the consumption of such information by different agents can be considerably eased. The ontology for economic and financial information presented in the previous section covered all the contents generated by TIF, but not contents like investment funds information, aggregated from information received from other parties. Therefore, we have accomplished the definition of a domain model for this type of information.

---

[24] See http://www.invertia.com/fondos/default.asp for an example

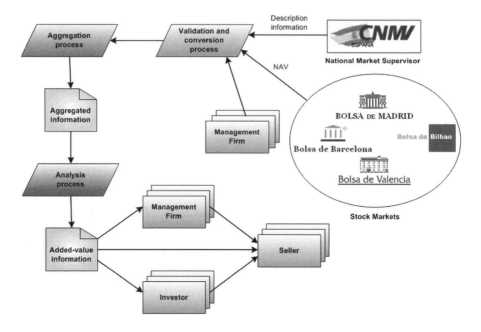

Figure 3-4. Investment funds information life cycle

The Spanish market supervisor (the CNMV) is considering the definition of XBRL (Engel et al. 2005) taxonomies for the descriptive and regulatory information on investment funds, which would have to be naturally adopted by all agents in the Spanish market. However, these models would not initially include analytical information. Furthermore, a semantic language such as OWL has not been considered so far as an alternative for defining shared information models for investment funds. In this setting, we have worked on: a) an XBRL taxonomy that includes not only descriptive but also analytical information of funds and that can serve as a basis for possible future developments led by the CNMV or for their extension, and b) on the evaluation of OWL as an alternative to XBRL. The reason for building an XBRL taxonomy first is that XBRL is being promoted as the language of choice for the modelling of financial information. However, it lacks one of the key features the Semantic Web has: information has formal semantics. Therefore, we evaluate in which way OWL ontologies and XBRL taxonomies are related, how XBRL taxonomies can be translated into OWL ontologies, and what benefits and limitations have OWL ontologies with respect to XBRL taxonomies.

3.2 Creation of a domain model based on XBRL

3.2.1 XBRL in a nutshell

XBRL is a language that builds on top of XML, XML Schema and XLink to provide users with a standard format in which information can be exchanged, enabling the automatic extraction of information by software applications (Engel et al. 2005). For that purpose, XBRL defines **taxonomies**, which provide the elements that will be used to describe information, and **instances**, which provide the real content of the elements defined. These are introduced below.

3.2.1.1 XBRL taxonomies
An XBRL taxonomy is constituted by an **XML Schema** and the **XLink linkbases** contained in or directly referenced by that schema. In XBRL terminology, the XML schema is known as the taxonomy schema.

Concepts describing reporting facts are exposed as XML Schema element definitions. A concept is given a *name* and a *type*. The type establishes the kind of data allowed for those facts described according to the concept definition. For example, the NAV concept of an investment fund would typically have a monetary type, declaring that when a NAV is reported, its value will be monetary. On the other hand, the legal name of the fund would usually have a string type so that, when it is reported in an XBRL instance, its value is interpreted as a string of characters. Besides these two attributes, additional constraints on how concepts can be used (e.g. instant/duration *period*, debit/credit *balance*) are documented by other XBRL attributes on the XML Schema element definitions.

Linkbases in a taxonomy provide further information about the meaning of the concepts by expressing relationships between concepts (inter-concept relationships) and by associating concepts to their documentation. Taxonomies make use of five different types of XLink linkbases, namely: definition linkbases, calculation linkbases, presentation linkbases, label linkbases and reference linkbases. The first three types contain different kinds of relations between elements, whereas the last two types contain documentation of elements.

Definition links describe relations among concepts in a taxonomy, such as generalisation and specialisation relations, that provide information on what an element actually is e.g. the specialisation of some other concept. Calculation linkbases provide information on how some elements are calculated in terms of some other elements, which can be exploited for data validation. Presentation linkbases contain relations such as parent-child that are exclusively used for presentation purposes e.g. a given element will be shown as the child of some other.

The last two types of links do not define relations among elements but document elements in a taxonomy. Label links provide labels in natural language with the purpose of facilitating the understanding of data by a human user. XBRL is equipped with multilingual support and enables the user to associate labels in different languages to the same element. Reference links point to legal or other type of documentation that explains the meaning of a given taxonomy element.

Usually, it is necessary to consider multiple related taxonomies together when interpreting an XBRL instance. The set of related taxonomy schemas and linkbases is called a Discoverable Taxonomy Set (DTS). The bounds of a DTS are determined by starting from some set of documents (instance, taxonomy schema, or linkbase) and following DTS discovery rules. Taxonomies are interconnected, extending and modifying each other in various ways.

3.2.1.2 XBRL instances

A taxonomy defines reporting concepts but does not contain the actual values of facts based on the defined concepts. These fact values are included in XBRL instances. The way XBRL organises the reporting information within a certain instance is based on two main elements: **XBRL items** and **XBRL tuples**.

- **XBRL items**. Defined as extensions of primitive data types (String, Integer, Boolean, etc.), XBRL items represent atomic information elements of an XBRL instance. Items can also reference XML Complex Types in the XBRL Instance Schema[25], or extensions of these types defined in existing taxonomies. In XBRL taxonomies, complex types are typically used to provide the set of possible values a data type can hold.
- **XBRL tuples**. In XBRL, a data model is built through tuples or blocks of information. While most business facts can be independently understood, some facts are dependent on each other and they must be grouped for a proper and/or complete understanding. For instance, in reporting the information of an investment fund, each deposit entity name has to be properly associated with a correct deposit entity identifier. Such sets of facts (deposit entity name, deposit entity identifier) are called tuples. Tuples have complex content and may contain both items and other tuples.

---

[25] http://www.xbrl.org/2003/xbrl-instance-2003-12-31.xsd

In addition to the actual values of a fact, such as "NAV is 50", XBRL instances provide contextual information necessary for interpreting such values e.g. "NAV is 50 today". Furthermore, for numeric facts, XBRL instances can also document measurement units e.g. "NAV is $50".

- **XBRL context elements**. Context elements include information about the entity being described, the reporting period and the reporting scenario (additional metadata taxonomy designers might want to associate to items), all of which are necessary for understanding a business fact captured as an XBRL item. The *period* element contains the instant or interval of time for reference by an item element. The sub-elements of the period element are used to construct one of the allowed choices for representing date intervals. For an item element with *periodType* attribute value equal to "instant", the period must contain an instant element that indicates the particular point in time in which the fact is valid. For an item element with the *periodType* attribute value set to "duration", the period must contain "forever" or a valid sequence of *startDate* and *endDate* elements, indicating the start and end points of the interval of time in which the value is valid.
- **XBRL unit elements**. Unit elements specify the units in which a numeric item has been measured. The content of a unit element must be either a simple unit of measure expressed with a single *measure* element, a ratio, or a product of units of measure. Some examples of simple units of measure are EUR (Euros), meters and kilograms. Some examples of complex units of measures are Earnings per Share or Square Feet.

3.2.2 Description of the XBRL taxonomy of investment funds

The lack of explicit and shared models for exchanging information in the investment funds market and the promotion and increasing adoption of XBRL by Spanish regulators and supervisors, e.g. Bank of Spain and CNMV, led us to consider XBRL as an interesting language for creating an explicit information model for the Spanish funds market and to create a taxonomy of investment funds.

For building this taxonomy we started by evaluating and reviewing the information model used by TIF and AFINet Global in order to define a revised model that could meet the needs of different agents in the market. For that purpose, we counted on the cooperation of Analistas Financieros Internacionales[26], a leading company in the analysis of the Spanish financial

---

[26] http://www.afi.es

market, and Gestifonsa[27], a firm that manages a number of funds commercialised in Spain.

The resulting model, agreed and approved by all parties, has been described using XBRL. For that purpose, the possible reuse of existing XBRL taxonomies was evaluated. In particular, the IPP[28] taxonomy from CNMV, the DGI[29] taxonomy, and the ES-BE-FS[30] taxonomy from Bank of Spain were evaluated. The result of the evaluation has been that parts of the DGI taxonomy can be reused for the description of certain elements of the investment funds information model, especially those elements describing the entities that commercialise or manage a given fund. Figure 3-5 shows the DTS of the taxonomy built, where *dgi-lc-es-2005-03-10.xsd* contains the information elements of the imported DGI taxonomy in Spanish and its respective linkbases, and *dgi-lc-int-2005-03-10.xsd* contains the international elements of the DGI taxonomy.

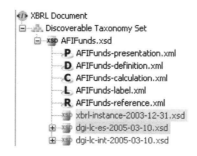

Figure 3-5. DTS of the investment funds taxonomy

The information elements of the created taxonomy have been divided into the following groups:

- **Descriptive information**: models all the descriptive aspects of a fund, such as the name of the fund, the entity managing the fund, the data relative to the registration by the CNMV, etc.
- **Relevant facts information**: models relevant facts about a given fund, such as changes in its investment policy. They allow for keeping historical track of the relevant changes of the fund.

---

[27] http://www.cajacaminos.es/
[28] http://www.xbrl.org.es/informacion/ipp.html
[29] http://www.xbrl.org.es/informacion/dgi.html
[30] http://www.xbrl.org.es/informacion/es_be_fs.html

- **Periodic descriptive values**: model descriptive information that is periodically updated, such as the NAV of the fund or the number of investors that own some shares of the fund.
- **Analytic information**: models the analytic values associated to a fund, such as performance measures, the rating of the fund in its category, its ranking, or different types of ratios (volatility, risk-profitability relation, etc).

The reason for identifying these four distinct groups of information (being the root of each group an XBRL tuple) is that the information they contain has a different nature, the sources providing the information are different, and the periodicity with which each group of information is produced is diverse. Besides the information elements created, the following linkbases have been defined:

- **Presentation linkbase** (*AFIFunds-presentation.xml* in Figure 3-5) defines how the information elements are presented. An extended link has been created for each of the information groups, and a parent-child hierarchy has been defined for the presentation of the elements of each of the groups.
- **Label linkbase** (*AFIFunds-label.xml* in Figure 3-5) defines labels for each information element. Only labels in Spanish have been defined so far, as the taxonomy is intended to be used in the Spanish market.
- **Calculation linkbase** (*AFIFunds-calculation.xml* in Figure 3-5) only links to validate that the percentage of the different types of assets sums up a 100% have been created. As it will be explained in the next subsection, other links could not been defined as the current version of XBRL does not provide enough expressivity for it.
- **Reference linkbase** (*AFIFunds-reference.xml* in Figure 3-5) associates references to information elements, providing a detailed explanation of their meaning.
- **Definition links** have not been used because: a) the use of links of type *requires-child* is not recommended in (Hamscher 2005), b) there are no equivalent elements in the taxonomy, so links of type *essence-alias* have not been used, c) no use was found for links of type *general-special*, and d) there are no similar tuples for which a link of type *similar-tuples* makes sense.

The last version of the taxonomy can be found at http://www.tifbrewery.com/tifBrewery/resources/XBRLTaxonomies.zip.

3.2.3 Limitations of calculation links

XBRL provides calculation links that allow for the description of the mathematical relation between different (numerical) information items. However, the current version of the XBRL specification has some important limitations in what can be expressed by such links.

First, the investment funds taxonomy should include validations that involve the evaluation of information items in different contexts. For example, we want to validate that a given NAV is not more than a 15% higher or lower than the previous NAV known for that fund. That requires expressing some mathematical relation between the same information element e.g. NAV at different points in time given by XBRL contexts. However, the current XBRL specification does not allow for this kind of validation, and calculation links are defined between information items independently of their context.

Second, XBRL calculation links only allow for the summation of items. However, there are some analytical values whose calculation from descriptive values is much more complex, involving the use of a wider range of mathematical operators. This is the case of, for example, the calculation of most of the performance measures used.

Future versions of XBRL are expected to overcome these limitations, and the requirements for future formula linkbases that extend the current calculation linkbases are already an XBRL candidate recommendation (Hamscher 2005).

3.3   Translating XBRL taxonomies into OWL ontologies

OWL is a potential alternative to the use of XBRL which presents some features that are of practical interest in the investment funds market. For this reason, we have developed a generic translation process from XBRL taxonomies to OWL ontologies so that existing and future taxonomies can be easily converted into OWL ontologies with the purpose of exploring the advantages of models with formal semantics with respect to XBRL taxonomies. In this section, we present the translation process designed and a discussion on the advantages and disadvantages of using OWL.

3.3.1 Description of the translation process

XBRL taxonomies provide explicit and shared information models and, thus, they are very similar to ontologies except that they do not have a formal semantics for all the aspects of the model. Similarly, XBRL instances can be seen as ontology instances and expressed as such. Therefore, we have designed a translation process of XBRL taxonomies into OWL ontologies, and of XBRL instances into OWL instances. In the following, we will restrict ourselves to the translation of taxonomies into ontologies.

An automatic translator has been implemented based on the process that will be presented. It has been tested by translated not only our funds taxonomy but also other XBRL taxonomies available at the International[31] and Spanish[32] XBRL official Web pages. Specifically, DGI, IFRS-GP[33], ES-BE-FS and IPP taxonomies have been translated. The last version of the obtained ontologies can be found at http://www.tifbrewery.com/tifBrewery/resources/OWLOntologiesv2.zip.

In Figure 3-6 we show the architecture of the translator. As XBRL is an XML[34] based technology, the first step in the translation process is to parse the XML elements. Using JDOM[35], the XML parsing module obtains the XML elements in the XBRL taxonomies, instances, and links to be translated. The translation steps that will be described below are then applied to the obtained elements, resulting in a Jena[36] model that provides us with a programmatic environment to OWL. The model, corresponding to the OWL ontologies and instances derived from the XBRL taxonomy and instances, is finally saved to text files.

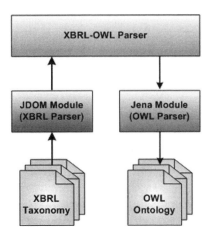

Figure 3-6. Syntactic translator architecture

[31] http://www.xbrl.org
[32] http://www.xbrl.org.es
[33] http://xbrl.iasb.org/int/fr/ifrs/gp/2005-05-15
[34] http://www.w3c.org/XML
[35] http://www.jdom.org
[36] http://jena.sourceforge.net

The different types of XBRL elements, the hierarchy and relationships between elements within a common taxonomy, and the relationships among several taxonomies will establish their order of translation in our proposal. In the following we describe the steps involved in the automatic translations, which are summarised in Table 3-1. For the sake of simplicity, we will reference the DGI taxonomy in the explanations. The transformation process for other taxonomies follows the same structure.

Table 3-1. Summary of parsed taxonomy element translations

Parsed taxonomy element	Root OWL class	Direct OWL subclasses
XML complex type	DGI_ComplexType	A subclass for each complex type
XBRL tuples	DGI_Element	DGI_Tuple
XBRL items		DGI_Item
XLink links	DGI_Link	DGI_LabelLink
		DGI_PresentationLink
		DGI_CalculationLink
XBRL contexts	Context (the ranges of its properties are subclasses of ContextElement)	Subclasses of ContextElement: ContextEntity ContextEntityElement (Identifier) ContextPeriod ContextScenario
XBRL units	Unit (the ranges of its properties are subclasses of UnitElement)	Subclasses of UnitElement: UnitMeasure

1. **Declaration of a root OWL class Element** from which complex (tuples) and simple (items) information parts of the taxonomy will inherit, named DGI_Element for the DGI taxonomy. This class has associated a property *xbrl_id*, corresponding to the XBRL attribute *id* common to all XBRL elements.

2. **Declaration of DGI_Tuple and DGI_Item, subclasses of DGI Element**. XBRL tuples and items correspond to OWL subclasses of DGI_Tuple and DGI_Item, respectively. The attributes of XBRL Item are translated into the OWL properties: *xbrl_balance*, with possible values "credit" and "debit"; *xbrl_periodType*, with possible values "instant" and "duration"; *xbrl_contextRef*, whose range is the OWL class Context (step 11); and *xbrl_unitRef*, whose range is the OWL class Unit (step 12).

3. **Declaration of a root OWL class DGI ComplexType**. XML complex types are translated into subclasses of DGI_ComplexType, having OWL properties: *xml_name* to store the name of the complex type,

xbrl_periodType, with possible values "instant" and "duration", and *xbrl_contextRef*, whose range is the Context class.

4. **Syntactic translation of XML complex types into OWL subclasses of DGI_ComplexType**. The names of the obtained subclasses are those stored in the XML attribute *name* of the complex type elements. Each subclass of DGI_ComplexType has a property whose name is the concatenation of the complex type name and the word "value", and whose type is the primitive data type associated to the complex type (xsd:string, xsd:integer, xsd:boolean, etc.). Additionally, they contain those properties defined in the primitive XBRL data types (xbri:stringItemType, xbrli:integerItemType, xbrli:booleanItemType, etc.). For example, in the DGI taxonomy, the class AddressFormatCodeItemType has the property *length* with a fixed value of 2, indicating that the possible values of the data type can only have 2 characters.

5. **Syntactic translation of XBRL Items into OWL subclasses of DGI_Item**. The names of the obtained subclasses are those stored in the XML attribute *name* of the item elements. Each subclass of DGI_Item has a property for storing the value of the item, and whose range is the type of the XBRL Item.

6. **Record XBRL Tuples as OWL subclasses of DGI_Tuple**. Initially, the classes are created empty, and their properties are added in step 7. The reason is that tuple properties will reference other tuples, which might be not yet created and which will have to exist in the OWL model that is being built.

7. **Syntactic translation of the XBRL tuple attributes into OWL object properties**. The attributes of the tuples are added to the subclasses of DGI_Tuple as OWL object properties. These properties will have as range a class associated to a complex type of step 4, a class created in step 5 or a class recorded in step 6.

8. **Declaration of a root OWL class DGI_Link**. Its instances, which correspond to the XLink links of the XBRL taxonomies, contain the properties: *xlink_from*, created for the translation of the XLink attribute *from*, stores the origin element of the link; *xlink_to*, created for the translation of the XLink attribute *to*, indicates the destination element of the link; *xlink_role*, created for the translation of the XLink attribute *role*, indicates the role assigned to the link: "label", "calculation", "presentation", etc.

9. **Declaration of OWL subclasses of DGI_Link**. Subclasses of DGI_Link are built for each type of link: DGI_LabelLink, DGI_PresentationLink, DGI_CalculationLink, DGI_ReferenceLink, and DGI_DefinitionLinks.

10. **Syntactic translation of XBRL linkbases into instances of the corresponding subclasses of DGI_Link**. Links in XBRL linkbases are translated into OWL instances of the different subclasses of DGI_Link (for reasons of space, only the translation of label, presentation and calculation linkbases is presented):

- Label links are translated into OWL instances of DGI_LabelLink. In addition to the common link properties (*from*, *to*, *role*), label links have properties: *xbrl_label*, obtained from the translation of the XBRL attribute *label* and used to store the text of the label, and *xml_lang*, obtained from the translation of the XML attribute *lang* and used to indicate the language of the label.

- Presentation links are translated into instances of DGI_PresentationLink. Besides common link properties, presentation links have properties: *xbrl_order*, from the translation of the attribute *order* and used to store the relative position of the destination element within the presentation of the origin element, and *xbrl_preferedLabel*, obtained from the translation of *preferedLabel*.

- Calculation links are translated into OWL instances of DGI_CalculationLink. Additionally to common link properties, calculation links have properties: *xbrl_order*, obtained from the translation of the XBRL attribute order and used to store the relative position of the destination element value within the calculation of the origin element value, and *xbrl_weight*, obtained from the translation of the XBRL attribute weight and used to store the weight of the destination value within the calculation of the origin element value.

11. **Syntactic translation of XBRL contextRef elements**. In order to translate XBRL contexts, a new ontology has been created, which will be imported by the ontologies resulting from the translation of XBRL taxonomies. This ontology contains a main class Context. The Context class has the following properties: a) *xbrl_id*, of type xsd:ID, for the translation of the XBRL attribute *id* to identify each context, b) *xbrl_entity*, of type ContextEntity, defined for the translation of *entity*, c) *xbrl_period*, of type ContextPeriod, defined for the translation of *period*, and d) *xbrl_scenario*, of type OWL Thing, and defined for the translation of *scenario*. Other classes such as ContextEntityElement, ContextPeriod (with subclasses ContextForeverPeriod, ContextInstantPeriod, and ContextStartEndPeriod), and ContextScenario are defined corresponding to the types of values that define an XBRL context.

12. **Syntactic translation of XBRL unitRef elements**. For the translation of units defined in an XBRL taxonomy, an independent OWL ontology has been created. This ontology will be imported by ontologies resulting from the translation process. Its main class is Unit, which has a property

xbrl_unitMeasure of type UnitMeasure and whose content is the definition of the associated unit. The UnitMeasure class, used to define the units added in a given context, does not have properties. Its subclasses distinguish the different types of units:

- **Divide** for units defined by means of a ratio (with properties *xbrl_unitNumerator* and *xbrl_unitDenominator*).
- **Measure** for simple units (with property *xbrl_measure*).

As mentioned before, besides the order of steps presented above, the hierarchy and relationships between elements within a taxonomy, and the relationships among different taxonomies, will define their translation order.

3.4 Comparison

The translation process presented in the previous sections helps to identify similarities and differences between XBRL taxonomies and OWL ontologies, which are described below.

1. *XBRL items and tuples*. There is a natural correspondence between XBRL items, and tuples and OWL classes. While XBRL items correspond to classes that only have one value (besides information such as the period, context, etc.), XBRL tuples correspond to classes with object properties that store the constituent parts of the tuple. In this sense, XBRL items and tuples can be naturally represented by OWL classes.
2. *XBRL contexts and units*. An important feature of XBRL is the possibility of associating contexts and units to XBRL elements. This can also be done in OWL by creating ontologies for contexts and units, as presented in the previous subsection, and by including appropriate object properties in OWL classes representing XBRL items and tuples. Therefore, we conclude that this type of information can be easily ontologically represented.
3. *Reference and label links*. Reference and label links can be represented in OWL by creating appropriate classes and instances, as it has be done by our translation process. Notice that these links are intended for documentation purposes, and no formal semantics is associated to them. Furthermore, no application of a possible formal semantics for this type of links envisioned.
4. *Definition links*. Definition links can be represented by creating instances of the classes introduced in the previous subsection. Special attention deserves the representation of *general-special* definition links which, even though they are currently translated into instances of definition link classes, naturally correspond to subclass relations in ontologies.

However, existing taxonomies e.g. IPP, DGI, or IFRS-GP hardly make use of general-special definition links. A reason for this is that this type of links is not exploited by current XBRL tools to infer additional information, as this kind of relation does not currently have a formal semantics. We believe that the formalisation of subclass relations can be of interest in practical applications, and that general-special definition links could be given formal semantics by using OWL.

5. *Calculation links.* Calculation links can be represented in the way outlined in the previous section. However, these links have a formal, mathematical semantics in XBRL, while in OWL this semantics is not supported. Therefore, we believe that for OWL ontologies to be adopted in the financial domain in general and in the investment funds market in particular, where mathematical relations are highly relevant for data validation, linking OWL to some form of mathematical support would be required.

6. *Presentation links.* Presentation links can be represented as described by our translation process. However, OWL tools should exploit this presentation information for data visualisation. Therefore, visualisation tools should be adapted to take into account presentation information, not currently available in OWL.

7. *Open-World Assumption (OWA) vs. Closed-World Assumption (CWA).* The semantics of OWL is based on classical First-Order Logic, FOL (Fitting 1996), and the OWA is made, i.e., information is not assumed to be false if it cannot be proven to be true. However, in an industrial setting the CWA is widely made e.g. in relational databases. In fact, XBRL users are expected to intuitively make the CWA when, for example, querying for particular information of an investment fund. Due to his background, an average user would most likely see natural a "no" answer to the question "Is the investment fund *myFund* classified in category *myCategory*?" if, according to the available information, the investment fund is not classified under this category. Locally closing the world using an epistemic operator for OWL could be a solution to this problem (Donini et al. 1998; Heflin et al. 2002). In addition, OWL does not define constraints but restrictions, as explained in (de Brujin et al. 2005b). However, for validation purposes we believe that the use of constraints, and not of restrictions, is required.

Summarising, the major advantage we see from the use of OWL is its formal semantics, which can be exploited for the automatic classification of funds if general-special relations are used and represented as OWL subclass (or subsumption) relations. As implicit subsumption relations can be automatically inferred using Description Logics reasoners (Nardi et al.

2003), customers or analysts can e.g. formally define the characteristics of funds they are interested in and appropriate funds will automatically and precisely be found. In particular, we are investigating the application of formal semantics to personalisation in the reception of information in the investment funds market and to the automated classification of funds. For this purpose, we can analyse subsumption relations present in current taxonomies but not explicitly declared. However, the Open-World semantics of OWL and the use of restrictions instead of constraints can hamper the use of OWL for querying investment funds information and for validating information reported.

Extensions of OWL to incorporate and automatically validate mathematical relations in the style of XBRL should be built, and current OWL tools should incorporate presentation information in ontologies so that they can be visualised according to different presentation specifications.

Other alternative languages for the formal description of investment funds can be considered, like the WSML family of languages (de Brujin et al. 2005a), which provides a basic interoperability layer and extensions in the direction of Description Logics and in the direction of Logic Programming.

4.   CONCLUSIONS

Semantic Web technologies promise an improvement in how information is currently described, managed, integrated, searched and exchanged based on the definition of explicit, shared and formal models of a given domain. The financial domain, in which information is complex and valuable, and where big volumes of information are daily exchanged, can naturally benefit from the use of explicit domain models, shared by all actors in different financial markets, and for which standard inference mechanisms can be applied for e.g. improve search results or better adapt information to investor profiles.

We have presented in this chapter the results of two investigations we have conducted: the development of an ontology-based platform for enhancing current practices in the management of economic and financial information, and the definition of a domain model for the investment funds market. These investigations have demonstrated some of the benefits of using semantic technologies, which are not exclusive for the financial domain but of which businesses in different fields can take advantage of.

While semantic technologies offer improvements in different aspects of information integration, management and exchange, these improvements are not possible without the definition of a shared and explicit model. However, the task of building such a model is challenging, especially if the model is meant to be shared beyond organisational boundaries to improve information exchange and (data) interoperability with external systems.

In fact, the biggest benefit of a semantic approach to information management is the construction of a model shared and agreed by all actors in the market. In this sense, models not necessarily semantic such as XBRL taxonomies being developed in finance are a valuable outcome; bringing commercial banks, financial institutions, central banks and other actors together to define shared models, as the XBRL community is doing, is good news for the achievement of an improvement in current information management and exchange practices. In fact, XBRL is being promoted by public institutions such as the Committee of European Banking Supervisors (CEBS)[37], which includes high level representatives from the banking supervisors and central banks of the European Union. CEBS has promoted the creation of working groups that have the mission of defining XBRL taxonomies to be later adapted and used for the financial reporting that banks and other institutions have to submit periodically to the banking supervisors.

While the models created by the XBRL community lack formal semantics, they possibly reflect the most difficult think to achieve when using semantic technologies: building a model most parties in a business domain can agree upon. Translation processes from non-semantic models to formal ontologies, such as the one we have presented in this chapter, become crucial in this context, as we can *ontologise* agreed models (Hepp et al 2006) and, thus, apply semantic search, visualisation, etc. to these models.

We can see, by following the activities of the XBRL community, how the awareness of the need of explicit and agreed domain models is dramatically increasing in the financial domain. This can ease the uptake, in the near future, of semantic technologies in finance. However, there are some barriers for such uptake, mainly:

1. the formal semantics of current languages such as OWL is not straightforward neither for business users in finance nor for IT staff; especially, the Open World Assumption made by the OWL language, while reasonable in the context of an open and distributed source of information like the Web, it is a bit unnatural in a more closed context like financial markets,
2. tool support and expertise in semantic technologies by IT developers is still not sufficient,
3. the Semantic Web community has not paid so far enough attention to the achievements of other communities, especially of the XBRL community, in building shared models; while the languages used by these

---

[37] www.c-ebs.org

communities are different, they share the goal of building explicit models enabling a better processing of information,

4. semantic languages such as OWL have been designed as general purpose languages, i.e., as languages to cover the description of any possible domain. However, domain-specific extensions are required in the financial domain, such as the support of complex calculation relations.

In a nutshell, companies and other institutions in the financial domain, as well as customers, can benefit from the advantages of using semantic technologies, namely: a better processing, management, search, visualisation and exchange of information. However, for such benefits to be achieved, and for semantic technologies to be widely adopted in the financial field, the problems discussed above have to be overcome.

5. QUESTIONS FOR DISCUSSION

Beginner:

1. Why are current content management systems not semantic?
2. How would you currently find e.g. an investment fund or a mortgage meeting your needs? How could this search be improved if firms commercialising these products would describe them using an ontology?
3. What kind of information does your company (or school/university/institution) manage? Is there an explicit model of this information which can be (or is) communicated to users? What kind of language is used to represent it?

Intermediate:

1. What are the differences and similarities between an XML Schema, an XBRL taxonomy, and an OWL ontology?
2. How do tagging, taxonomies, ontologies and Semantic Web relate? What role can these different concepts/technologies play in improving e.g. the search of a loan meeting certain requirements? And in improving the exchange of information?
3. What initiatives exist for improving regulatory reporting to central banks by using shared, explicit models? How can these initiatives be extended beyond regulatory reporting and semi-formal models? TIP: visit www.xbrl.org.

Advanced:

1. What type of applications/domains can benefit from the Open World Assumption (OWA) made by languages such as OWL? And from the

Closed World Assumption (CWA)? Is the OWA or the CWA made by XBRL?

2. Do you think banks and investment firms will be willing to semantically annotate their products and make these descriptions publicly available? What reasons would they have for and against this initiative? How would you convince these institutions to follow this initiative? Are intermediate solutions possible?

3. How would you extend OWL to incorporate XBRL calculation links?

Practical exercises:

1. Imagine you are a financial analyst who wants to launch a new Web-based service to guide users on where to invest their money depending on their profile (especially on how much risk they are willing to assume and for how long they are willing to put their money in some investment instrument):

    a) Find sites and companies who supply information about different investment products (investment funds, pension plans, stock markets, deposits, etc.)

    b) Analyse how you can integrate information from all these sources in order to have a complete knowledge base of investment products you can use for your investment recommendations to users.

    c) Describe how your integration approach would react to changes in the structure of the information provided by one of your sources.

    d) Describe how would you model and manage user profiles, and how you would match them against product descriptions.

    e) Analyse how the definition of a model of investment products shared by all your information sources would improve your new service and its profitability.

    f) Define a simple ontology of investment products.

    g) Think of applications of the formal semantics of your ontology to improve your investment recommendation service.

6.   SUGGESTED ADDITIONAL READING

*   Alexiev, V., Breu, M., de Bruijn, J., Fensel, D., Lara, R. and Lausen, H. (2005). *Information Integration with Ontologies: Experiences from an Industrial Showcase*, Wiley, 2005. This book describes the application of semantic technologies in the automotive industry, including the annotation of information, the modelling of the domain, and the benefits achieved by the use of semantic technologies.

- Singh, M. P. (2004). *The Practical Handbook of Internet Computing*, Chapman & Hall/CRC, 2004. The third part of this book is devoted to different information management techniques, giving a good overview of different approaches, including the use of formal semantics.

7.   REFERENCES

Alexiev, V., Breu, M., de Bruijn, J., Fensel, D., Lara, R. and Lausen, H. (2005). Information Integration with Ontologies: Experiences from an Industrial Showcase. Wiley, 2005.

Bechhofer, S., Harmelen, F. V., Hendler, J., Horrocks, I., McGuinness, D. L., Patel-Schneider, P. F. and Stein, L. A. (2004). OWL Web Ontology Language Reference. Technical report, W3C\ recommendation. http://www.w3.org/TR/2004/REC-owl-ref-20040210.

Berners-Lee, T., Handler, J., Lassila, O. (2001). The Semantic Web, Scientific American, **64**(5):34-43.

Brickley, D. and Guha, R. V. (2004). RDF Vocabulary Description Language 1.0: RDF Schema. W3C Recommendation, 10 February 2004.

de Brujin, J., Lausen, H., Krummenacher, R., Pollers, A., Predoiu, L., Kifer, M. and Fensel, D. (2005a). The Web Service Modelling Language WSML. Technical report, WSML, 2005.

de Bruijn, J., Polleres, A., Lara, R. and Fensel, D. (2005b). OWL DL vs. OWL Flight: Conceptual Modelling and Reasoning for the semantic Web. In Proceedings of the 14th World Wide Web Conference (WWW 2005), Tokyo, Japan, May 2005.

Castells, P. and Macías J. A. (2001). An Adaptive Hypermedia Presentation Modelling System for Custom Knowledge Representations. World Conference on the WWW and Internet (Web-Net'2001). Orlando, 2001.

Castells, P., Foncillas, B. and Lara, R. (2004). Semantic Web Technologies for Economic and Financial Information Management. In Proceedings of the 1st European Semantic Web Symposium (ESWS 2004), Heraklion, Greece, May 2004.

Ding, Y. and Fensel, D.: Ontology Library Systems (2001). The key to successful Ontology Re-Use. In Proceedings of the 1st Semantic Web Working Symposium (SWWS 2001). California, USA, July 2001.

Donini, F. M., Lenzerini, M., Nardi, D., Nutt, W. and Schaerf, A. (1998). An Epistemic Operator for Description Logics. Artificial Intelligence, **100**(1-2):225-274.

Engel, P., Hamscher, W., Shuetrim, G., Kannon, D. V. and Wallis, H. (2005). XBRL eXtensible Business Reporting Language. Technical report, XBRL International recommendation. http://www.xbrl.org/Specification/XBRL-RECOMMENDATION-2003-12-31+Corrected-Errata-2005-11-07.htm.

Fast, K., Leise, F. and Steckel, M. (2002). What Is A Controlled Vocabulary? Boxes and Arrows, December 2002.

Fitting, M. (1996). First Order Logic and Automated Theorem Proving. Springer Verlag, 2nd edition, 1996.

Green, S. L., Delvin, S. J., Cannata, P. E. and Gómez, L. M. (1990). No Ifs, ANDs or Ors: A study of database querying. International Journal of Man-Machine Studies, 32 (3), pp. 303-326, 1990.

Gruber, T. (1993). A Translation Approach to Portable Ontology Specifications. Knowledge Acquisition, **5**(2):199-220.

Hamscher, W., Shuetrim, G. and Kannon, D. V. (2005). XBRL Formula Requirements. Technical report, XBRL International candidate recommendation. http://www.xbrl.org/technical/requirements/Formula-Req-CR-2005-06-21.htm.

Hearst, M. (1999). User Interfaces and Visualization. In Modern Information Retrieval. Addison-Wesley, pp.257-323, 1999.

Hearst, M., Elliott, A., English, J., Sinha, R., Swearingen, K. and Yee K. (2002). Finding the Flow in Web Site Search, Communications of the ACM, 45 (9), September 2002.

Heflin, J. and Muñoz-Ávila, H. (2002). LCW-based Agent Planning for the Semantic Web. In Proceedings of the AAAI Workshop on Ontologies and the Semantic Web, Palo Alto, CA, USA, July 2002.

Hepp, M., Lytras, M. D., and Benjamins, V. R. (2006). Preface for OIS 2006. In: John F. Roddick et al.: Advances in Conceptual Modelling - Theory and Practice, ER 2006 Workshops. Springer Verlag LNCS 4231, 2006, pp. 269-270.

Lara, R., Cantador, I. and Castells, P. (2006). XBRL Taxonomies and OWL Ontologies for Investment Funds. In the 1st International Workshop on Ontologizing Industrial Standards at the 25th International Conference on Conceptual Modelling (ER2006), Tucson, AZ, USA, November 2006.

Nardi, D., Baader, F., Calvanese, D., McGuinness, D. L. and Patel-Schneider, P. F. (eds.). (2003). The Description Logic Handbook. Cambridge, 2003.

Seaborne, A. (2004). RDQL - A Query Language for RDF. W3C Member Submission, 9 January 2004.

Chapter 4

INTELLIGENT SEARCH ENGINE FOR ONLINE ACCESS TO MUNICIPAL SERVICES

Jose Manuel Gómez-Pérez[1], Richard Benjamins[1], Mercedes Blázquez[1], Jesús Contreras[1], María Jesús Fernández[2], Diego Patón[1] and Luis Rodrigo[1]

[1]iSOCO, Pedro de Valdivia 10, Madrid, Spain – {jmgomez, rbenjamins, mblazquez, jcontreras, dpaton,lrodrigo}@isoco.com

[2]City Government of Zaragoza, Plaza de Ntra. Señora del Pilar nº18, 50071 Zaragoza, Spain – mjferuiz@zaragoza.es

1. INTRODUCTION

Since some years, most Spanish local city governments offer their citizens the possibility to access and execute government services such as for changing ones address, obtaining a permit for reconstruction of ones house or for disposing of large furniture. As of 2006, citizens have the possibility to perform 80 % of the city government services from their homes. However, when a citizen is looking for a particular service, it turns out not so easy to find the appropriate service in the website of the City. First of all, many city website simply enumerate the available services in a list organized by categories. In case there are 500 or 1000 services (see UK's Local Government Service List) to choose from, it may be hard to find the right one. Other city websites offer a traditional search engine that retrieves services based on co-occurrence of words in the query and the description of the services. However, the language used by Public Administrations is not always the same as the way citizens refer to services, and there may be many ways to ask for the same thing. For instance, when a citizen wants to throw a way an old washing machine, it needs to know that the government service is called "special collections for large items".

In order to stimulate the uptake of eGovernment (eEurope 2005, Liikanen 2005, Hagen et al. 2000, Tarabanis et al. 2002, Tambouris et al. 2004) it is therefore very important to make access to online services as easy as possible. Disappointed citizens are not likely to return to their local municipality website for other services and information.

We have applied emerging Semantic Web technology to improve citizens' access to online services. Two important improvements concern:

- City governments should not force citizens to learn their jargon
- When citizens look for a particular service, it is useful to find also related services (e.g. if I change home address, I may want to apply this change also to my car).

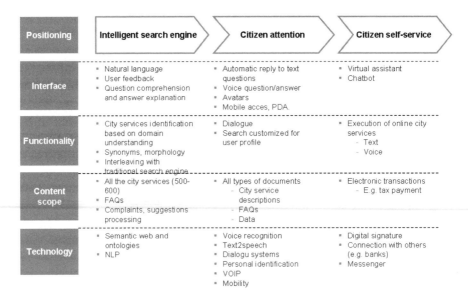

Figure 4-1. From attention to citizens to citizen self-service

Figure 4-1 shows our roadmap towards automation of city government service offering to citizens. The stage that we are currently aiming is related with the intensive use of intelligent search engines where Semantic Web and NLP technology are used to detect services that the user needs information about. This stage is still intertwined with interaction with traditional search engines. The next step, attention to citizens, introduces mobility and voice interfaces in order to facilitate user interaction. Avatars are used to increase user-friendliness of the system. Finally, not only would services be recognized by the user utterance but also, execution of these services would be possible. Thus, interaction with third parties like e.g. banks would also be necessary. This chapter describes the work done towards implementing the first stage of this roadmap.

As shown in Figure 4-2, the city of Zaragoza is pioneer in the adoption of this initiative, being a reference for the Spanish municipalities in this regard. In fact, it has been selected as the most innovative city government for the second consecutive year (2005-06) by the Spanish renowned national newspaper El País (El País 2006).

Figure 4-2. Intelligent search engine deployed in the city of Zaragoza

The following figures reflect the different ways in which Semantic Web technology is applied in order to match citizen needs with services. In this case, the application consisted of an online answer service for Frequently Asked Questions (FAQ) in the legal domain (Benjamins et al. 2003).

The first approach (see Figure 4-3) is based on a statistical recount of occurrences of all relevant concepts of the user question among different conceptualizations of the domain, i.e. ontologies (Gruber 1993, Guarino 1995, Borst 1997, van Heijst 1997). In the second approach (Figure 4-4), the user question is word-like tokenized and the system tries to match each token with the description of the available online city services. Different types of matching (exact, synonymy and morphological) are used. As a result, a narrower list of candidate FAQ items is supplied. Although this might seem similar to other standard searching systems using keywords or metadata, here the difference lies in the use of morphological parsing of the user question that discards non-relevant words, and the use of synonymy and morphology for matching.

Finally, Figure 4-5 represents a scenario in which semantic distance (Casellas et al. 2005) is applied in order to relate how semantically close the meaning of the user expression is to the description of a service (or in the example, a FAQ). Grammatical patterns are detected in the user request, in terms of the ontology which describes the domain, to build a graph path or trace connecting the different concepts present in the question. The system matches this graph against smaller graphs each representing one the target services. Such graphs are calculated offline in a previous stage.

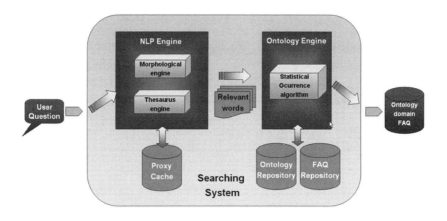

Figure 4-3. Statistical approach to interpretation of citizen request

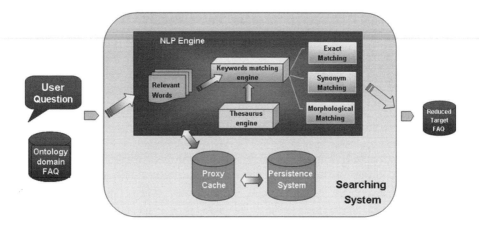

Figure 4-4. Enhanced keyword-based approach to interpretation of citizen request

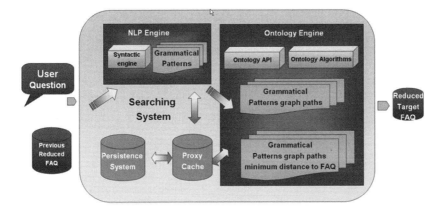

Figure 4-5. Applying semantic distance to interpreting citizen request

All these approaches can be combined, and in fact they are, exploiting their benefits and reducing the effects of their disadvantages. For example, the first approach is the least powerful but it is also the one which consumes less resources. On the contrary, the third approach is very powerful but costly. Applications like the one deployed in the city of Zaragoza arrange them following a pipe architecture where each stage, from less to more resource consuming, is triggered only when the previous stages did not return satisfactory results.

2. HOW DOES IT WORK?

In contrast to traditional search engines that retrieve documents based on occurrences of keywords, our product has some understanding of online services. It knows for instance that persons can change address, car owners need to pay taxes, certain business may cause hinder (such as bars and discotheques), and that there are different kinds of reconstruction works each requiring different permits. All this information is stored in a so-called ontology (described in next section): a computer-understandable description of what e-government services are. This ontology allows our product to "understand" what citizens ask and return the relevant services. In addition, it returns related services to the one requested. Apart from the ontology, our product uses natural language understanding software to translate free text queries of citizens into the ontology.

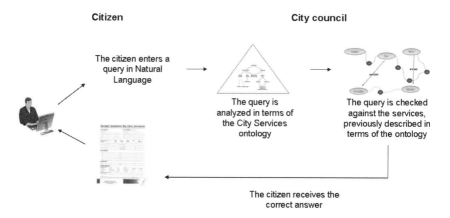

Figure 4-6. Citizen-city government interaction

Figure 4-6 shows the overall interaction between citizen and city government, which takes place when a given user asks the system, by means of a free text question, about a particular service provided by the municipality. In this workflow, the next three components are key. The domain ontology provides vocabulary for the description of city services which Knowledge Tagger (KT), a Natural Language Processing (NLP) system, uses to analyze user utterance. KT classifies the terms contained within as occurrences of ontology terms. Finally, the Semantic Distance component checks these terms against others, previously stored, which describe the services supported by the system. The three of them will be described in more detail in following sections.

This process allows answering questions to citizens which standard search engines can not satisfy with the same level of accuracy, providing uniform access to data or service information. Table 4-1 and Table 4-2 compare the approach described in this chapter with that represented by standard search engines. In general, the intelligent search engine is able to "understand" questions expressed in a richer language as standard search engines do. This allows providing answers which are much more precise with respect to the questions formulated by the user, hence offering a higher level satisfaction.

Table 4-1. Characteristics of traditional search engines

Characteristics	Examples
- Search for keywords or complete text - Result is a ranked list of documents - Limitations: false positives - Users need to invest time and effort to filter the right piece of information out of the overall results	- "residence change" - "visit city guided"

Table 4-2. Characteristics of the intelligent search engine

Characteristics	Examples
- Search for keywords, complete text, lemmas, synonyms, semantic concepts, related concepts - Real-time detection of relevant words - Result is not a list of documents but the actual data whose relevance is explained in terms of the question. - Language dependent and bound to the domain of application - Perceived as a search engine which "understands" the user - Tradeoff between question understanding and performance	- "I'm moving. What do I need to do?" - "What guided tours are available in this city?"

3. THE CITY GOVERNMENT SERVICE ONTOLOGY

The development of the ontology started with a detailed study of the services that the city government offers to the citizens of Zaragoza. The objective of this study is to extract all the relevant terms that belong to this domain which, given the diversity of the terms that can be found in the textual description of a service, is considerably large. This ontology contains four main classes, described as follows:

Table 4-3. Taxonomy of the city government Service ontology

Agent participating in an action

Process: A series of actions that a citizen can do using the on line services offered by the city government.

Event: Any social gathering or activity.

Object: Any entity that exists in the city, which can be used for or by a service offered by the city government.

Our approach uses this ontology to establish the semantic similarity between a question provided by a citizen and a city government service usually offered to the citizen as a Frequently Asked Question (FAQ). Hence, the ontology needs to be complete in order to contain all the necessary terms to satisfy this kind of requests.

This ontology is complemented with a number of thesauri that allow us to refer a term in different ways by means of synonymy relations. For example, the ontology term *baby* can be complemented with the thesaurus entity *infant*, i.e. in practice, whenever a user requires information regarding any of these terms the system will consider all possibilities related with the term *baby* described in the ontology. For the sake of completeness, Figure 4-7 shows a sample of the instances contained in the ontology.

Figure 4-7. Instances in the City Services Ontology

An important issue to deal with is ambiguity. For example, in Spanish, the term *casar* can be interpreted as the act of marrying or as a type of building. If a citizen asks the system: *qué debo hacer para casarme en el ayuntamiento?* i.e. *what must I do to get married in the city hall?,* the system will recognize the terms *casar* and *ayuntamiento* because they belong to the ontology and might use both interpretations of *casar* to build a reply. Context information can be used to avoid this kind of ambiguity.

4. NATURAL LANGUAGE PROCESSING FOR ONLINE CITY SERVICES

The innards of the search engine consist of a series of technology and algorithms among which Knowledge Tagger (KT), which automatically annotates text according to a domain ontology (see Figure 4-8), has a prominent role. It relies on a series of linguistic analyzers, ranging from simple tokenizers or sentence splitters to more complex spell checkers or morphological databases. As a result, it provides a list of all the references it can find in the text to elements of the ontology, including classes, attributes and instances, taking into account the input text as well as their lemmas, spelling corrections and synonyms. KT is built upon the Gate architecture (Cunningham et al. 1995).

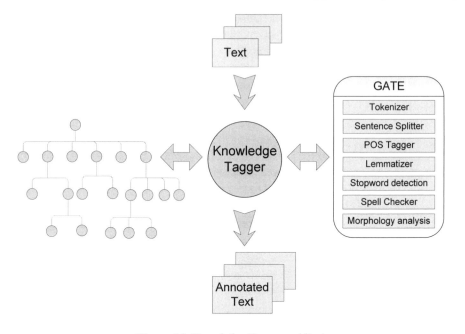

Figure 4-8. Knowledge Tagger architecture

The annotated text obtained from KT can be used in various applications. Figure 4-9 shows one of them. In this case, the KT2queries component receives the elements that KT could identify in the input text (that should be a natural language question about a city service, in this context). From this set of independent elements, it calculates the shortest path in the ontology that connects all the annotations. Once a connected sub-graph has been found, it can be translated to a query language (W3C 2006), to retrieve from the ontology the answer to the question posed by the user. This same scenario will be described more in detail further in the chapter.

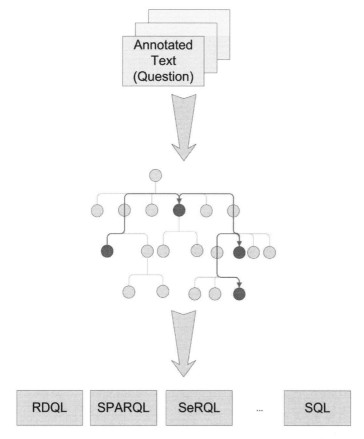

Figure 4-9. Query synthesis in terms of a domain ontology

5.   SEMANTIC ANNOTATION OF CITY SERVICES

As described above, user requests on information about city services need that information on services themselves be acquired in a preliminary stage in order to allow their semantic descriptions to be checked against these queries. This pre-processing is described in Figure 4-10, comprising four different stages:

1. The description of the original city service is fetched, and the relevant terms, according to the ontology and the existing thesauri are identified.
2. These terms go through the next stage, a morphosyntactic analysis, which provides information about the linguistic category of the identified terms, i.e. whether they are verbs, nouns, singular, plural, etc.

3. This information is semantically processed and, as a result, a number of semantic graphs are produced. Their nodes are the ontology entities (concepts, instances, attributes, and relations) identified in the previous stage and the edges represent proximity relations between them, defined by the ontology. For example, an ontology concept detected in the service description will appear in one of these semantic graphs as a node with edges which relate it with all its attributes, relations and instances appearing in the service description.

4. As output of the overall process, services are semantically described and ready to be checked against citizen requests for information.

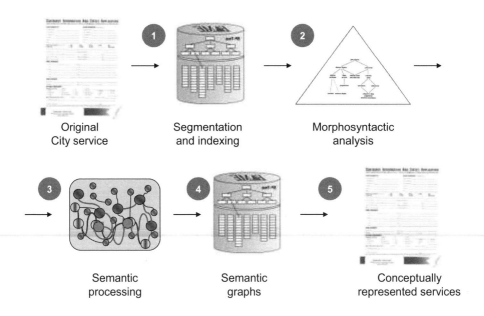

Figure 4-10. Semantic annotation of city government services

Among the problems typically found during this process it is relatively frequent that municipalities do not count with comprehensive descriptions of the online services that they offer to citizens. In other occasions, these descriptions are expressed in a technical language which largely differs from the language used by the average citizen. This has to be corrected by applying richer thesauri. On the other hand, in these situations it is harder to reflect the domain in the ontologies which are the basis of this approach. Hence, more iterations with domain experts, usually representatives from the city municipalities, are required for a complete formalization of the domain.

6.   SEMANTICALLY-ENABLED SEARCH OF CITY SERVICES

Users type questions about city services which need to be automatically confronted with the highest degree of accuracy, determined by standard measures for search engines, i.e. precision and recall, against the service descriptions managed by the system. The application of advanced techniques allows our system to achieve a precision degree of 98%, while recall is up to 80%.

Several searching and score algorithms have been designed to achieve this goal. They can be applied consecutively in a multistage. Several non-functional considerations have been taken into account during system design:

- Exhaustive search can be very time consuming.
- Multistage searching system lets the system stop when the city service target set has been reduced considerably. Therefore not all stages are exhausted and the computational cost is reduced and adapted to search features.
- Besides, multistage searching allows configuring the system to show the best score results before completing all available searching stages, so users can decide to accept the result or continue with the remaining search stages.

The matching stages mentioned above can be described as follows:

- **Ontology domain detection stage**. The main purpose of this stage is to determine the domain of the target service set, based on user question analysis, for use at a later stage. A complete service database is made up over existing service repositories as building blocks. Reducing the target is the first consideration to take into account, so the first search stage focuses on it. This goal is achieved by a statistical recount of occurrences of all relevant concepts of the user question in the ontology.
- **Keyword matching stage**. At this stage, the user question is word-like tokenized and system tries to match each token with each service description token. Both exact and synonymy matching are used. As a result of this stage, a narrower list of candidate service items is supplied. This might seem similar to other standard searching systems using keywords or metadata. Here, the difference lies on the use of morphological parsing of the user question that discards non-relevant words and the use of synonymy.

- **Ontology concept graph path matching stage**. This is the most time consuming stage, and therefore it is left to the final stage, when the service target database has already been very reduced by previous searching stages. At this stage, grammatical patterns will be detected from user question. Then, these patterns are searched in the ontology to build a graph path or trace. Finally, the system tries to match this user question ontology graph path with a reduced service target subset graph paths previously calculated in the background using some semantic distance algorithms.

Next, we show some examples of questions satisfied by the intelligent search engine deployed in the city of Zaragoza.

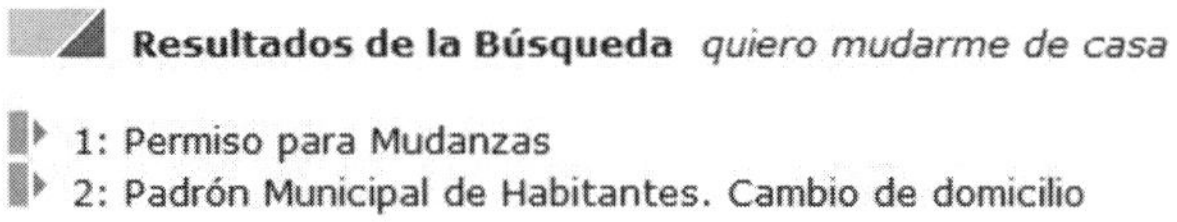

Resultados de la Búsqueda *quiero mudarme de casa*

▮▶ 1: Permiso para Mudanzas
▮▶ 2: Padrón Municipal de Habitantes. Cambio de domicilio

Figure 4-11. Sample question 1: I want to change my residence

In the first consult, a user expresses interest about the city procedures related with a change of residence. Note that the language in which the question is formulated is informal, certainly far from the technical language used in official public administration documents. In this case, the relevant terms of the question with respect to the ontology and the thesauri are *mudarme* as a synonym of *mudar*, i.e. to move, and *casa (house*, in English*)*. As a reply, the system identifies two services focused on how to obtain permission from the city to actually move and the steps necessary to take in order to update the new postal address in the city registry, respectively.

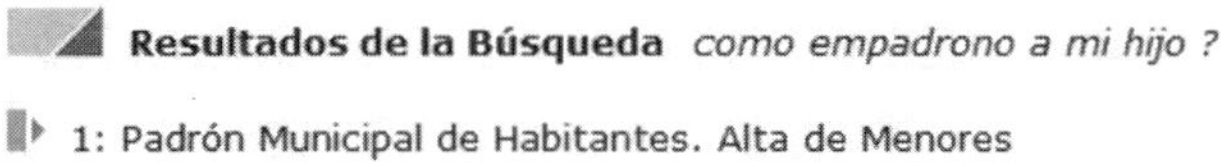

Resultados de la Búsqueda *como empadrono a mi hijo ?*

▮▶ 1: Padrón Municipal de Habitantes. Alta de Menores

Figure 4-12. Sample question 2: How can I register my baby in the city records?

The second sample consult refers to the registry of a newborn into the city records. The relevant terms are *empadrono*, as a synonym of *padrón*, i.e. *census*, and *hijo*, as a synonym of *menor de edad*, i.e. a person who is not yet of age. In this case the system reply is extremely precise, as the question used very specific terms, consisting of a single city service.

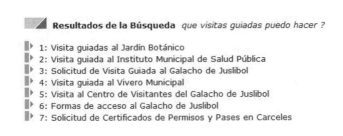

Resultados de la Búsqueda *perros peligrosos*

▌▶ 1: Licencia para Tenencia de Perros Potencialmente Peligrosos
▌▶ 2: Tramite de salud publica. Campaña de Vacunación Antirrábica para Perros (en Barrios Rurales), 2005
▌▶ 3: Campaña de Vacunación Antirrábica para Perros (en Barrios Rurales), 2005
▌▶ 4: Alta en el Censo Canino Municipal
▌▶ 5: Baja en el Censo Canino Municipal
▌▶ 6: Inscripción en el Registro de Perros Potencialmente Peligrosos
▌▶ 7: Recogida de perros, gatos y demás animales abandonados
▌▶ 8: Trámite por pérdida o rotura de chapa identificativa del perro en el Censo Canino Municipal

Figure 4-13. Sample question 3: dangerous dogs

The third consult aims at obtaining all the information about city procedures dealing with dangerous dogs. The relevant terms are *perro* (dog) and *peligroso* (dangerous). The system reply contains all the city procedures and services related with dangerous dogs. Note that the results are ordered by their relevance with respect to the user query.

Resultados de la Búsqueda *que visitas guiadas puedo hacer ?*

▌▶ 1: Visita guiadas al Jardín Botánico
▌▶ 2: Visita guiada al Instituto Municipal de Salud Pública
▌▶ 3: Solicitud de Visita Guiada al Galacho de Juslibol
▌▶ 4: Visita guiada al Vívero Municipal
▌▶ 5: Visita al Centro de Visitantes del Galacho de Juslibol
▌▶ 6: Formas de acceso al Galacho de Juslibol
▌▶ 7: Solicitud de Certificados de Permisos y Pases en Carceles

Figure 4-14. Sample question 4: What guided visits are available?

The last example shows a question about the guided visits offered by the municipality of Zaragoza. The list of results includes all the procedures and services related with visits, ranging from museums to prisons.

7.   SYSTEM ARCHITECTURE

Scalability, efficiency and memory issues have led to a distributed architecture with different components in order to support user search request. The main building blocks of this architecture are the following:

- One or more components for NLP processing.

- One or more components for Ontology processing.
- One component to gather user requests as a main dispatcher.

All components exhibit their services by means of web services public interfaces. All connections between components are compliant with this assumption. This allows improving system efficiency in terms of global memory and processing to fit itself to increasing demand of services. It is important to note that NLP and especially ontology processing tend to be very memory consuming processes. The architecture is described in Figure 4-15.

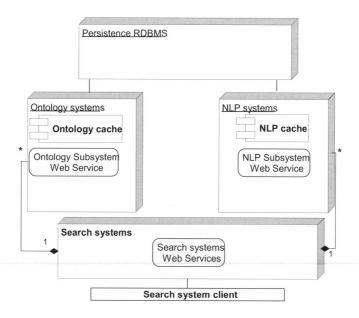

Figure 4-15. Overall system architecture

This distributed architecture allows decoupling the user interface from the system core and straightforward exploitation in Application Service Provider (ASP) mode. The application provider cares for the maintenance of the system resources for the different municipalities which contract the service. This allows one-time maintenance of common resources like the ontology or the underlying NLP technology. Additionally, city governments are released from the tedious need of applying software patches whenever updates are necessary as happens in more traditional business models. This is the business model that the next generation Web 2.0 is aiming for.

8.   CONCLUSIONS

The intelligent search engine, based on intensive use of Semantic Web technology (Ontologies, NLP, etc), increases machine understanding of the queries of a citizen in terms of relevant concepts for online services provided by city governments. This understanding enables it to significantly improve performance and coverage, of traditional search technology.

Even though our product understands to some extent what citizens ask, it is important to notice that this is *not* the same as *human* understanding. We – persons- have an infinite amount of background and common sense knowledge that we bring to bear when understanding questions from other people. Our product has to do it with "just" an ontology representing eGovernment services (Adams 2002). Moreover, the system has to understand correctly the query typed by the citizen, which in itself is a hard problem; natural language software and specific synonym lists are therefore important.

The objective of the system is to offer a concrete solution for city governments whose aim is to stimulate wider uptake of online services. However, on top of already available ontologies, it is possible to provide intelligent access to other content than online services with little additional effort. As a final remark, the problem of retrieving content is not limited to public administrations. Any organization where interaction with final customers (or internal users) abounds, and where customer satisfaction is critical, could significantly benefit from this technology modulo the construction of appropriate ontological resources. iSOCO has experience in taking this technology to sectors such as the legal domain, culture, finances, news, cultural heritage and international relations (geo-politics).

9.   QUESTIONS FOR DISCUSSION

Beginner:
1. Why does the search provided by the intelligent search engine have higher quality results as conventional search engines like Google or Yahoo!?
2. What is the roadmap towards automation of citizen service offering?

Intermediate:
1. What are the different stages into which semantic search is structured?
2. Why is it convenient to structure search into such pipeline?

Advanced:
1. What are the advantages and disadvantages of the intelligent search engine?

10.   SUGGESTED ADDITIONAL READING

- V. Richard Benjamins, Pompeu Casanovas, Joost Breuker, Aldo Gangemi (Eds.): Law and the Semantic Web: Legal Ontologies, Methodologies, Legal Information Retrieval, and Applications. This book is the outcome of the Workshop on Legal Ontologies and Web-Based Legal Information Management.

11.   ACKNOWLEDGEMENTS

This work is partially funded by EU-IST projects 2003-506826 SEKT and 2002-507967 HOPS.

12.   REFERENCES

Casellas, N.; Blázquez, M.; Kiryakov, A.; Casanovas, P.; Benjamins, V.R. (2005). "OPJK into PROTON: legal domain ontology integration into an upper-level ontology". R. Meersman et al. (Eds.): *OTM Workshops 2005*, LNCS 3762. Springer-Verlag Berlin Heidelberg, pp. 846-855.

V. Richard Benjamins, Pompeu Casanovas, Joost Breuker, Aldo Gangemi (Eds.): Law and the Semantic Web: Legal Ontologies, Methodologies, Legal Information Retrieval, and Applications [outcome of the Workshop on Legal Ontologies and Web-Based Legal Information Management, June 28, 2003, Edinburgh, UK & International Seminar on Law and the Semantic Web, November 20-21, 2003, Barcelona, Spain]. 3369 2005, ISBN 3-540-25063-8.

T. R. Gruber. A translation approach to portable ontology specifications. Knowledge Acquisition, 5:199–220, 1993.

N. Guarino. Formal ontology, conceptual analysis and knowledge representation. International Journal of Human-Computer Studies, 43(5/6):625–640, 1995. Special issue on The Role of Formal Ontology in the Information Technology.

W. N. Borst. Construction of Engineering Ontologies. PhD thesis, University of Twente, 1997.

G. van Heijst, et al. Using explicit ontologies in KBS development. International Journal of Human-Computer Studies, 46(2/3):183–292, 1997.

W3C SPARQL Query Language for RDF http://www.w3.org/TR/rdf-sparql-query/ 2006.

El País. "Todos los grandes ayuntamientos tienen web". http://www.elpais.com/articulo/portada/Todos/grandes/ayuntamientos/tienen/web/elpcibpo r/20060713elpcibpor_1/Tes

Cunningham, H., Wilks, Y., Gaizauskas, R.J. "GATE-a General Architecture for Text Engineering", Technical Report CS-95-21, Sheffield, UK, 1995.

European Commission, eEurope 2005 Action Plan. Available at http://europa.eu.int/ information_society/eeurope/2005/all_about/action_plan/index_en.htm

"e-Gov and the European Union" Speech by Mr Erkki Liikanen (Member of the European Commission, responsible for Enterprise and the Information Society) at the Internet and the City Conference "Local eGovernment in the Information Society" Barcelona - 21 March 2003.

Hagen M., Kubicek H. (editors), "One-Stop-Government in Europe: Results of 11 national surveys", University of Bremen, Bremen, Available at http://infosoc2.informatik.unibremen.de/egovernment/cost/one-stop-government/home.html, 2000.

Tarabanis K. and Peristeras V. "Requirements for Transparent Public Services Provision amongst Public Administrations", in EGOV 2002, LNCS 2456, pp. 330-337, 2002.

Tambouris E. and Wimmer M. "Online one-stop government: a single point of access to public". Chapter of the book Digital Government: Strategies and Implementations in Developed and Developing Countries, which has been scheduled to be published by Idea Publishing Group, USA in 2004 (ed. Dr. Wayne Huang).

Adams N. et al. "Towards an Ontology for Electronic Transaction Services", Proceedings of ES 2002, Cambridge, UK, December 2002.

PART III – HEALTHCARE AND LIFE SCIENCES

Chapter 5

ONTOLOGY-BASED DATA INTEGRATION FOR BIOMEDICAL RESEARCH

Vipul Kashyap[1], Kei-Hoi Cheung[2], Donald Doherty[3], Matthias Samwald[4], M. Scott Marshall[5], Joanne Luciano[6], Susie Stephens[7], Ivan Herman[8] and Raymond Hookway[9]

[1]*Partners Healthcare System, Clinical Informatics R&D, 93 Worcester St, Suite 201, Welleley, MA, USA – vkashyap1@partners.org*
[2]*Yale Center for Medical Informatics, Yale University School of Medicine, 300 George Street, Suite 501, New Haven, CT, USA – kei.cheung@yale.edu*
[3]*Brainstage Research, 5001 Baum Blvd, Suite 725, Pittsburgh, PA,USA – donald.doherty@brainstage.com*
[4]*Medical Expert and Knowledge Based Systems, Medical University of Vienna,Spitalgasse 23 A-1090, Vienna, Austria – matthias.samwald@meduniwien.ac.at*
[5]*University of Amsterdam, Kruislaan 403, 1098 SJ, Amsterdam, The Netherlands – marshall@science.uva.nl*
[6]*Department of Genetics, Harvard Medical School, NRB Room 238, 77 Louis Pasteur Ave, Boston, MA 02115, USA – jluciano@gmail.com*
[7]*Oracle Corporation, 10 Van de Graaf Drive, Burlington, MA, USA – susie.stephens@gmail.com*
[8]*World Wide Web Consortium (W3C),c/o Centrum voor Wiskunde en Informatica, Kruislaan 413, 1098 SJ, Amsterdam, The Netherlands – ivan@w3.org*
[9]*Hewlett Packard, Marlborough, USA.*

1. INTRODUCTION

The healthcare and life sciences sector is playing host to a battery of innovations triggered by the sequencing of the human genome as well as genomes of other organisms. A significant area of innovative activity is that of translational medicine which aims to improve the communication between basic and clinical science so that more diagnostic and therapeutic insights may be derived. Translational research (Translational Medicine

2007) goes from bench to bedside, where the effectiveness of results from preclinical research are tested on patients, and from bedside to bench, where information obtained from patients can be used to refine our understanding of the biological principles underpinning the heterogeneity of human disease.

A large extent of the ability for biomedical researchers and healthcare practitioners to work together – exchanging ideas, information and knowledge across organizational, governance, socio-cultural, political and national boundaries – is currently mediated by the internet and its exponentially-increasing digital resources. These digital resources embody scientific literature, experimental data, and curated annotation (metadata) whether human- or machine-generated. This is the digital part of the scientific "information ecosystem" (Davenport and Prusak 1997). Its structure, despite the revolution of the web, continues to reflect a degree of domain hyper-specialization, lack of schematization, and schema mismatch, which works against information transfer.

The key requirement is to enable organization of knowledge on the web by its meaning, purpose and context of use; and to effectively bridge and map meanings across specialist domains of discourse. We want the expression of this meaning to be digital, machine readable, capable of being filtered, aggregated and transformed automatically. We want it to be seamlessly embedded in the structure of web documents. And we would like to provide built-in visibility of information change – provenance – and explanation. In sum, we would like to make the context of information – which is established by both use and meaning - available with information content.

Modern biomedical science produces vast amounts of data that is produced by practitioners and researchers in finely subdivided sub-specialties. It is common for biologists in different sub-specialties to be completely unaware of the key literature in each other's domain. Yet, particularly in applying research to curing and preventing diseases - the bench to bedside transition - an integrated understanding across sub-specialties becomes essential. In complex diseases this is a difficult task, inadequately supported by the current information ecology of science. This difficulty applies with the most force to highly controversial and rapidly evolving areas of research, such as the understanding and cure of neurodegenerative diseases (Parkinson's Disease (PD), Alzheimer's Disease (AD), Huntington's disease, Amyotrophic Lateral Sclerosis (ALS) or Lou Gehrig's disease, and others).

As an example, AD affects four million people in the United States and causes both great suffering and enormous costs to society. Yet there is still no agreement on exactly how it is caused, or where best to intervene to treat it or prevent it. The Alzheimer Research Forum records fifty significant hypotheses related to aspects of the etiology of AD, most of them combining supporting data and interpretations from multiple specialist areas of biomedicine. One typical recent hypothesis on the etiology of AD (Lesne' et. al. 2006) combines data from research in mouse genetics, cell biology, animal neuropsychology, protein biochemistry, neuropathology, and other areas.

Many areas of biomedical research including drug discovery, systems biology, and personalized medicine rely heavily on integrating and interpreting data sets produced by different experimental methods, in different groups, with heterogeneous data formats, and at different levels of granularity. Research in other neurodegenerative disorders such as PD, the second most common neurodegenerative disorder, is also quite frequently multimodal, and like AD research often includes interpretations based on clinical phenotype data collected from different patient populations.

There is a need for a synthesis of understandings across disciplines, and across the continuum from basic research to clinical applications. This applies to most complex diseases and too many healthcare issues. A useful synthesis must combine not only data, but also interpretations of the data. It must support both, the well-structured standardized presentation of data as well as the discovery and fusion of convergent and divergent interpretations of data. With advances in hardware instrumentation and data acquisition technologies (e.g., high-throughput genotyping, DNA micro arrays, and mass spectrometry), there is an exponential growth of healthcare as well as life science data. In addition, the results of these experimental approaches are typically stored in heterogeneous formats in disparate data repositories. Over time, it has become increasingly difficult to identify and integrate these data sources. Even if we assume that the data is stored in the same format, the complex nature of healthcare and life science data makes deep domain knowledge a prerequisite to understand and integrate the data in a meaningful way. The problem is becoming more acute, both due to continuing increases in data volumes and the growing diversity in types and formats of data that need to be interpreted and integrated.

In this chapter, we illustrate by the means of a real world use case based on PD, how ontologies can be used to enable data integration and information synthesis across various data repositories belonging to various biomedical research areas. We begin with a brief description of the disease and an illustrative query example in Section 2. This is followed by a discussion on development of domain ontologies to characterize information and knowledge about the disease in Section 5. A discussion of the data sources is presented in Section 6 including a discussion of pragmatic issues related to data integration in Section 4.3. Conclusions and future work are presented in Section 5.

2.   USE CASE: PARKINSON'S DISEASE

The neuroscience domain provides a rich and diverse set of scientific studies (involving both biomedical and clinical research) with associated datasets. In this section, we present a use case pertaining to PD, which is the focus of research and activity of a broad collection of neuroscience researchers, practitioners and neurologists. The use case provides an example to illustrate how semantic web technologies can potentially be used to enable the bench-to-bedside vision and support the ability to cross-link, aggregate and interpret the information across various perspectives (Parkinsons Use Case 2007). In this chapter, we will focus on the systems physiology, cell and molecular biology perspectives on PD.

2.1   Systems physiology perspective

A scientist researching PD from a systems physiology perspective wants to know the structures (anatomy) involved in the disease and the ways those structures interact (physiology) or fail to interact resulting in the disease state. For instance, it is well known that brain cells that cluster together to form a brain structure known as the substantia nigra degenerate and die in PD patients. These particular brain cells, or neurons, contain a chemical substance called dopamine. Neurons in the substantia nigra communicate with other neurons in other brain structures through the transmission of dopamine. Neurons that are able to listen and respond to signals from dopamine containing neurons must have dopamine receptors. A scientist interested in a systems physiology perspective knows that there are fewer dopamine containing neurons in a PD patient's brain than normal so they may reasonably ask if the neurons in the brain that receive dopamine may have something to do with disease related behaviors. The scientist may ask a semantic web enabled search engine "what neurons in the brain have dopamine receptors and what anatomical structure do they belong to?"

   A part of the substantia nigra is composed of neurons that transmit the chemical dopamine. It's when these dopamine transmitting neurons in the substantia nigra die, that the amount of dopamine released into another part of the basal ganglia known as the striatum decreases and PD symptoms appear. The striatum connects to a third part of the basal ganglia known as the pallidum. In fact, there are two distinct connections that form parallel anatomical pathways from the striatum to the pallidum. One connection is known as the direct pathway and the other the indirect pathway. Each pathway is activated in a different way by the dopamine released from the substantia nigra. Activating the direct pathway facilitates movement, for instance moving your arm or legs. In contrast, activating the indirect pathway inhibits movement. At the systems physiology level it is the balance of activity between the indirect and direct pathways from the striatum to the pallidum that at one extreme leads to PD (over-activity in the indirect pathway results in over-inhibited movement in the D1 receptor) and at the other extreme leads to Huntington's disease (over-activity in the direct pathway results in too much movement in the D2 receptor).

2.2   Cellular and molecular biology perspective

Studies identifying genes involved with PD are rapidly outpacing the cell biological studies that would reveal how these gene products are part of the disease process. The alpha synuclein and Parkin genes are two such examples. The discovery that genetic mutations in the alpha synuclein gene could cause PD has opened new avenues of research in PD. When it was also discovered that synuclein was a major component of Lewy bodies, the pathological hallmark of PD in the brain, it became clear that synuclein may be important in the pathogenesis of sporadic as well as rare cases of PD.

More recently, further evidence for the intrinsic involvement of synuclein in PD pathogenesis was shown by the finding that the synuclein gene may be duplicated or triplicated in familiar PD, suggesting that simple over expression of the wild type protein is sufficient to cause disease. Since the discovery of synuclein, studies of genetic linkages, specific genes, and their associated coded proteins are ongoing for PD research - transforming what had once been thought of as a purely environmental disease into one of the most complex multigenetic diseases of the brain. Studies of genetic linkages, specific genes, and their associated coded proteins are ongoing for PD research. Mutations in the Parkin gene cause early onset PD, and the Parkin protein has been identified as an E3 ligase, suggesting a role for the proteasomal pathway of protein degradation in PD. DJ-1 and PINK-1 are proteins related to mitochondrial function in neurons, providing an interesting genetic parallel to mitochondrial toxin studies that suggest disruptions in cellular energetics and oxidative metabolism are primarily responsible for PD.

Other genes, such as UCHL-1, tau, and the glucocerebrosidase gene, may be genetic risk factors, and their potential role in the sporadic PD population remains unknown. Mutations in LRRK2, which encodes for a protein called dardarin, is the most recently discovered genetic cause of PD, and LRRK2 mutations are likely to be the largest cause of familial PD identified thus far.

Dardarin is a large complex protein, which has a variety of structural moieties that could be participating in more than a dozen different cellular pathways in neurons. As the cellular pathways that lead to PD is not fully understood, it is currently unknown, how, or if, any of these pathways intersect in Parkinson's disease pathogenesis.

2.3   Example query

Based on the current research in PD, a neuroscience researcher or practitioner might be interested in asking a query, such as the following:

> *Show me the neuronal components of receptors that bind to a ligand which is a therapeutic agent in {Parkinson's, Huntington's} disease in reach of the dopaminergic neurons in the {pars compacta, pars reticularis} substantia nigra.*

The above query can be visualized in the context of a biomedical researcher trying to propose and validate (or invalidate) research hypotheses. Hypothesis validation involves either trying to conduct bench experiments or re-use existing scientific results available on the web. These results are typically available in the form of scientific publications through a widely available repository such as PubMed. In the context of this project, we seek to demonstrate the value of structured scientific facts describing experiments, hypotheses, etc. Consider the following use case scenarios where the above query might be submitted to the semantic web:

- A researcher interested in anatomy/physiology trying to hypothesize the location of various components on a neuron might want to look at scientific data or hypotheses on the presence of certain type of receptors on a neuron.
- A researcher interested in molecular biology trying to hypothesize the location of some receptors on neurons might want to look at scientific data or hypotheses on the anatomical structure of a neuron or the pharmacology of chemical compounds that bind to a receptor.
- A clinical researcher interested in developing new therapies for a disease may be interested in understanding the mechanisms of how chemical compounds or ligands bind to receptors.

Common to these scenarios is the ability of a researcher to access information from different knowledge domains and correlate it with data and information from his or her information domain. This can form the basis for various decision making activities such as forming new hypotheses or validating old ones.

The information query discussed above, requires the synthesis and integration of data and data interpretations across the following specializations in biomedical research:

- Anatomy/Physiology relating to the compartments of neurons
- Molecular Biology relating to the receptors on neurons
- Pharmacology relating to chemical compounds that bind to receptors.
- Clinical information relating to ligands that are associated with a disease.

Ontologies and semantic web technologies play a critical role in enabling the synthesis and integration of data and data interpretations. The key role played by ontologies is that they provide a common language to express the shared semantics and consensus knowledge developed in a domain. This shared semantics is typically captured in the form of various domain specific ontologies and classifications such as MeSH, GO and the Enzyme Commission. Ontological concepts provide the shared semantics to which various data objects and data interpretations can be mapped to enabling integration across multiple biomedical data sources and domains. We now discuss issues related to creation and modeling of ontologies.

3. ONTOLOGIES

In this section, we present our approach to creating a domain ontology that provides the basis for data integration. The design and creation of the domain ontology is based on the description of the use case and the sample query presented in the previous section. Different modeling alternatives and choices that emerged when creating the ontology are presented; and issues relating to re-use of pre-existing ontologies are also discussed.

3.1 Ontology design and construction

Various ontology creation methodologies have been proposed in (Cardoso and Sheth 2006, Matteo and Cuel 2005). Most of them have primarily focused on the manual processes of interaction between subject matter experts and ontologists. We propose a methodology for iterative creation of ontologies based on available resources such as textual descriptions of subject matter knowledge; information needs and queries of the users; and cross-linking to pre-existing ontologies whenever there is a need for more extensive coverage. Our approach complements the approach adopted in (Kashyap 1999), where the ontology creation process is driven by the underlying database schemas. It may be noted that in the semantic web scenario; a large number of web repositories contain semi-structured (e.g., XML-based) data and typically their underlying schemas are not available. A brief illustration of the ontology design process is illustrated in Figure 5-1.

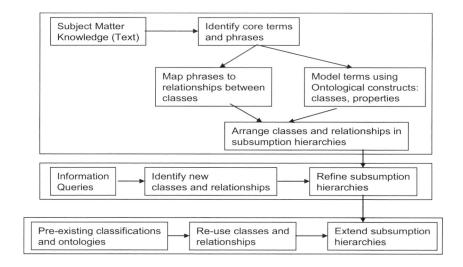

Figure 5-1. Ontology Design and Creation Approach

We begin by looking at the textual description of the PD use case descriptions and (manually) extracting the key concepts that relate to the disease. For pragmatic reasons, we decided to focus on creating ontology specifically for the use case and then expanding it later as information needs and usage becomes clearer. We will also cross-link to pre-existing ontologies wherever there is a need for more extensive coverage instead of "re-inventing the wheel".

3.1.1 Identifying concepts and subsumption hierarchies

The first step in designing the PD ontology was to characterize the core vocabulary in terms of the classes and the subsumption hierarchy that describes the information related to the use case. Consider the following textual description:

*Studies identifying **genes** involved with **PD** are rapidly outpacing the cell biological studies which would reveal how these gene products are part of the disease process in PD. The **alpha synuclein** and **Parkin** genes are two examples.*

The discovery that ___genetic mutations___ in the ___alpha synuclein gene___ could cause PD has opened new avenues of research in the PD field. Since the discovery of ___synuclein___, studies of genetic linkages, specific genes, and their associated coded proteins are ongoing in PD research field - transforming what had once been thought of as a purely environmental disease into one of the most complex multigenetic diseases of the brain.

Mutations in the Parkin gene cause early onset Parkinson's disease, and the ___parkin___ protein has been identified as an ___E3 ligase___, suggesting a role for the proteasomal pathway of protein degradation in PD. ___DJ-1___ and ___PINK-1___ are proteins related to mitochondrial function in neurons, providing an interesting genetic parallel to mitochondrial toxin studies that suggest disruptions in cellular energetics and oxidative metabolism are primarily responsible for PD. Other genes, such as ___UCHL-1, tau___, and the ___glucocerebrosidase___ gene, may be genetic risk factors, and their potential role in the sporadic PD population remains unknown. ___Mutations in LRRK2___, which encodes for a protein called ___dardarin___, is the most recently discovered genetic cause of PD, and LRRK2 mutations are likely to be the largest cause of familial PD identified thus far. ___Dardarin___ is a large complex protein, which has a variety of structural moieties that could be participating in more than a dozen different cellular pathways in neurons.

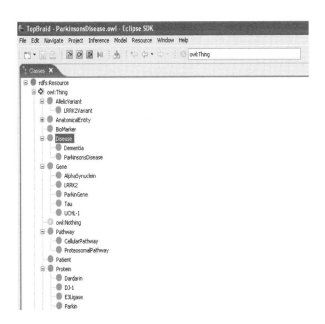

Figure 5-2. Parkinson's disease ontology: concepts and subsumption hierarchy

Based on the above analysis, one can begin to identify some important ontological concepts relevant to PD:

- Genes, such as alpha synuclein, Parkin, UCHL-1, tau and glucocerebrosidase
- Proteins, such as synuclein, Parkin, Dardarin, DJ-1 and PINK-1
- Allelic Variations or Genetic mutations such as in the LRRK2 gene
- Diseases, such as PD.

These and some of the other identified concepts are illustrated in Figure 5-2.

3.1.2 Identifying and extracting relationships

The next step was to identify and represent relationships between the concepts identified in the ontology above. Consider the following textual description:

> *The discovery that genetic mutations in the alpha synuclein gene could cause PD has opened new avenues of research in PD. When it was also discovered that synuclein was a major component of **Lewy bodies, the pathological hallmark of PD in the brain**, it became clear that synuclein may be important in the pathogenesis of sporadic as well as rare cases of PD.*
>
> *DJ-1 and PINK-1 are proteins related to mitochondrial function in neurons, providing an interesting genetic parallel to mitochondrial toxin studies that suggest disruptions in cellular energetics and oxidative metabolism are primarily responsible for PD. **Other genes, such as UCHL-1, tau, and the glucocerebrosidase gene, may be genetic risk factors,** and their potential role in the sporadic PD population...*

Based on the above analysis, the following relationships may be added to the PD Ontology:

- Lewy Bodies is_pathological_hallmark_of PD.
- UCHL-1 is_risk_factor_of PD.

The representation of these relationships and their inverses is illustrated in Figure 5-3.

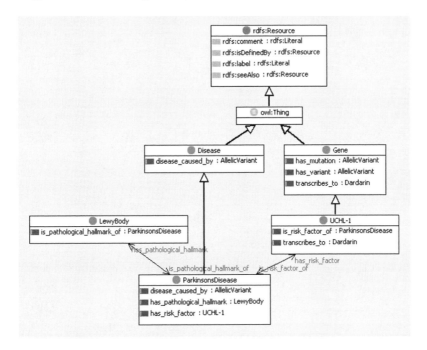

Figure 5-3. Parkinson's disease Ontology: Relationships between Concepts

3.1.3 Extending the ontology based on information queries

We next considered various information queries and identified concepts and relationships that needed to be part of the Parkinson's disease ontology. This was important as, otherwise, without these concepts and relationships it would not have been possible for a biomedical researcher to specify these queries for retrieving information and knowledge from the system. Consider the following queries:

- What ***cell signaling pathways*** are implicated in the pathogenesis of Parkinson's disease? In what cells?
- What proteins ***are involved*** and in which pathways?

The above queries lead to addition of new concepts and relationships illustrated in Figure 5-4.

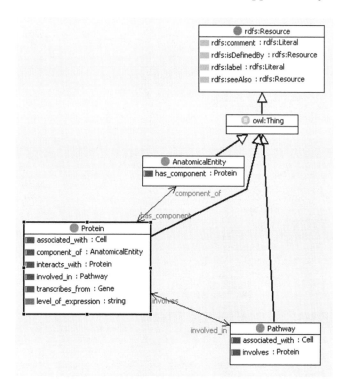

Figure 5-4. Parkinson's disease ontology: adding concepts and relationships to support information queries

3.1.4 Ontology re-use

As we expand and refine our use case, it became clear to us that we needed a methodical way of extending our ontology. Clearly our intention is to re-use various ontologies and vocabularies being developed in the healthcare and life science fields. Some of the dimensions along which the ontology could be extended and the associated re-usable ontologies are as follows:

- **Diseases:** Over time, we could anticipate addressing information needs related to other related diseases such as Huntington 's disease or AD. Some ontologies/vocabularies we are considering reuse of are the International Classification of Diseases (ICD 2007) and a subset of Snomed (SNOMED 2007).
- **Genes:** Over time, we may want to add more genes and other genomic concepts such as proteins, pathways, etc. to the ontologies. We are considering linking to Gene Ontology (Gene Ontology 2007).

- **Neurological Concepts**: We may need to add more concepts related to brain structures and parts to extend our ontology if required. We are considering the use of NeuroNames (Neuro Names 2007), a nomenclature of primate brain structures and related terms that describe the superficial features of these structures.
- **Enzymes:** Concepts for various enzymes and other chemicals may be required, for which purpose, we will consider linking to the Enzyme Nomenclature (Enzyme Nomenclature 2007).

Some criteria that need to be investigated for re-use of ontologies are as follows:

- How specific or general should the ontology be that is being re-used? For instance, do we choose ontology of neurological diseases or do we choose a generalized ontology of diseases and include an appropriate subset?
- At what level of granularity do we include concepts from ontology? For instance, we can include ontologies at a very shallow level, with just the concepts being included. A deeper level of inclusion may entail inclusion of associated properties, relationships and axioms as well.

Depending on the level of inclusion, ontology re-use could lead to circularities and inconsistencies. We propose to use pragmatic approaches to handle these situations. For instance, we may choose to include certain concepts at a "shallow" level to avoid potential inconsistencies or give priority to a concept from one ontology over another

3.2   Ontology Design Choices

We now discuss various design choices that came up in the process of ontology design and discuss possible criteria that might help choose one representation over another.

Use of Relationships versus Classes for Modeling Knowledge: Suppose we want to represent the knowledge of transcription of a particular gene, such as UCHL-1 into a protein such as Dardarin. Two possible choices for representing this are:

- UCHL-1 transcribes_into Dardarin
- Represent a class called transcription with properties has_transcription = Dardarin, has_gene = UCHL-1.

The former could be chosen if usage scenarios are just interested in gene products, whereas the latter would be preferable if a researcher is interested in the laboratory conditions under which the transcription takes place. Information about these lab conditions could be modeled as object properties associated with the transcription class. It should be noted that the former alternative is preferable from the point of view of storage and querying.

Modeling of Diseases: Diseases could be modeled in an ontology as static classes or as dynamic processes. The former is probably more suitable in the context where a researcher is interested in the association of diseases and genes, but on the other hand, if someone is interested in understanding the change in physiological states due to administration of a drug.

Use of Instances versus SubClasses: A generic/specific relationship can be modeled by using instances or subclasses. Consider the following examples:

• Parkinson's Disease may be viewed as a subclass or an instance of the class Disease
• UCHL-1 may be viewed as subclass or an instance of the class Gene.

The appropriate modeling choice depends on the usage scenario. In general if one were interested in counting the occurrence of diseases or alleles in a population, the subclass modeling choice would be needed. However, if the usage scenario just requires annotation for the sake of search and query expansion, then the instances choice might suffice.

Granularity of representation of relationships: Relationships could be represented at different levels of genericity or specificity. For example, one could represent the relationship between an allelic variant and disease at the following levels of granularity:

• AllelicVariant causes Disease
• LRR2KVariant causes Parkinson's Disease

The latter representation might be preferred if the usage scenarios are focused on only causes for Parkinson's disease or if only very few and specific allelic variants are known to cause Parkinson's disease.

Representation of uncertainty: Current semantic web specifications are silent when it comes to representation and reasoning with uncertain information. For instance, consider the following statement from the use case in Section 2.

The discovery that genetic mutations in the alpha synuclein gene **could cause** *Parkinson's disease in families has opened new avenues of research in the Parkinson's disease field.*

Even though the underlying meta-models and tools do not support representation and manipulation of uncertainties, pragmatic approaches such as using reification and using the query language operators to retrieve information satisfying certain threshold constraints.

Domain/Range polymorphism: Relationships can have multiple domain and range classes and the current RDF/OWL semantics of combining these classes may not accurately reflect the intended meaning. For example:

• *associated_with(Pathway, Cell)*
• *associated_with(Protein, Biomarker)*

The associated_with relationship has two domain classes, Pathway and Protein; and two range classes, Cell and Biomarker. It may be necessary to represent specific OWL constraints (Kashyap and Borgida 2003) to make sure that the proper semantics are identified and represented.

Default Values: In some cases, it is important to represent default values of object properties, for e.g., consider the statement:

• *The default function of proteasomal pathway is protein degradation*

Currently, SW tools do not support the representation of and reasoning with default values. In the context of data integration, it can help us retrieve information or identify mappings in the absence of availability of data from the underlying data sources. In certain cases, certain implicit assumptions can be made explicit using default values.

Ternary and other Higher Order Relationships: Typically, a biomedical discovery, such as an association between a particular gene and a disease could be at the same time be established to be true in the context of one study and could be established to be false in another. This requires the representation of a ternary relationship between genes, diseases and studies as follows:

• *established_in(Disease, Gene, Study)*

There is a need for representation of ternary and other higher order relationships, which is typically implemented by representing them as a class (SWBPDWG 2006).

3.3   Summary

In this section, we presented our approach for creating a domain ontology for data integration and high lighted some modeling and representation choices that need to be made. From a pragmatic perspective, the semantic web is not at a stage whether standardized ontologies for various domains are freely above. So, there is a need for creating ontologies based on well defined use cases and functional requirements on one hand; and also to link to pre-existing classifications and ontologies available for more complete coverage. Multiple modeling and representation choices emerge when designing these ontologies and there is no one good answer for all situations. A pragmatic approach should be adopted and modeling choices should be based on the use cases and functional requirements at hand.

4.   DATA SOURCES

In Section 3, we discussed our approach for modeling and representing the domain ontology. In particular, we used the collection of information queries identified as being useful to our user group, i.e., biomedical researchers. We now discuss with the help of the example query discussed above in Section 2.3, how the query can be answered based on retrieval and integration of data from different biomedical data sources. We first describe a set of data sources that are relevant to the use case. We then describe how the use case query illustrated in Section 2 can be answered using these data sources. Some of the elements of our solution such as conversion of the data sources into RDF, the ability to map RDF graphs to ontological concepts and the ability to merge RDF graphs based on declaratively specified mapping rules are then highlighted.

4.1   Relevant data sources to the query

A list of data sources that are being integrated using semantic web technologies are as follows:

- **Neuron Database:** Neuron DB (Morenco, Tosches, et. al. 2003) provides a dynamically searchable database of three types of neuronal properties: voltage gated conductances, neurotransmitter receptors, and neurotransmitter substances. It contains tools that provide for integration of these properties in a given type of neuron and compartment, and for comparison of properties across different types of neurons and compartments.

- **PDSP KI Database:** The PDSP KI Database (PDSP KI 2007) is a unique resource in the public domain which provides information on the abilities of drugs to interact with an expanding number of molecular targets. The KI database serves as a data warehouse for published and internally-derived Ki, or affinity, values for a large number of drugs and drug candidates at an expanding number of G-protein coupled receptors, ion channels, transporters and enzymes.

- **PubChem:** PubChem (PubChem 2007) is organized as three linked databases within the NCBI's Entrez (Entrez 2007) information retrieval system. These are PubChem Substance, PubChem Compound, and PubChem BioAssay. PubChem also provides a fast chemical structure similarity search tool. Links from PubChem's chemical structure records to other Entrez databases provide information on biological properties. These include links to PubMed (PubMed 2007) scientific literature and concepts from the MeSH taxonomy (MeSH 2007).

Now consider the use case query presented in Section 2. The answer to this query can be constructed by correlating data retrieved from underlying data sources as follows:

- Data that identifies *Distal Dendrite* as a compartment on the *dopaminergic neuron* and the receptor *D1* belonging to the *Distal Dendrite* can be retrieved from the Neuron Database.
- Data that identifies *5-Hydroxy Tryptamine* as a ligand that can bind to the *D1* receptor can be retrieved from the PDSP KI database
- Data that identifies that the ligand *5-Hydroxy Tryptamine* is associated with *Parkinson's disease* can be retrieved from PubChem. The ligand *5-Hydroxy Tryptamine* is cross-linked to the MeSH concept related to *Parkinson's disease*.

Correlation of the data results in: The ligand *5-Hydroxy Tryptamine*, a therapeutic agent for *Parkinson's disease* binds to the receptor *D1* in the *Distal Dendrite* area of the dopaminergic neuron in the substantia nigra.

Details on how this is implemented using semantic web technologies are presented next.

4.2   Implementing the data integration solution

The data integration solution can be implemented using two broad architectural approaches:

- A centralized approach where the data available through web-based interfaces is converted into RDF and stored in a centralized data repository.
- A federated approach where the data continues to reside in the existing data repositories. An RDF-based mediator or gateway converts the underlying data into the RDF format.

Common to both these approaches are the functionalities required for converting non-semantic web data such as relational or XML data into RDF; mapping ontological concepts into RDF graphs, possibly via association with appropriate SPARQL queries; and merging of RDF graphs based on matching of IDs and URIs and declaratively specified mapping rules.

4.2.1 Conversion into RDF graphs

An approach for converting XML-based data into RDF has been presented in (Sahoo, Bodenreider, et. al. 2006). Typically, queries requiring navigation of multiple relationships across multiple objects requires writing complex SQL and applications programming code when using relational databases. The RDF format allows us to focus on the logical structure of the information in contrast to only representational format (XML) or storage format (relational database).

There are many issues involved in the conversion of XML data into RDF format including the use of unique identifiers, preservation of original semantics of the converted data, resolution of bidirectional relationships and filtering of redundant element tags from the original XML record. Unlike traditional XML to XML conversion, XML to RDF conversion should take into account the advantages of the RDF model in representing the logical structure of the information and the modeling of the relationships between concepts. The underlying objective of converting XML data into RDF is to capture the semantics of the data and leverage such semantics in querying the repository to not only retrieve the explicit but also the implicit knowledge through inference. Some issues that need to be considered in the conversion are:

- The use of a specific identifier allows the unique identification of the nodes (*subject* and *object*) and *predicates* in an RDF repository. But, there is no globally accepted biomedical identifier schema that may be used. The bioinformatics community is currently debating this issue and there are many candidate schemas that may be used including the Life Science Identifier (LSID) (LSID 2007) and solutions based on the HTTP protocol (i.e., URIs (Universal Resource Identifiers), URLs (Universal Resource Locators) and URNs (Universal Resource Names)). NLM resources such as the Unified Medical Language System (UMLS 2007) could provide the basis for the identification of biomedical entities.

- It is important to decide whether to reflect the native nesting of elements in the original XML format or modify the structure to reflect one of the many possible perspectives on the data.
- In case there is an existing domain ontology, the RDF structure can be based on the domain ontology. However, if different ontologies need to be mapped to the same set of data, one may need to specify mappings between ontological concepts and a given choice of an RDF representation.

We now discuss issues related to mapping ontological concepts to their associated RDF Graphs.

4.2.2 Mapping ontological concepts to RDF graphs

As presented in Section 4.1, the use case query is satisfied by correlating fragments of data retrieved from the individual data sources. These fragments correspond to the following concepts and relationships from the ontology:

- Compartment located_on Neuron
- Receptor located_in Compartment
- Ligand binds_to Receptor
- Ligand associated_with Disease

In order to enable this data integration, we need to map these concepts and relationships to RDF graphs in the underlying data sources. We assume that there is a wrapper which transforms the results retrieved from these data sources into RDF graphs. We would need to capture the following information in these mappings:

- **Ontological Element:** This would represent the ontological concept mapped to the RDF graphs in a given data source. One may also chose to specify the properties or edges that the given data source supports. In some precise cases, one may want to specify the actual triplet which a data source may support.

- **Data Source:** This would represent the data source which would support the retrieval of data corresponding to the concepts in the ontology
- **Target SPARQL Query:** This would represent the SPARQL query which would need to be executed on the underlying data source to retrieve the required RDF graph.
- **Identifier Scheme:** This would represent the identifiers for the nodes and edges for a particular RDF graph. We adopt the approach of using URIs to identify "object" nodes in an RDF graph, i.e., those that are not "literals". Each URI is constructed on a set of base URIs corresponding to each data source that delineates the respective name spaces.

An example table illustrating the representation of mappings is illustrated in Table 5-1 below:

Table 5-1. Mapping table

Ontological Element	Data Source	SPARQL Condition	Namespace
Neuron	Neuron Database	?x rdf:type Neuron	Neuron DB
Neuron, {located_in}	Neuron Database	?x located_in ?y, ?x rdf:type Neuron	Neuron DB
Neuron located_in Compartment	Neuron Database	?x located_in ?y, ?x rdf:type Neuron, ?y rdf:type Compartment	Neuron DB
Receptors located_on Compartment	Neuron Database	?x located_on ?y, ?x rdf:type Receptor, ?y rdf:type Compartment	Neuron DB
Ligand binds_to Receptor	PDSP KI Database	?x binds_to ?y, ?x rdf:type Ligand, ?y rdf:type Receptor	PDSPKI DB
Ligand associated with Disease	PubChem	?x associated_with ?y, ?x rdf:type Ligand, ?y rdf:type Disease	PubChem DB
...	...	...	...

The above table represents some of the possibilities for representing some of the information required to enable data integration. This table is referenced by the system to invoke the appropriate queries on the underlying data sources to retrieve RDF graphs for display to the biomedical researcher.

An interesting omission is standardized ontologies that might be used by a given data source to represent some information, for e.g., the PubChem data source uses MeSH concepts to represent diseases. We currently make the assumption that there are certain standardized ontologies included in the domain ontology and that the RDF wrapper "maps" concepts from one ontology to another. For instance, if the domain ontology uses Snomed for representing disease concepts, and the local data source uses MeSH, the RDF wrapper will map the MeSH ID corresponding to Parkinson 's disease to the Snomed ID corresponding to Parkinson 's disease. Alternatively this can be done by invoking a specialized "terminology mapper" program at the global level.

4.2.3 Generation and merging of RDF graphs

As discussed earlier, RDF wrappers perform the function of transforming information as stored in internal data structures in LIMS and EMR systems into RDF-based graph representations. We illustrate with examples (Figure 5-1), the RDF representation of neurological and chemical data from the various datasources.

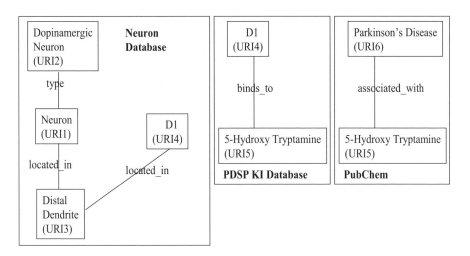

Figure 5-5. RDF Representation of neurological and chemical data

Each box is labeled with the name of the data source from which the associated RDF Graph can be generated. In the box corresponding to the Neuron Database, the RDF graph generated in response to the query may consist of nodes corresponding to instances of a Neuron which is linked with edge labeled *type_of* to the node representing the concept of a Dopinamergic Neuron; and with an edge labeled *located_in* to the node representing the Distal Dendrite region. The node corresponding to the D1 receptor is in turn linked with the edge labeled *located_on* to the node corresponding to the Distal Dendrite region. In the box corresponding to the PDSP KI database, the edged labeled *binds_to* represents the relationship between the ligand 5-Hydroxy Tryptamine and the D1 receptor. The box corresponding to the PubChem database uses the edge labeled *associated_with* to represent the association between the ligand 5-Hydroxy Tryptamine and Parkinson 's disease.

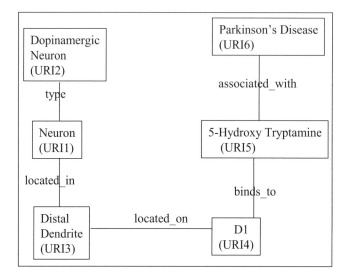

Figure 5-6. The Integrated RDF Graph

The data integration process is an interactive one and involves the end user, who in our case might be a *biomedical researcher*. RDF graphs from different data sources are displayed. The steps in the process that lead to the final integrated result (Figure 5-6) are enumerated below.

1. RDF graphs are displayed in an intuitive and understandable manner to the end user in a graphical user interface.
2. The end user previews them and specifies a set of rules for linking nodes across different RDF models. An example of linking rule could be something as simple as matching IDs of nodes in the various graphs.
3. Merged RDF graphs that are generated based on these rules are displayed to the user, who may then decide to activate or de-activate some of the rules displayed.
4. New edges may be added to the merged graph and be added back to the system. For instance, one may choose to add an edge *promising_candidate* between the nodes corresponding to the ligand 5-Hydroxy Tryptamine and Parkinson 's disease.

4.3 Approaches for data integration

As discussed in the beginning of this section, there are two primary approaches to implement the data integration solutions presented above:

- **Centralized approach:** In this approach the data sets are extracted from various data sources converted into the RDF representation and stored in a single RDF data store. The advantage of this approach is that it is likely to be very efficient and can be simply and quickly implemented. The disadvantage of this approach is that there are a huge number of biomedical data repositories on the web and it is infeasible to load them into one big data store. Furthermore, as the data and structures in the underlying data sources change, the centralized data store is likely to become out of date and will need to be periodically refreshed and restructured.
- **Federated approach:** In this approach, the data sets sit in their native locations. An RDF wrapper is responsible for converting SPARQL queries into the native query language of the database, e.g., SQL. Results returned, e.g., in the tabular form are mapped into a RDF graph representation. The advantage of this approach is that it is more likely to scale to cover the large number of biomedical data repositories on the web. Furthermore and change in the underlying data collections are immediately reflected as, data is retrieved only in response to a query and is not pre-stored. The disadvantages of this approach are that the performance can be slow as data is fetched and possibly joined over the network and changes in the organization and structure of the data repository on the web will require the RDF wrapper to be reconfigured or rewritten. A mitigating factor is that changes in a RDF wrappers can be isolated to a local site and can be handled via reconfiguration by the local developer.

5. CONCLUSIONS AND FUTURE WORK

Semantic Web technologies provide an attractive technological and informatics foundation for enabling the Bench to Bedside Vision. Many areas of biomedical research including drug discovery, systems biology, and personalized medicine rely heavily on integrating and interpreting data sets produced by different experimental methods, in different groups, with heterogeneous data formats, and at different levels of granularity. Further more, there is a need for evolving synthetic understandings across disciplines, and across the continuum from basic research to clinical applications, applies to most complex diseases and many healthcare issues. A useful synthesis must combine not only data, but interpretations. Ontologies play a critical role in integrating data. They are also used to represent interpretations in the form of mappings to the underlying data on one hand and definitions and axioms on the other.

In this chapter, we present a real world use case related to Parkinson's disease and discuss with the help of an illustrative example how ontologies and semantic web technologies can be used to enable effective data integration. We first present pragmatic issues and design choices that arise while designing ontologies. A discussion of real world biological data repositories represented in our approach is presented and steps for implementing data integration solutions are discussed with the help of illustrative examples.

This is part of ongoing work in the framework of the work being performed in the Healthcare and Life Sciences Interest Group chartered by the W3C. The examples presented in this chapter are a part of broad set of use cases that will be implemented as demonstrations of Semantic Web technology for the healthcare and life sciences. We will evaluate different approaches for data integration, viz., centralized vs. federated in this context.

6.   QUESTIONS FOR DISCUSSION

Beginner:
1. Why is Google, Yahoo! or MSN search not good enough for searching biological data?
2. There are various Web 2.0 approaches based on collaborative annotations of various web resources such as in Flickr. Explain why or why not these approaches are able to capture semantics.

Intermediate:
1. There have been various approaches to using Taxonomies on the Web, for example, Yahoo! and the International Classification of Disease, Medical Subject Headings (MeSH), etc. Explain how these classifications can help in the data integration process.
2. Explain if the classifications identified above are enough to support data integration or more sophisticated ontologies are required.

Advanced:
1. Explain why you think there is value in creating an ontology? Shouldn't the ability to link RDF graphs via URIs be enough to achieve data integration?
2. Explain why you think a Semantic-Web/RDF-based approach is better than current relational database and web based solutions? If not, why not?
3. Compare and contrast the following: classifications and taxonomies, database schemas, ontologies; with respect to the knowledge expressed and their utility in the context of data integration.

7. ADDITIONAL SUGGESTED READING

- Baker, C. J. O., and Cheung, K-H. (Editors); *Semantic Web: Revolutionizing Knowledge Discovery in the Life Sciences*, Springer 2007, 450 pp; This book is a nice collection of articles illustrating the application of semantic web and ontology-based techniques in the domain of biomedical informatics
- Ruttenberg, A., Clark, T., Bug, W., Samwald, M., Bodenreider, O., Helen C., Doherty, D., Forsberg, K., Gao, Y., Kashyap, V., Kinoshita, J., Luciano, J., Marshall, M. S., Ogbuji C., Rees, J., Stephens, S., Wong, G., Wu, E., Zaccagnini, D., Hongsermeier, T., Neumann, E., Herman, I., and Cheung, K-H. *Advancing Translational Research with the Semantic Web*, BMC Bioinformatics, Vol. 8, suppl.2, 2007. This paper is a nice overview paper of various semantic web technologies such as RDF, OWL and Rules to important informatics problems in the area of Translational Medicine.

8. ACKNOWLEDGEMENTS

A significant portion of this work was performed within the framework of the Health Care and Life Sciences Interest Group of the World Wide Web Consortium. We appreciate the forum and the resources given by this Interest Group. We also acknowledge the feedback provided by Alan Ruttenberg at the HCLSIG Face to Face in Amsterdam. Kei-Hoi Cheung was supported in part by NSF grant DBI-0135442.

9.   REFERENCES

Cardoso, J. and A. Sheth (Eds.) (2006). "Semantic Web Services, Processes and Applications", Springer, Hardcover, ISBN: 0-38730239-5.

Davenport, T. H. and L. Prusak (1997). Information Ecology: Mastering the Information and Knowledge Environment, Oxford University Press.

Entrez (2007). http://www.ncbi.nlm.nih.gov/gquery/gquery.fcgi

Enzyme Nomenclature (2007), http://www.chem.qmul.ac.uk/iubmb/enzyme/

Gene Ontology (2007). The Gene Ontology, http://www.geneontology.org/

ICD   (2007).   International   Classification   of   Diseases   (ICD), http://www.who.int/classifications/icd/en/

Kashyap, V (1999). Design and Creation of Ontologies for Environmental Information Retrieval, In the 12th International Conference on Knowledge Acqusition, Modeling and Management, Banff, Canada.

Kashyap, V. and A. Borgida (2003). Representing the UMLS Semantic Network in OWL (Or "What's in a Semantic Web Link?"), Proceedings of the Second International Semantic Web Conference (ISWC), October.

Lesne' et al. (2006). Nature 16;440(7082):352-7

LSID (2007). Life Sciences Identifier (LSID) Resolution Project, http://lsid.sourceforge.net/

Marenco L, N. Tosches, et. al. (2003). Achieving evolvable Web-database bioscience applications using the EAV/CR framework: recent advances. J Am Med Inform Assoc. 10(5):444-53.

Matteo, C. and R. Cuel (2005). A Survey on Ontology Creation Methodologies. Int. J. Semantic Web Inf. Syst. 1(2): 49-69.

MeSH (2007). Medical Subject Headings, http://www.nlm.nih.gov/mesh/

Neuro Names (2007). Bowden DM, Martin RF (1995) NeuroNames brain hierarchy. *Neuroimage* 2:63–83.

Parkinsons Use Case (2007), http://esw.w3.org/topic/HCLS/ParkinsonUseCase

PDSP KI (2007). The PDSP KI Database, http://pdsp.med.unc.edu/kidb.php

PubChem (2007). http://pubchem.ncbi.nlm.nih.gov/

PubMed (2007). http://www.ncbi.nlm.nih.gov/entrez/query.fcgi?db=PubMed

Sahoo, S., O. Bodenreider et. al. (2006). Adapting resources to the Semantic Web: Experience with Entrez Gene, First International Workshop on the Semantic Web for the Healthcare and Life Sciences

SNOMED (2007). http://www.snomed.org

SWBPDWG (2006). Semantic Web Best Practices and Deployment Working Group, http://www.w3.org/2001/sw/BestPractices/

Translational Medicine (2007). Journal of Translational Medicine, http://www.translational-medicine.com/info/about/

UMLS (2007). Unified Medical Language System, http://umlsinfo.nlm.nih.gov/

Chapter 6

ACTIVE SEMANTIC ELECTRONIC MEDICAL RECORDS
An application of Active Semantic Documents

A. Sheth[1], S.Agrawal[2], J. Lathem[1], N.Oldham[2], H.Wingate[2], P.Yadav[2] and K. Gallagher[2]

[1]*LSDIS Lab, University of Georgia, Athens, GA, USA – {amit,lathem}@cs.uga.edu*
[2]*Athens Heart Center, Athens, GA, USA – {subodh, noldham, ppyadav, kgallagher}@athensheartcenter.com*

1.   INTRODUCTION

The most cumbersome aspect of healthcare is the extensive documentation which is legally required for each patient. For these reasons, physicians and their assistants spend about 30% of their time documenting encounters. Paper charts are slowly being phased out due to inconvenience, inability to mine data, costs and safety concerns. Many practices are now investing in electronic medical records (EMR) systems which allow them to have all patient data at their fingertips. Although current adoption by medical groups (based on a 2005 survey (AHRQ 2005)) is still below 15% with even less adoption rate for smaller practices, the trend is clearly towards increasing adoption. This trend will accelerate as regulatory pressures such as "Pay-4-Performance" become mandatory thus enhancing the ROI sophisticated systems can achieve. This paper focuses on the first known development and deployment[38] of a comprehensive EMR system that utilizes semantic Web and Web service/process technologies. It is based on substantial collaboration between practicing physicians (Dr. Agrawal is a cardiologists and a fellow of the American Cardiology Association, Dr. Wingate is an

---

[38] Preliminary deployment in September 2005, full deployment in January 2006.

emergency room physician) at the Athens Heart Center and the LSDIS lab at UGA. More specifically, we leverage the concept and technology of Active Semantic Documents (ASDs) developed at the LSDIS lab. ASDs get their *semantic* feature by automatic semantic annotation of documents with respect to one or more ontologies. These documents are termed *active* since they support automatic and dynamic validation and decision making on the content of the document by applying contextually relevant rules to components of the documents. This is accomplished by executing rules on semantic annotations and relationships that span across ontologies.

Specifically, Active Semantic Electronic Medical Record (ASEMR) is an application of ASDs in healthcare which aims to reduce medical errors, improve physician efficiency, improve patient safety and satisfaction in medical practice, improve quality of billing records leading be better payment, and make it easier to capture and analyze health outcome measures. In ASMER, rules specified in conjunction with ontologies play a key role. Examples of the rules include prevention of drug interaction (i.e., not allowing a patient to be prescribed two severely interacting drugs, or alerting the doctor and requiring his/her to make specific exceptions when low or moderate degree of interactions are acceptable) or ensuring the procedure performed has supporting diagnoses. ASDs display the semantic (for entities defined in the ontologies) and lexical (for terms and phrases that are part of specialist lexicon, specific items related to the clinics, and other relevant parts of speech) annotations in document displaced in a browser, show results of rule execution, and provide the ability to modify semantic and lexical components of its content in an ontology-supported and otherwise constrained manner such as through lists, bags of terms, specialized reference sources, or a thesaurus or lexical reference system such as WordNet (http://wordnet.princeton.edu/). This feature allows for better and more efficient patient care and because of the ability of ASDs to offer suggestions when rules are broken or exceptions made.

ASEMR is currently in daily and routine use by the Athens Heart Center (AHC) and eight other sites in Georgia. ASEMRs have been implemented as an enhancement of AHC's Panacea electronic medical management system. Panacea is a web-based, end to end medical records and management system, and hence it is used with respect to each patent seen at AHC. This has enhanced the collaborative environment and has provided insights into the components of electronic medical records and the kinds of data available in these systems. The preliminary version was implemented during Summer 2005 and tested in early fall. The current version was deployed and has been fully functional since January 2006. Parts of ASMER we will focus on in this paper are:

- the development of populated ontologies in the healthcare (specifically cardiology) domain
- the development of an annotation tool that utilizes the developed ontologies for annotation of patient records
- the development of decision support algorithms that support rule and ontology based checking/validation and evaluation.

The remainder of this chapter is organized as follows. Section 2 makes a case for semantics through a motivating scenario (for brevity, only one example is given). Section 3 describes the knowledge and rules representation. The application is detailed in Sections 4 and the implementation details are given in Section 5. Section 6 evaluates the approach and provides statistics which support the growth of the practice since the use of the EMR. Section 7 lists related work and Section 8 concludes with future work.

2. MOTIVATING SCENARIO AND BENEFITS

In addition to the complexity of today's healthcare, medical practitioners face a number of challenges in managing their practices. One of the challenges is the need to improve the quality of care, adhere to evolving clinical care pathways, reduce waste and reduce errors (with associated need to develop and report quality of care measures). Another challenge is that of medical billing. Let's investigate the latter further. Each insurance company follows Local Medical Review Policy (LMRP) which are policies specifying which diagnosis justify the medical necessity of a procedure. If the appropriate codes are not given in accordance with these LMRPs, the insurance will not pay for the charge. Because of these rigid requirements many claims are rejected and the amount of time for receiving a payment is prolonged and in many cases the physicians are not reimbursed for their services. If correct coding compliance is enforced by the system at the point of charge entry on the superbill (the bill of all charges and diagnoses for a visit) the problem of procedures without supporting diagnosis codes is eliminated. Table 6-1 contains a partial list of ICD9CM codes that support medical necessity for CPT 93000 EKG which were taken from the Centers for Medicare and Medicaid Services (CMS 2006)[39].

---

[39] ICD9-CM stands for "The International Classification of Diseases, 9th Revision, Clinical Modification"; these codes are used to denote the diagnosis. CPT (Current Procedural Terminology) codes are used to denote treatments. Payment is done based on the treatment, but the bill must contain acceptable diagnosis for that treatment.

Table 6-1. Medical necessity for EKG

ICD9CM	Diagnosis Name
244.9	Hypothyroidism
250.00	Diabetes Mellitus Type II
250.01	Diabetes Mellitus Type I
242.9	Hyperthyroidism
272.2	Mixed Hyperlipidemia
414.01	CAD-Native
780.2-780.4	Syncope and Collapse – Dizziness and Giddiness
780.79	Other Malaise and Fatigue
785.0-785.3	Tachycardia Unspecified – Other Abnormal Heart Sounds
786.50-786.54	Unspecified Chest Pain – Precordial Pain
786.59	Other Chest Pain

The primary diagnosis code selected for the EKG must be one of the supporting diagnosis codes listed above. There are additional complex rules such as certain ICD9CM codes should not be selected together and certain procedures should not be billed for in the same claim. In section 4.2, we will present our approach which uses a combination of OWL ontologies and rules to validate data in a superbill to ensure coding compliance by presenting the appropriate subset of linking diagnosis codes when a procedure is selected. Due to the creation of more accurate and compliant claims, this approach has the potential to eliminate coding errors which would result in improved financials.

In addition to greater facilitation of billing process, physicians benefit from the clinical decision support that can be provided by a system which has rich domain understanding through the use of ontologies and rules. Patients benefit as well as this ability allows better patient care, increased safety and satisfaction. Checks such as preferred drug recommendations lead to prescription drug savings for patients leading to improved satisfaction. The most important benefit we seek from ASEMR with its proactive semantic annotations and rule-based evaluation is the reduction of medical errors that could occur as an oversight. Ultimately the proof of these support features will be manifest by improved outcome data for example better Medpar scores (Medicare beneficiary morbidity and mortality data) for Physicians.

3.   KNOWLEDGE AND RULES REPRESENTAION

We employ a combination of OWL (OWL 2004) ontologies with RDQL (A. Seaborne 2004) rules in order to supply the document with rich domain knowledge. The rules provide additional domain knowledge and compensate for the limitations of the OWL language.2.1 Ontologies. A more complex rule specification (and corresponding rule processing) capabilities may be needed in future, but for our current purpose this was more than adequate and this choice also provided efficient implementation alternative. We utilize three ontologies to represent aspects of the domain. The practice ontology contains concepts which represent the medical practice such as facility, physician, physician assistant, and nurse. The infrastructure of the medical practice is given by the concepts and relationships. The practice ontology was created in conjunction with experts in the medical field. Parts of our own databases were the source for populating this ontology.

The Drug ontology contains all of the drugs and classes of drugs, drug interactions, drug allergies, and formularies. Capturing such information reduces medical errors and increases patient safety. Furthermore, prescribing drugs from the formularies of the patient's insurance plans improves patient satisfaction. License content (Gold Standard Media) equivalent to physician's drug reference was the primary source for populating this ontology which is shown, in part, in Figure 6-1.

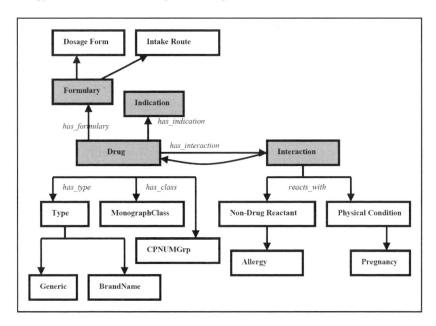

Figure 6-1. Partial view of drug ontology

The Diagnosis/Procedure ontology includes concepts such as medical conditions, treatments, diagnoses (ICD-9), and procedures (CPT). Licensed SNOMED (Systematized Nomenclature of Medicine--Clinical Terms) SNOMED® (http://www.snomed.org/) content is used for populating this ontology. A key enhancement involved linking this ontology to the drug ontology. This allows powerful decision support by giving the system specialized domain knowledge. We will use this representation to enable the system to suggest treatments and drugs based on the patient's condition or diagnosis. User or user group specific frequently used codes lists are supported by this ontology. This allows customizability such that each area of the practice will be given procedures and diagnosis codes which frequently apply to their area.

For example, procedures such as Dipiridamol injections and Muga scans are generally administered in the area of Nuclear medicine and should therefore the remainder of the clinical staff should not be bothered with those procedures cluttering their view. Each area has customizable frequent lists such as Nuclear, Pacemaker Evaluation, Echocardiograph, etc.

Medical records of patients are automatically annotated using the ontologies listed above and are displayed in a browser. Drugs, allergies, physicians and facilities (e.g., physicians or facilities the patient is referred to), treatments, diagnosis, etc. are automatically annotated. The physician has the ability to pull up a contextual list or even a visual subset of the relevant ontology and pick alternative choices. In some cases, alternatives are provided in ranked order list (e.g., other physicians with the same specialty in the same area and accepting the same insurance as the patient).

3.1   Rules

ASEMRs support active features by executing relevant rules over semantic annotations to support the following initial sets of capabilities:

- drug-drug interaction check,
- drug formulary check (e.g., whether the drug is covered by the insurance
- company of the patient, and if not what the alternative drugs in the same class of drug are),
- drug dosage range check,
- drug-allergy interaction check,
- ICD-9 annotations choice for the physician to validate and choose the best possible code for the treatment type, and
- preferred drug recommendation based on drug and patient insurance information

The benefits of combining the use of ontologies and rules are two-fold. First, the rules allow the system to make decisions. Second, using rules the system can become declarative to the extent that additional relationships and facts can be added at any time without changing the code. For example, if the relationship "cancels_the_effect" is added to the ontology coupled with a rule indicating which drug or combinations of drugs cancel the effect of drugX, then the capability of the system is enhanced without any code modifications. This allows for a great deal of extensibility and flexibility such that one could even define classes of drugs, such as blood thinners, which cancels the effects of other classes of drugs. Rules allow for more flexibility, enhanced reasoning power and extensibility.

4. APPLICATION

The following section details two components which utilize semantic web technologies and are currently deployed and in use by at least eight beta sites. The evaluation section contains an analysis of the effect of this semantic health record application on one practice.

4.1 Active Semantic Documents

Physicians are required to thoroughly document each patient encounter. Reports usually contain a problem list, family history, history of present illness, review of symptoms, impressions and plans. Data acquisition and data entry is a painstaking process which usually results in late hours for the physician. One alternative is dictation. While dictation maybe faster for the physician, it has many negative drawbacks including lack of structured data for analysis and mistakes in transcription that have to be corrected. It is clear from our experience that a better solution is an application which "understands the domain" thus facilitates the structured entry of data by offering relevant suggestions in a customizable point and click interface generating complete and coherent reports. The Active Semantic Documents (ASD) EMR both expedites and enhances the patient documentation process. The support and speed provided by them enables physicians and physician assistants to complete all of their patient documentation while the patient is still in the room allowing the physician to provide better care with a greater volume of patients.

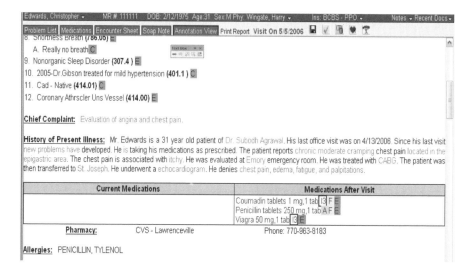

Figure 6-2. An application of Active Semantic Documents

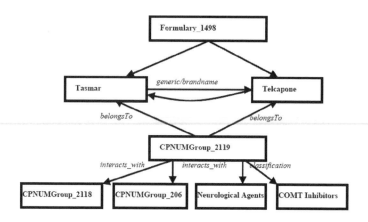

Figure 6-3. Exploration of the neighborhood of the drug Tasma

The annotation view pictured in Figure 6-2 is an Active Semantic Document. The annotations facilitate the creation of the document by performing annotations of ICD9s, words and sentences within the report, and drugs. Three drug related annotations can be seen in Figure 6-2 under the "Current Medications" section. The drug Coumadin has a level three interaction warning. Holding the cursor over this warning displays the name of the drug with which it interacts. The yellow *F* annotation warns that the drug is not covered under the patient's insurance formulary. The annotations can also be extended to also semantically enhance the monograph. The green

A annotation warns that the patient is allergic to this drug. Clicking on the *E*xplore button allows the user to write a prescription for this drug, change quantities, or view the monograph for this drug. Exploring the drug allows for semantic browsing, querying for such details as how many patients are using this class of drug, and for performing decision support. Figure 6-3 shows the exploration of the drug Tasmar.

4.2   Coding of impressions

Section 2 described a scenario in which the complexity of medical billing is remedied by enforcing correct coding at the point of data entry by the nurse, physician, or assistant. As a patient is seen, orders and diagnoses are marked by the healthcare provider on an 'encounter sheet' or 'superbill'. It is imperative at this time that a diagnosis which supports medical necessity for a procedure be given in order to facilitate the billing process. This application employs a novel semantic approach for entering charges into the encounter sheet based on domain knowledge taken from the procedure and diagnosis ontology. This application allows for diagnoses to be taken directly from the documentation described in the previous section. Furthermore, when orders are placed the subset of diagnoses codes which are defined to support medical necessity for that order are shown.

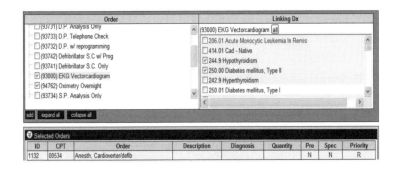

Figure 6-4. Semantic Encounter Sheet

This method ensures that the charges will be entered correctly at the very beginning of the process. The semantic encounter sheet is shown in Figure 6-4. As users select orders from the right column, the left column automatically populates with the linking diagnosis codes which support medical necessity. The doctor is required to validate this choice, and ontology enables him/her to easily consider alternatives.

5.   IMPLEMENTATION DETAILS

The Panacea database holds all information about a patient and the patient's visits including the patient demographics, medications before the visit, medications added during the visit, past and present problems, diagnoses, treatment, doctors seen, insurance information, and a text description of the visit. The method of data entry and data storage ensures that it is well structured and can trivially be converted into a single large XML. It is important to note that the text description is not simply stored as one large string but as a tree structure which can be lexically annotated far faster and with better accuracy compared with using natural language processing. A detailed discussion of this is out of the scope of this paper.

After the XML is created annotations must be applied in order to assert the rules. Since the structure and schema of the XML is known a priori, annotation is simply performed by adding metadata to the correct tags. The correct tags are identified using XPath. This approach has a much higher accuracy them most types of semantic annotation techniques. This is a result of knowing the structure of the XML prior to the annotation.

The module that creates the XML and the module that annotates the XML are separate entities on different servers and implemented in different languages. This was necessary as the legacy code is in ASP and most wide spread tools for XML and ontology querying are written in Java. The two modules communicate by passing the XML from the ASP to the Java server via a REST based web service. The addition of Web 2.0 technologies such as REST services allows much of the requests to generate from the client instead of the server. This gives the application the ability to mask latency and allow easy integration in to client side scripting. This solution offers much more than fixing the heterogeneity created by the two languages. This solution also offers scalability and extensibility. Allowing the memory and IO intensive ontology querying to be done independently of the application server frees up resources which may be used elsewhere.

After annotation a third module applies rules to the annotations. The rules used are written in RDQL. A rule either checks for the existence of an edge or its absence. For example, an 'interaction' relationship should not exist between two drugs or there should be a relationship, 'covered', between a drug and patient's insurance. When these rules are broken metadata is added to the previously added annotations in the form of properties. Once all of the annotations have been applied and the rules are asserted, the annotated XML makes its way back to the client where an XSLT is applied. The XSLT turns the XML into HTML which can be made interactive and presented to the user for review and edits. Currently Panacea annotates doctors, problems, diagnosis, drugs, and patient demographics semantically. The rest of the document is annotated lexically. Queries that could be run against these annotation include but are not limited to:

- drug-drug interaction check,
- drug formulary check (e.g., whether the drug is covered by the insurance company of the patient, and if not what the alternative drugs in the same class of drug are),
- drug dosage range check,
- drug-allergy interaction check,
- ICD-9 annotations choice for the physician to validate and choose the best possible code for the treatment type, and
- preferred drug recommendation based on drug and patient insurance information

Figure 6-5 depicts the architecture of the Active Semantic Document component of Panacea.

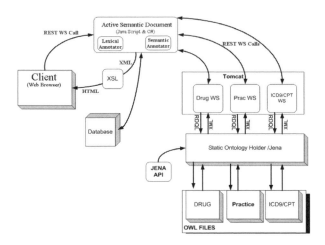

Figure 6-5. ASEMR architecture

6. DEPLOYMENT AND EVALUATION

At AHC, the main site of deployment, the application accommodates between 78 and 80 patient encounters per day, most of which are seen within a four hour time frame. The AHC, with two physicians, two to four mid-level providers, eight nurses, and four nuclear and echo technicians, relies on Panacea/ASEMR for fully Web-based paperless operations for all functions except for billing (which is currently under development). The semantically annotated document creation in conjunction with workflow solutions such as patient tracking has allowed the AHC to operate in 'real time' mode such that the physicians and their assistants are able to complete all documentation for the patient's visit during the encounter. Prior to deploying ASEMR, majority of charts were completed in Panacea after patient hours, often requiring mid-level providers to complete them over the weekend.

As a result of Panacea deployment first, followed by its ASEMR extension, the AHC has greatly increased the volume of patients which they are able to care for, and importantly, without increasing its clinical staff. Figure 6-6 shows the growth of the AHC since March of 2004. This data was obtained by querying the database for the number of appointments scheduled.

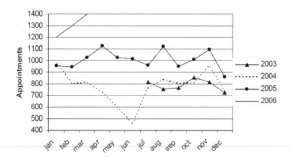

Figure 6-6. Athens Heart Center practice growth

The development of Panacea began in the year 2002 and the ASEMR was deployed in December 2005; it became fully operational in January 2006. In other words, data prior to December 2005 reflects pre-semantic situation (as Panacea did not have any semantic/ontological/rule support, and the data after January 2006 reflect situation after deploying the semantic technology. The number of clinical staff members and facility remained relatively consistent throughout the entire sample period. The AHC saw growth in 2005 as they scheduled around 1000-1200 patients per month. The patient volume for the year 2006 has started at a consistent growth rate of 25-30%, with March peaking around 1400 appointments scheduled per month. Even with this increase in patient volume, the physician assistants are able to accompany the physicians to the hospital immediately after clinic hours instead of charting until late evening hours. Before the deployment of the new annotation view supported in ASEMR the mid-level providers remained in the office an additional 4-5 hours charting after the clinic closed. Main reason for the work remaining after clinical hours related to the need to insure consistency, completeness and correctness of the patient record (e.g., the CPT and ICD9 codes that form parts of billing information captured as part of coding of impressions). Since ASEMR addressed these issues through semantics and rules. Since the time we completed the training of clinical staff, all charts are completed before the clinic closes, and in most cases a chart is completed while the patient is still in the office.

Even with this increase in patient volume, the physician assistants are able to accompany the physicians to the hospital immediately after clinic hours instead of charting until late evening hours. Before the deployment of the new annotation view supported in ASEMR the mid-level providers remained in the office an additional 4-5 hours charting after the clinic closed. Figure 6-7 and Figure 6-8 show the dramatic change in the number of charts completed on the same day versus the number of charts backlogged at the end of the day for pre-deployment and post-deployment months respectively.

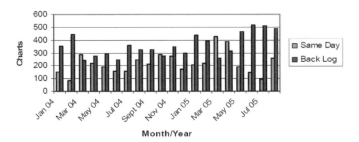

Figure 6-7. Chart completion before the preliminary deployment of the ASMER

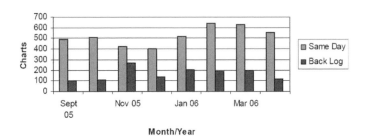

Figure 6-8. Chart completion after the preliminary deployment of the ASMER

We have observed improvement in the patient satisfaction such as through the use formulary check as this could reduce patient costs through the check for medication with lower co-payments and insurance coverage, and the benefits associated with the use coding impression on improved billing as the basis of improved medical records and billing. Our next challenge is to measure these improvements and benefits quantitatively as part of an effort to develop and share return on investment (ROI) measures. As an aside, this work has in part enabled us to be an active member of W3C's interest Group on Semantic Web for Heath Care and Life Sciences, and provide the perspective of semantic Web applications and deployments in healthcare arena with a focus on smaller practices (W3 2005).

Given that this work was done in a live, operational environment, it is nearly impossible to evaluate this system in a "clean room" fashion, with completely controlled environment – no doctors' office has resources or inclination to subject to such an intrusive, controlled and multistage trial. Evaluation of an operational system also presents many complexities, such as perturbations due to change in medical personnel and associated training. In this context, we believe we have been able to present convincing evaluation of the benefits of a semantic technology.

7.   RELATED WORK

Some other healthcare applications have benefited from the use of ontologies. Chen et al. have experimented with step-wise automation of clinical pathways for each patient, in particular, according to the patient's personal health condition at the time of consultation in (H. Chen, D. Colaert and J. De Roo 2004). Their approach uses ontologies and web services; however, this approach does not propose the use of rules to supplement domain knowledge to compensate for the limitations of OWL. BioDASH (E. Neumann and D. Quan, BioDASH 2006) is a Semantic Web prototype of a Drug Development Dashboard that associates disease, compounds, drug progression stages, molecular biology, and pathway knowledge for a team of users. This work mentions use of rule-based processing using off-the-shelf RDF inference engines, and the use of rules to filter and merge data. Kashyap et al present a semantics-based approach to automate structured clinical documentation based on a description logics (DL) system for ontology management in (V. Kashyap, A. Morales et al. 2005). This paper describes the use of document and domain ontologies. Onto-Med Research Group has designed Onto-Builder[40], a tool designed to support the construction and administration of Data Dictionaries in the field of clinical trials. This standard Data Dictionary is then used in the collection and

---

[40] http://www.openclinical.org/dm_ontobuilder.html

analysis of clinical trials data. Quality assurance in carrying out clinical trials and uniformity are some benefits to such ontology.

We also note that as a "SW in Use" track paper, we focus on discussing a deployed system demonstrating the use of semantic web, rather than attempt to distinguish research contributions with respect to years of research in AI and decision support in healthcare, some of which took much longer to mature and find operational use than the new newer technologies. The newer technologies encompassing Semantic Web, SOA and Web 2.0 offer many practical advantages, including ease of use, deployment and maintenance, which we have not discussed in detail due to space limitations. Resources such as OpenClinical (http://www.openclinical.org/), where this system is also listed, provide extensive complementary material covering research, applications and demonstrations.

8.   CONCLUSION AND FUTURE WORK

The approach proposed in this paper combines three ontologies with rules in order to enhancing the accuracy of EMRs both by providing clinical decision support and improving the correctness of medical coding therefore reducing the number of rejected claims. We have presented a semantic approach which improves patient care and satisfaction, and enables healthcare providers to complete all charge entry and documentation before the patient has left the office. At this time, we are unaware of any application similar to ASEMR that is in daily use, especially at small practices in any field of healthcare. During ISWC 2006, we have planned to organize group visits to AHC (which is 5 minutes from the conference venue) to enable all interested persons to observe the use of ASEMR in person (a canned demo is at http://lsdis.cs.uga.edu/projects/asdoc/). This work also demonstrates successful collaboration between academic research and small medical clinics. For business and legal reasons, we are unable to present some details such as error detection and reduction in this paper.

The ASEMR approach can be extended to provide decision support on a deeper level. For example, semantic associations (K. Anyanwu and A. Sheth 2003) can be discovered to find even obscure relationships between symptoms, patient details, and treatments. Semantic alerts will also be explored in future versions such as when a physician scrolls down on the list of drugs and clicks on the desired drug, any study, clinical trial, or news item about the drug and other related drugs in the same category can be displayed. In addition ontologies can be utilized to find contradictions and mistakes in the medical report. Another key area of extension that we are also working on include coupling this system with a billing system with higher degree of automation (e.g., with better workflow and better validation of billing data) than current state of the art in medical billing.

9.   QUESTIONS FOR DISCUSSION

Beginner:
1. Review the on-line demo of the application at http://lsdis.cs.uga.edu/projects/asdoc/ and discuss the usability issues, and the technology that makes that possible (e.g., the use of AJAX technology).
2. Review "Semantic Web in Health-care and Life Sciences - Applications and Demonstrations" at: http://www.w3.org/2005/04/swls/ .

Intermediate:
1. Discuss what features or characteristics of a domain make it more ready for application of Semantic (Web) technologies? Especially discuss why there is more interest and examples in applying Semantic (Web) technologies in life sciences (including biomedical science and healthcare) and biological science domains.
2. Review OpenClinical at http://www.openclinical.org/ and discuss use of knowledge bases and ontologies in Clinical applications.

Advanced:
1. Review/Discuss how the three ontologies used in ASEMR are different, especially in terms of source of data/knowledge used to populate them. Use this as a case study to discuss issues in Ontology Management, such as the need and frequency of updating ontologies.
2. Write the rules described in this chapter in RDQL and SWRL. Discuss architectural choices in efficient implementation of these rules.

10.   SUGGESTED ADDITIONAL READING

- E. Neumann (2005). *"A Life Science Semantic Web: Are We There Yet?"* Sci. STKE 2005 (283), 10 May, p.22. This is an excellent short introduction on the opportunities and challenges in applying Semantic Web in Life Science domain.
- D. Quan, S. Martin, and D. Grossman (2003). *"Applying Semantic Web Techniques to Bioinformatics,"* unpublished manuscript at:

http://theory.csail.mit.edu/~dquan/iswc2003-bioinformatics.pdf . This work presents very good insights into unifying diverse bioinformatics resources, and in the process identifies integration challenges many efforts may face.

- D. Wang, M. Peleg, S. Tu, E. Shortliffe, and R. Greenes (2001). *"Representation of clinical practice guidelines for computer-based implementations,"* Medinfo. 10(Pt 1):285-9. More formal and comprehensive support for clinical guidelines is one of the key next steps to a rather limited workflow ASEMR supports; this paper provides a background on this subject.
- C. Baker, K. Cheung, (Eds.) (2007). *"Semantic Web Revolutionizing Knowledge Discovery in the Life Sciences"*, Springer, 450p. ISBN: 0-387-48436-1. At the time of writing this chapter, this book has the best collection of chapters dealing with technical and applications issues of Semantic Web techniques and technologies in Life Science.

11. ACKNOWLEDGEMENTS:

We thank M. Eavenson, C. Henson, and D. Palaniswami at LSDIS for their effort in ontology design and population. Note: This chapter is largely a reprint of the paper published in the International Semantic Web Conference, 2006 with copyright permission.

12. REFERENCES

AHRQ (2005). Agency for Healthcare Research and Quality - http://www.ahrq.gov/news/press/pr2005/lowehrpr.htm

E. Neumann and D. Quan, BioDASH. (2006). A Semantic Web Dashboard for Drug Development, Pacific Symposium on Biocomputing 11:176-187 Also, http://www.w3.org/2005/04/swls/BioDash/Demo/

CMS (2006). Centers for Medicare and Medicaid Services http://www.cms.hhs.gov/

H. Chen, D. Colaert, J. De Roo (2004). Towards Adaptable Clinical Pathway Using Semantic Web Technology, W3C Workshop Semantic Web for Life Science, 2004.

V. Kashyap, A. Morales, T. Hongsermeier and Q. Li (2005). Definitions Management: A semanticsbased approach for Clinical Documentation in Healthcare Delivery Industrial Track, Proceedings of the 4th International Semantic Web Conference, November 2005

OWL (2004). D. McGuinness, and F. Harmelen, eds. OWL Web Ontology Language Overview http://www.w3.org/TR/owl-features/

A. Seaborne (2004), RDQL - A Query Language for RDF. W3C Member Submission 9 January 2004, http://www.w3.org/Submission/RDQL/

W3 (2005), <u>Semantic Web in Health-care and Life Sciences - Applications and Demonstrations</u>, www.w3.org/2005/04/swls/

K. Anyanwu and A. Sheth (2003). <u>The ρ Operator: Discovering and Ranking Associations on the Semantic Web</u>, The Twelfth International World Wide Web Conference, Budapest, Hungary, May 2003, pp. 690-699.

PART IV – EDUCATION

Chapter 7

TARGETING LEARNING RESOURCES IN COMPETENCY-BASED ORGANIZATIONS
A Semantic Web-based Approach

Anne Monceaux[1], Ambjörn Naeve[2], Miguel-Angel Sicilia[3], Elena Garcia-Barriocanal[3], Sinuhé Arroyo[3] and Joanna Guss[4]

[1]*EADS-Innovation Works,18, rue Marius TERCE, Toulouse, France – anne.monceaux@eads.net*
[2]*Royal Institute of Technology (KTH), Stockholm & University of Uppsala. Uppsala Learning Lab (ULL), Kyrkogårdsgatan 2 C Uppsala, Sweden;– amb@nada.kth.se*
[3]*University of Alcalá de Henares. Polytechnical Building (Computer Science Dept.).Ctra. Barcelona km. 33,600. Alcalá de Henares, Spain – msicilia@uah.es , elena.garciab@uah.es, sinuhe.arroyo@alu.uah.es*
[4]*EADS France – Innovation Works, Learning Systems - CTO-IW-SE-LE, 12, Rue Pasteur - BP76 - 92150 Suresnes Cedex, France – joanna.guss@eads.net*

1. MOTIVATION AND PROBLEM DESCRIPTION

Recent standardization and specification efforts in the area of learning technology (Friesen, 2005) have resulted in a considerable improvement in the interoperability of learning resources across different Learning Management Systems (LMS) and Learning Object Repositories (LOR). Examples are the ADL SCORM and IMS Learning Design specifications, which provide shared languages to express the packaging of learning contents and learning activity designs respectively, among other elements. The central paradigm of such reuse-oriented technology is the notion of *learning objects* (LO) as digital reusable pieces of learning activities or contents. This represents an opportunity for organizations to devise more effective mechanisms for targeting learning activities internally as a way of improving their capacity to respond to the changing business and technological environments and also to the evolving customer needs.

However, transportability of digital learning objects across platforms is only a basic step towards higher levels of automation and possibilities of delegation of tasks to software agents or modules. Such advanced technology requires richer semantics than those offered by current metadata specifications for learning resources (Sicilia and García-Barriocanal, 2005). Semantic Web technology and the use of ontologies are able to provide the required computational semantics for the automation of tasks related to learning objects as selection or composition. In general, they enable new possibilities to enhance organizational learning or even fostering systemic learning behavior inside the organization (Sicilia and Lytras, 2005). In addition, Semantic Web Services (SWS) provide the technical architecture and mediation facilities for semantic interoperability required for selection and composition of learning objects in a distributed environment in which there are potentially many heterogeneous repositories (Lama et al., 2006).

Within the context described, the dynamic search, interchange and delivery of learning objects within a service-oriented context represent a major challenge that needs to be properly addressed. In short, this entails the technical description of the solution in terms of SWS technology, and also the provision of the ontologies, facilities and components required to extend and enhance existing learning technology systems with the advanced capabilities provided by computational semantics. Semantic Web Services provide the required conceptual representations, along with the capabilities to translate and integrate diverse systems that share the common goal of reusing learning objects. A Semantic Web Service engine integrated with existing standardized LMS technology will extend the possibilities of learners, tutors and instructional designers with semantic search tools capable of asking for and retrieving learning objects from any provider that registers itself as a Semantic LOR.

Semantic Web Services, as conceived in the WSMO framework[41] provide the required ontology-based representation flexible enough to specify realistic learning needs and exploit domain or specialized knowledge in the process of search for learning objects (Lama et al. 2006). A key feature of WSMO is the ontological role separation between user/customer (goal) and Web Service. This matches the concept of learning tasks being separate concept in learning literature. However, before a SWS architecture can be fully exploited, there is a need to devise the underlying framework for the expression of learning needs and their subsequent use for selecting learning resources. This chapter addresses one concrete way of expressing such learning needs in terms of competencies, which are especially adequate for organizational learning.

---

[41] http://www.wsmo.org/

Competencies have been defined in terms of observable human performance, (Rothwell and Kazanas, 1992) encompassing several elements: (1) the work situation is the origin of the requirement for action that puts the competency into play, (2) the individual's required attributes (knowledge, skills, attitudes) in order to be able to act in the work situation, (3) the response which is the action itself, and (4) the consequences or outcomes, which are the results of the action, and which determine if the standard performance has been met. This kind of definitions leads to a paradigm of *competency computation* in which both organizational needs and the expected outcomes of learning resources are expressed in terms of competencies, thus enabling numerical or symbolic accounts of the *competency gap*, i.e. the (amount of) competencies that are required to fulfil some give needs or to reach a more desirable status in organizational terms. Existing work on engineering competency ontologies (Sicilia, 2005) has resulted in flexible models that can be used for the critical task of targeting learning activities inside the organization, personalized to the competency record of each employee. This chapter reports on the early implementation of such approach in a concrete organizational context.

With the aim of exploiting the advantages of a Semantic Web Service Architecture to make richer and more flexible the processes of query and specification of learning needs in the context of Learning Management Systems and Learning Object Repositories, a use case centered on competency-based selection in the Aeronautic field is depicted in the following. Based on this analysis, the viability and benefits of the approach are presented and briefly discussed at the end of the chapter.

2.   COMPETENCY DRIVEN TRAINING SELECTION IN THE AERONAUTICAL FIELD

Training significantly contributes to the companies' ability to react on requirements of fast changes markets, customer needs and successful business process. Nowadays, aeronautical industries have a high demand for well-trained teams. At the same time they face continuous changes in their work processes and tools. Not only is continuous education an important process but it is managed on a contractual basis. Therefore, training management activity is a common responsibility of Human Resources (HHRR) departments. Actions and decisions about training are taken by HHRR according to the company objectives. The important requirement for training management is that it supports developing and maintaining the right range of skills and competencies needed for the employees' jobs.

The present use case aims at improving the way in which Training Management can work towards this goal. More in detail, on how to better mediate among domains by reusing or integrating knowledge that results from competency management activities for training selection. Thus, it can be stated that the ultimate mission of Training management is to support Competency management.

In the following, a brief depiction of the main aspects of the use case is presented. Such depiction helps elaborating about the benefits of a Semantic Web-based approach to e-Learning, same for the particular Aeronautical scenario presented as for learning activities in general.

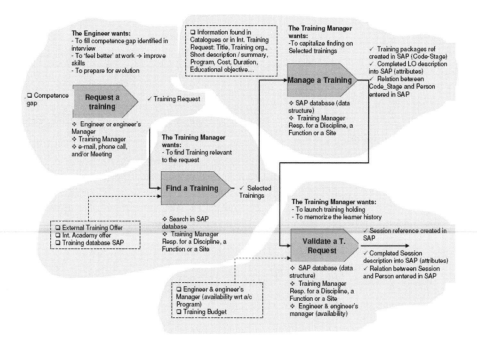

Figure 7-1. Main training processes

2.1   Actors and roles

Several actors participate in training management processes:

1. **Training Manager** from the Human Resource Training Department. The Training Manager takes responsibility for managing training plans

according to the business strategy, as well as training budgets and requests.

2. **Employees**, including Engineers and their Team Managers. They are the originators of training requests.
3. **Training organisms** provide the training offer, including training materials and courses.

In the following section the particularities of the use case are briefly depicted. Figure 7-1 provides an overall view of the main elements in the training management process. The concept of competency can be used in such processes as the language for expressing needs, match learning resources, record the employee profile and measure the effectiveness of the training activities.

2.2 Training related information objects

The HR Training Department activity uses and produces various training related information. In the following, the different categories of information objects of interest for the use case are presented.

- **Structured Training Packages.** HR manages some LO references and description in an SAP database. The granularity level under consideration is that of Structured Training Packages (Naeve et al 2005).
- **Core training catalogue.** Metadata elements are used for publishing purposes. Web training catalogues are rendered accessible through the various subsidiary companies' intranets. These training catalogues are online abstracts of the real SAP database.
- **People training history.** SAP database also allows the management of the people Training History. Human Resources keep track of requested, planned, rejected, accepted or completed training sessions for every Employee. Thus, it is possible to know about the training sessions followed by a given Employee or about the status of a given Training Request.

All these materials are currently stored in databases and independently maintained. A topic hierarchy (See Figure 7-2) is used to filter accesses to the SAP training database. By this means, specialized training engineers benefit for an accurate information access and are made responsible for such or such topics. It is also used to structure the display of the web training catalogue on the intranet.

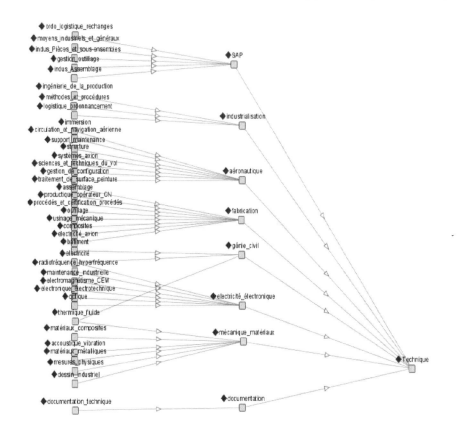

Figure 7-2. Training Topic thesaurus (excerpt)

Training packages can be assimilated to a very specific kind of learning objects, and in consequence, they can be annotated with the competencies that are the expected outcomes of the training. This is already considered in the IEEE LOM learning object metadata standard (in which classifications of learning objects may state competencies) and thus provide room for describing the resources in terms of complex models or ontologies of competencies.

2.3   Training requests

The employees' training requests are addressed to the Training Manager. Two different cases are considered when it comes to deal with training requests:

*   **Individual training request**: It involves an Engineer who wants to follow a particular training or express 'informal' need.

- **Competency driven training request**: The request is a result of an annual interview between an Engineer and her/his Team Manager. This interview results in the Engineer competency profile update, and an agreement on associated training needs.

The training history serves as a way to encode the competency record of employees, so that competency driven requests can use that information as input. This step can be supported by the use of ontologies of competencies, which can be used to "suggest" possible paths of competency acquisition and the associated resources/activities that could be used in each of them. After the eventual completion of the activities, their effectiveness can be used as input for future learning activities, thus closing the loop.

2.4   Competency index and profiles

Competency management, although in the sphere of Human Resources, is a parallel process generating its own information flow and data. The categories of information objects related to competency management are presented below:

- **Reference competency index**: Lists competencies, skills and knowledge involved in professions needed by the organization;
- **Position profile**: Resorts to the reference index to define scaled required competencies and skills at a given position. Several positions may come under the scope of a same reference profession, while requiring different proficiency levels.
- **Personal profile**: Resorts to the reference index to define scaled actual competencies and skills of a person holding the given position.

The use case intends to make them reusable for training retrieval and selection, allowing the calculation of a competency gap between a target position profile and an employee profile. Thus, job positions serve as stereotyped models of competency aggregations.

2.5   Viability and benefits

As shown above, various data and systems are involved in answering training requests taking in account the needed and available competencies. Resorting to Semantic Web-services for the selection and combination of training courses requires that:

- The training search function supports selection/combination and allows taking a competency gap description as criteria. This means:
- Handling queries with various concepts (competencies, professions, topics, etc.) from separated data sources: training database or other LCMS, (training history), profession competency index, etc.
- Handling position profiles and employee profiles to build competency gaps.
- Handling competency profiles and using them as criteria for selecting trainings.
- Handling LO target competency or pre-requisite and use them as criteria for combining trainings.
- LO-based training descriptions include competencies. The key point towards context-aware learning object delivery in the aeronautical context is that both, trainings goals and pre-requisites must be described in terms of competencies. This is where a different problem occurs, related to the cost of manual annotation in time and resources, especially when the training database is continuously evolving to reflect updated offers.
- A unified model applicable to the Training management and Competency management domains supports the indexing of Training Packages using Profession / competency referential; and the retrieval / selection / combination services over Training Packages.

Ontologies of competencies (Monceaux and Guss 2006) provide a rich description framework for the selection of resources, which can be extended with a organizational process view as that described in (Naeve and Sicilia 2006). The benefits in terms of increased decision support are evident from the above, and the organization could also benefit from the systematic approach to defining competencies required. However, an assessment of the viability also requires reflection on the technological challenges required. These entail the storage of competency databases and the development of query resolvers that handle the abovementioned elements. The results of the LUIS project provide the framework for these issues. In consequence, organizations that do actually have a "competency culture" can benefit from semantic technology directly, since the requirements on management and recording of competencies are currently covered by non-semantic technology, perhaps with the exception of some practices as the formal annotation of learning resources with a statement of the competencies they are intended to provide. This is thus a case of technological enhancement on existing practices.

3. THE OVERALL PROCESS VIEW: A COMPETENCY GAP APPROACH

In a service-oriented environment that aims for reusability of service components, the "process-object" – or "process-module" is of vital importance. In this section we will discuss how such process modules can be used as contextual units, e.g., connecting learning objects with learning objectives and competency gaps. Moreover, we will show how such process modules can be connected into service networks, whose overall service goals can be seen as aggregated from and composed of the sub-goals of the participating process modules.

3.1 The Astrakan™ process modelling technique

The basic ideas underlying the Astrakan™ process modelling technique[42] are depicted in Figure 7-3.

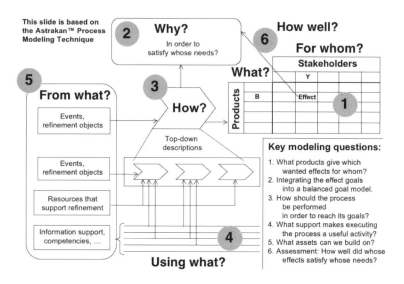

Figure 7-3. The Astrakan process modelling technique

A *Process Module* has certain *Process Goals*, produces *Output Resources* for different Stakeholders, refines *Input Resources* and makes use of Supporting Resources (Figure 7-4). The difference between an input- and a

---

[42] www.astrakan.se

supporting resource is that the former is refined in the process, while the latter facilitates this refinement.

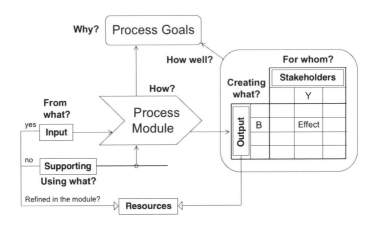

Figure 7-4. A process module with its goals, and its input-, output-, and supporting resources

Figure 7-5 depicts a kind of (= subclass of) Process Module, called a *Learning Process Module (LPM)* with its corresponding *Learning (Process) Goals,* and its *Input-, Output-,* and *Supporting Learning Resources.*

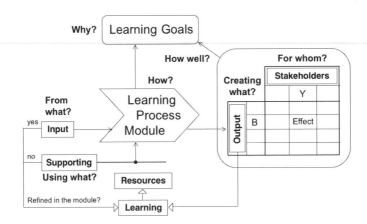

Figure 7-5. A learning process module with its learning goals, and its input-, output-, and supporting learning resources

Observe that, in Figure 7-5, the Learning Process Module (LPMs) provides the crucial connections between Learning Resources (LRs), which include so called Learning Objects (LOs)[43], and Learning Goals (LGs). Hence, it becomes possible to describe why we are using certain LO in a particular LPM, i.e. what pedagogical aspects that we are trying to support and what LGs that we are trying to achieve. Apart from the never-ending debate about their definition, a major criticism against LOs is that they are too often considered in isolation from the learning context within which they are supposed to be used. Hence it becomes difficult to connect LOs with the social and pedagogical dimensions of the learning process, and answer the crucial pedagogical/didactical questions of why LOs are being used and what one is trying to achieve by using them. By applying the modeling techniques introduced in (Naeve et al. 2005) and elaborated in (Naeve and Sicilia 2006), such questions can be answered in a satisfactory way.

3.2   Different types of competency gaps

Since individual competencies are refined and developed by learning, they can be considered as input and output data to learning processes. In fact, each Learning Process Module (LPM) can be considered as filling a Real Competency Gap (RCG), which is the difference between the *Input Competency (IC)*, i.e., what the learner knows before entering the LPM, and the *Output Competency (OC)*, i.e., what (s)he knows after having passed through it. The Formal *Competency Gap (FCG)* is the difference (as specified e.g., in a course manual) between the *Pre-Requisite Competency (PreRC)*, which is required to enter the LPM, and the Post-Requisite Competency (PostRC), which is the competency that the LPM aims to provide for learners that fulfill its corresponding PreRC.

In Figure 7-6, the ICs and OCs are modeled as a kind of Learning Resources, while PreRCs and PostRCs are modeled as a kind of *Learning Goals*. *Pre-assessment* can be used to investigate whether there is a Pre Competency Gap (PreCG), i.e. whether there is a difference between what a learner knows when entering the LPM, and what (s)he should have known in order to enter it. Post-assessment can be used to investigate if the learner has actually acquired the aspired PostRC. If not, then there is a *Post Competency Gap (PostCG)*, i.e., there is a difference between the PostRC and the actual OC for this learner. If there was no PreCG, then we can conclude that something went wrong in this LPM.[44]

---

[43] As well as other types of resources, such as human resources and physical resources (materials, tools, laboratories, etc.)

[44] This is analogous to a software principle called "design-by-contract", where only data that satisfies the pre-conditions are allowed to enter a software module. If the post-conditions are not fulfilled, then we can conclude that something went wrong in this module.

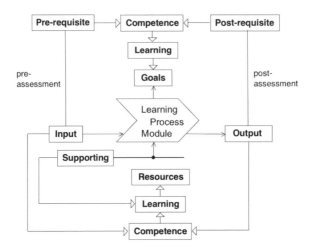

Figure 7-6. A learning process module with a formal and a real competency gap

A *Forward Competency Gap (FCG)* is a difference between what the learner knows and what (s)he plans to know, while a *Backward Competency Gap (BCG)* is a difference between what the learner knows and what (s)he should have known. Hence, with respect to an LPM, a BCG is identical to a PreCG.

In the EADS use case, the difference between an employee's *Personal Profile* and her/his *Present Position Profile* is her/his BCG. The difference between the employee's *Personal Profile* and her/his *Desired Position Profile* is her/his FCG.

In general, FCGs are more associated with strategic learning needs (what a company needs to learn in order to stay in business), while BCGs are more associated with operational learning needs (what a company needs to know in order to deliver in its present undertakings). BCGs often appear because employees leave the company and have to be replaced by others who do not quite know what they (ideally) should have known in order to serve as good replacements.

3.3   Competencies as connectors of learning process modules

A Learning Process (LP) can be modelled as a chain of successive LPMs, where the PostRC of the LPM_k is identified with the PreRC of the LPM_{k+1}. In this way, the large learning goal of the entire LP can be broken down into a sequence of smaller learning (sub)goals for each LPM. This map well to the concepts of goals and sub-goals in WSMO, where there are gg-mediators that are used to mediate between goals.

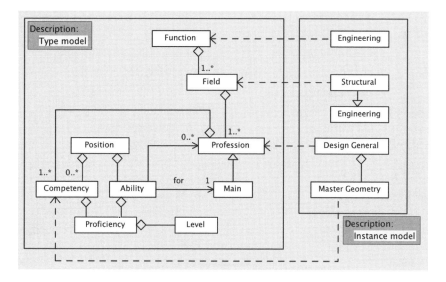

Figure 7-7. The EADS employee competency model

3.4 Modeling with a general competency ontology

Reuse-oriented learning technology emphasizes the role of metadata that describes the properties of learning resources as a mean to provide advanced support for the location and selection of learning resources. These properties are of a various kind, but one of its principal categories is that of describing the *learning needs* the resource facilitates in some way. In semantic approaches to learning technology, ontologies that enable the description of learning needs are thus a critical piece. Learning needs can be stated in many different ways and can be considered to be dependant on theories of learning to some extent. Among them, the concept of *competency* emphasizes the specification of external, observable behavior oriented to performance in activities. In organizational contexts, this entails that competencies are oriented to describe performance in concrete work situations.

The literature on formalizing competencies to date is scarce and fragmentary, and specifications dealing with competencies as *HrXML-Competencies*[45] or *RCDEO*[46], while useful for data interchange, do not provide the required computational semantics. A general purpose schema for competencies (call GCO –General Competency Ontology –) based on the

---

[45] http://www.hr-xml.org
[46] http://www.imsproject.org/competencies/

schema describe in (Sicilia, 2005) has been approached in an attempt to increase the re-usability and flexibility of the resulting technologies.

3.5 Addressing flexibility in the definition of the competency concept

Flexibility in competency specification is currently approached in the ontology in two ways. On the one hand, a competency definition is made up of competency elements, and competency elements are specialized in several components (skills, attitudes and knowledge elements in actual version), allowing for the inclusion of other elements in the future. On the other hand, current schema allow for incomplete definitions of competencies. A competency is completely defined if it is explicitly indicated as such, and this entails that the presence for an individual of all the elements that compose the competency is a necessary and sufficient condition to describe the competency. A competency can be partially defined if it is defined as a primitive competency (i.e. its elements are not defined) or if the described components do not define the competency completely.

The general competency model described in this section is used in the architecture of the LUISA project[47]. Figure 7-8 depicts an scenario inside LUISA, in which a search component talks to the Negotiation Layer (a part of the SWS infrastructure) to get matches for some given competency gap. The resources are stored in (one or several) LOMR (learning object metadata repositories), and the metadata in such repositories can be edited through SHAME tools[48].

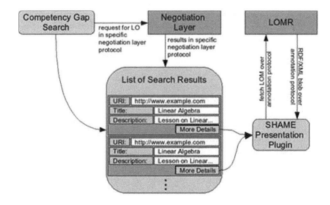

Figure 7-8. Scenario from the LUISA architecture

[47] http://www.luisa-project.eu
[48] http://kmr.nada.kth.se/shame/

See the following example (Figure 7-9): The competency "Programming Java with Eclipse" is composed by two knowledge elements "To know Eclipse environment" and "Programming Java". The competency has been explicitly defined as a *completely defined competency*. If a person P1 has acquired both knowledge elements, a reasoner can deduce that this person has the competency "Programming Java with Eclipse", although it is not expressly stated.

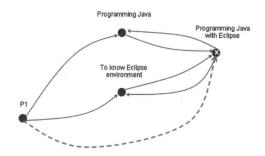

Figure 7-9. Example of completely defined competency

3.6   Competency components

One important issue to deal with in the ontology refers to the need of separate actual competencies, associated to particular individuals, and the definition of competencies as stereotypes. Given that the *Competency* concept represents a discrete competency of an individual generally portrayed as processors. Such processor provides room for software systems that are able to exhibit some competencies.

On top of that, the elements influencing competencies are of a various kinds, including *knowledge, skills, abilities,* and also *attitudes.* By using these concepts a clear separation about three types of traits that represent different aspects of competency is clearly achieved.

For example, an employee may have the knowledge about the different phases of a given internal process, since he or she has attended trainings about it. This is different than having the skill of implementing the process correctly. In fact, the knowledge about the internals of the process may not be necessary for its proper usage, and on the contrary, knowing the internals does not guarantee that the employee is able to use the process efficiently. In addition to that, attitudes represent elements that are not necessarily connected to specific knowledge or skills. For example, having good influencing skills does not always entail that an employee would have the attitude to make his/her opinion prevail. Figure 7-7 provides a screenshot of the modeling of EADS competency ontology. In that case, the terminology was slightly different, but after a mapping phase, they were assimilated to similar concepts in the GCO.

It should be noted that from an ontological perspective, attitudes are mostly domain independent, while knowledge items and skills are not. Examples are "service orientation" or "attentive to details" attitudes that are equally applicable to employees, irrespective of the industry. Some skills are also of a generic nature, like "social aptitude" or "leadership," but many others refer to concrete elements or artifacts that are specific of the industry. Typical examples are "PHP programming skill," "Unix administration," "repairing Aston Martin engines," and the like.

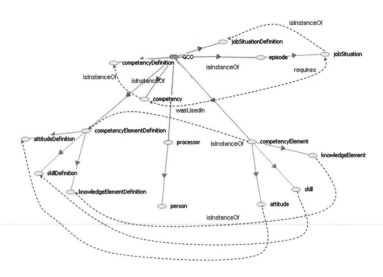

Figure 7-10. Graphical view of the ontology: competencies and competencies definition.

The part of the current version of the ontology that models competencies and competencies definitions is depicted in Figure 7-10. For the sake of clarity, not all the ontology properties are shown.

3.7   Work situations

Competencies are put into play in concrete job situations, which can be considered as a kind of *Episode* in the life of the organization that occurs at a concrete moment in time. The *consequence* attribute in the concept *JobSituation* simply represents the outcome of the episode, which can be used as a source of assessment for various purposes, including the revision of the beliefs the system has about the competencies of the participants.

Competencies and job situations are connected to their respective "definition" elements. These definitions are used to represent stereotypical competencies and job contexts, so that they can be used to describe, for example, job position characterizations in human resource selection processes, or as a way to state the needs of a project.

Each job situation definition requires a number of competencies as defined in *CompetencyDefinitions*. This is a way to describe work situations in terms of required competencies.

Figure 7-11 briefly depicts work situations in the current version of the ontology.

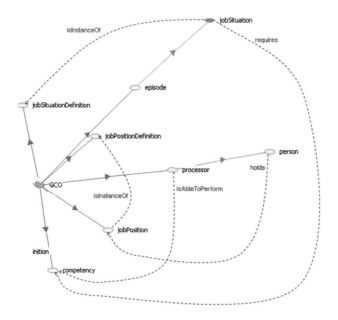

Figure 7-11. Partial graphical view of the ontology: work situations

3.8 Relationships between competency specifications

Competency specifications are implicitly related by the relationships among competency components. For example, if a competency c1 is considered to require some knowledge k1 then, the competency implicitly requires the knowledge of any k1 pre-requisite knowledge. This is represented through the *prerequisite* relationship (knowledge trees can be modeled this way). Skills can also have knowledge elements as prerequisites, and they could be considered to be composite (not in that version of the ontology).

Relationships between competencies can be of a diverse kind. Initially, we only deal with *prerequisite* and *details* relationships here. The latter is conceived as a form of "specialization" in the sense that a competency provides a more detailed description to an existing one. For example, "Administering Oracle databases in large installations" stays at a higher degree of abstraction than "Administering Oracle 9.0 databases in large installations." The specialized competency usually requires more specific knowledge elements. Both the "prerequisite" and "details" relationships entail some form of prerequisition, but the semantics are not exactly the same. For example, the *C1* ≡ *"relational database design"* competency is a prerequisite for *C2* ≡ *"Administering distributed Oracle databases in large installations"*, but it is not a detail, since it reflects only a previous component of knowledge. In other words, the competency *C2* cannot be considered as a specific kind of competency *C1*.

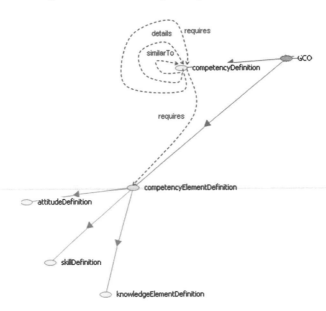

Figure 7-12. Partial graphical view of the ontology: relationships between competencies

Some other simple competency relationships are *equalTo* and *similarTo*. The former is a simple way to state that two competencies are the same, while the latter is a way to express different strengths of correlation or resemblance between competencies.

Figure 7-12 depicts relationships between competencies in the current version of the ontology.

3.9   Defining competency measurement scales

Measurement scales for competencies can also be of a diverse nature. Although the development of simple integer scales is common, other kind of scales could also be allowed. In the ontology, a Measurement is connected to competencies as an elaboration of the simple Level attribute of the *Competency* concept in Figure 7-12. Measurements are always related to a given *MeasurementScale*, and usually some *MeasurementInstruments* associated to such scales are available (e.g., questionnaires or interviews). From this basic level, several types of scales and their associated measurements can be defined. Specific scales can be defined as an instance of *IntegerMeasurementScale*. Each scale must provide some definitions that act as constraints on the description of the measurements.

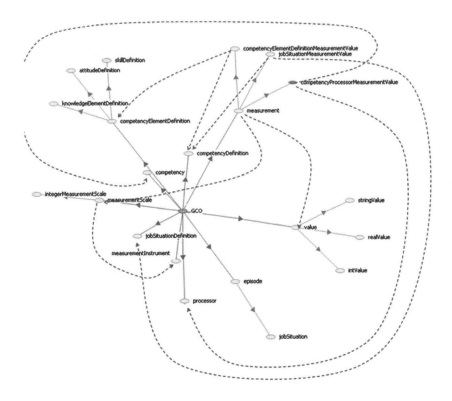

Figure 7-13. Partial graphical view of the ontology: measurements in ontologies

In the ontology, a *JobPosition* is described in terms of competency definitions by specifying a given *MeasurementLevel*, connected to the scale in which the level is expressed. This is an example of how other elements different from processors can be described using the ontology. The elements in current version of the ontology could be complemented with other ontology terms that better describe each measurement instrument, and also with "conversions" from one scale to another, when available.

Figure 7-13 depicts the part of the current ontology that represents measures. For the sake of clarity, properties have not been labeled.

4.   ARCHITECTURAL SOLUTION

In the following the architectural solution provided is putting in the context of the use of competencies. Firstly, the LUISA architecture is presented. Secondly, how it is applied to computing competency gaps is sketched. Finally, the particularities on how it tackles the use of training resources by means of a specialized *QueryResolver* are carefully depicted.

4.1   The LUISA architecture

Currently, the LUISA includes the following core building blocks that are directly related to the competency approach:

- **Competency Gap Search**: It provides the means for finding competencies and filling the competency gap. In short, given a target position and the employee profile, the competency gap search takes care of calculating the competency gap, requesting LO using a specific negotiation layer protocol and finding an appropriate set of learning objects that can in principle fill the competency gap.
- **Negotiation Layer**: The negotiation layer fulfils a two-fold purpose. It receives requests for LO expressed using the specific negotiation protocol. It also takes care of providing the results of a particular competency gap search. This layer is an interface for the WSMO-based SWS layer that integrates heterogeneous sources of LO by means of semantic description of conventional Web Services.
- **SHAME**: Taking as input the results of a competency gap search the SHAME plug-in takes care of presenting them as appropriate. In order to obtain all the necessary metadata it closely communicates with the LOMR module.
- **LOMR**: The LOMR receives LOM metadata from the SHAME plug-in. Additionally, it provides SHAME with RDF/XML blobs, also using the same annotation protocol for its presentation.

4.1.1 Computing competency gaps

Competency gaps are calculated by subtracting the training requirements from a particular target position from trainings already attended by a given employee as detailed on his profile. As a result a collection of metadata that needs to be mapped to learning objects descriptions is produced. Once such process has been achieved, it is the task of the negotiation layer to locate the most appropriate set of learning objects for filling the competency gap. Should that matching set of LOs be available, the competency gap, is indeed filled. Of course this is only one of the many possible competency gap analyzers that could be devised, but it serves as the ground for the future integration of other, perhaps more complex, analysis schemes.

4.1.2 Targeting training resources through an specialized QueryResolver

One of the main tasks of the specialized *QueryResolver* is to manage queries that affect multiple data sources. In short, it takes care of consolidating the results obtained from training repositories, training histories, LCMS or any other that needs to be checked in order to bridge a competency gap. Additionally, it provides indexing capabilities for easing and speeding the combination and location of materials. The idea of having a *QueryResolver* for gap analysis enables the design of several of these components that could be "pluggable" inside the LUISA architecture.

5. CONCLUSIONS

Competencies represent a paradigm of observable workplace behaviour that can be represented in terms of ontologies. These ontologies can be used for the expression of learning needs, and also for the expression of the expected outcomes of these activities. This creates a link between needs and resources that can be exploited for advanced targeting capabilities. A concrete case of organizational learning has been described, followed by a general conceptual model that details how competencies and learning resources can be mapped in a process-oriented framework. Competencies provide the organizational meaning to learning resources, and they can be used as input and outputs in learning process models. Finally, the results of project LUISA have been described as a technical solution using Semantic Web Service technology that uses a given, flexible and generic competency schema. The LUISA solution provides the required semantic technology to fulfil the needs of competency-centric approaches to organizational learning of any arbitrary complexity.

6.   QUESTIONS FOR DISCUSSION

Beginner:

1. Competencies are a model of observable human behavior that is widely used in the literature about organizational learning. However, the term "competency" (plural *competencies*) is used in the literature with different meanings. The GCO model presented in this paper provides a flexible definition of competencies but other ways of referring to the same things can be found. The following questions are oriented to:

   - It is common in the literature on theories of learning to refer to concepts as declarative knowledge, procedural knowledge and values as related to learning. How these three terms relate to the competency elements skills, knowledge items and attitudes?
   - The O*Net database[49], containing information on hundreds of standardized and occupation-specific descriptors. They include the concept of "skill". How does the O*Net concept of skill related to the GCO described in the chapter? And how the rest of the concepts in O*Net map to the GCO?

2. The key ingredient of competency-based approaches is a correct understanding of what competencies, their components and their relationships are. This is an understanding and analysis phase that requires reflection on how competencies are defined and measured inside the organization.

Intermediate:

1. Expressing organizational needs in terms of competencies requires some kind of forecasting or at least a consideration of the requirements for the short terms regarding the capacity of the employees. The competency gap then expresses the competencies (or competency components) currently not available among the employees, and then the process of matching and targeting learning resources (learning objects) takes the gap and attempts to select the best learning activities/contents that can be used to facilitate the learning process that eventually might result in the required increased human capacity. However, this process is not as simple at seems at first glance, and many issues that require the use of complex models – as those that can be expressed in terms of ontologies –

---

[49] http://www.onetcenter.org/

demand attention. The following questions are oriented to reflect on some of these issues:

- How can learning resources be described to facilitate search in terms of competencies?
- Once learning activities have been programmed and carried out by the target employees, there is a need to evaluate the acquisition of the required knowledge. How does this impact the assessment of the learning resources for future learning programs?
- How can the agenda and constraints of the employees be taken into account in the delivery of the learning activities resulting from a competency gap analysis process?

2. Learning object metadata in semantic form is an alternative for resolving question (1) – some answers can be found in (Sicilia, 2006). Question (2) points out to the possibility of using the evaluation of the activities to rate in some way the learning resources used, so that those that have effectively facilitated the required learning are considered best, and those that have not can be considered to be discarded or improved. Question (3) introduces the complex issues of time planning. Gap analysis can be combined with temporal (or spatial) constraints for a more informed way of targeting learning activities inside an organization.

Advanced:

1. There is not a single, universal approach for computing competency gaps from a given record of competencies. This is among other factors because the relationships between competencies can be of very different natures; there is not a universal method to assess competencies and competencies can be described at different levels of granularity. In consequence, competency ontologies as the GCO described in the chapter are "upper models" or general schemas that can be used and extended in several directions. The following questions pose some of the issues that could be considered for concrete applications.

2. How can competencies be measured for particular employees? Since competencies are related to workplace performance, which type of methods are more reliable? Peer assessment might be one of them?

3. How can competency components be aggregated into composite competencies? What is the difference between dependencies between competencies and competency components? What are the implications of these kind of issues for computing competency gaps?

4. When considering a concrete organizational need expressed in terms of competencies, the matching process should require an exact mix of competencies? In other words, if some employee possess competency

level 3 for competency X and the requirement is a level of four, could this be compensated, for example, by an "excess" in other of the required competencies?

All these questions are actually research questions and they do not have a unique answer. Many different approaches can be devised considering variants of the algorithms of gap analysis and/or tailored models of competencies. This is essentially the approach of the LUISA project, different *QueryResolvers* can be used to implement different (perhaps competing) approaches, creating opportunities for contrast and customization.

7.   SUGGESTED READINGS

- The recent book on competencies in organizational e-learning edited by Sicilia (2006) provides a selection of chapters about the competency approach for organizational learning. It includes chapters on the key organizational dimension, but also several chapters that describe concrete applications of Semantic Web technologies to managing competencies. As such, it is an excellent complement to the approach described in this chapter.
- The description of learning resources can be accomplished through metadata. Standards and specifications regarding different aspects of learning-oriented metadata are introduced in Friesen (2005). After a basic understanding of the specifications mentioned by Friesen is achieves, it is worthwhile to go through some papers that deal with the extension of such standards with Semantic Web technology. Many examples can be found in the "Applications of Semantic Web technologies for e-Learning" (SW-EL) workshop series[50], and Sicilia and García-Barriocanal (2005) can be used for a general understanding of the issues behind those approaches.

8.   ACKNOWLEDGEMENTS

This work has been supported by project LUISA (*Learning Content Management System Using Innovative Semantic Web Services Architecture*), code FP6–2004–IST–4 027149 and by project SERE-OC (Resource

---

[50]http://www.win.tue.nl/SW-EL/

selection in e-learning based on competency ontologies), code CCG06-UAH/TIC-0606 funded by UAH and the CAM (Comunidad Autónoma de Madrid).

9.   REFERENCES

Friesen, N., 2005, Interoperability and learning objects: An overview of e-learning standardization. *Interdisciplinary J. of Knowledge and Learning Objects.* **1**: 23-31.

Lama, N., Arroyo, S., Sicilia, M.A. and López Cobo, J.M., 2006, Making learning objects useful with semantic web services. *eChallenges Conf.*

Lytras, M. and Naeve, A., (eds), 2005, *Intelligent Learning Infrastructures for Knowledge Intensive Organizations: A Semantic Web Perspective,* IDEA publishing group.

McGreal, R., 2004, Learning objects: A Practical definition. *Int. J. of Instructional Technology and Distance Learning* **1**(9).

Monceaux, A., Guss, J., 2006, Training management system for aircraft engineering: indexing and retrieval of corporate learning object. *Industry Forum: Business applications of Semantic Web challenge Research in the European Semantic Web Conference ESWC'06.*

Naeve, A. and Sicilia, M-A., 2006, Learning processes and processing learning: From Organizational Needs to Learning Designs, *Invited paper for the ADALE workshop* (in conjunction with the Adaptive Hypermedia conference).

Naeve, A., Yli-Luoma, P., Kravcik, M., Lytras, M., Simon, B., Lindegren, M., Nilsson, M., Palmér, M., Korfiatis, N., Wild, F., Wessblad, R., Kamtsiou, V., Pappa, D. and Kieslinger, B., 2005, A Conceptual Modelling Approach to Studying the Learning Process with a Special Focus on Knowledge Creation. *Deliverable 5.3 of the Prolearn EU/FP6 Network of Excellence*, IST 507310.

Rothwell, W. and Kazanas, H., 1992, *Mastering the Instructional Design Process.* Jossey-Bass.

Sicilia, M. A., 2005, Ontology-based competency management: Infrastructures for the knowledge- intensive learning organization, in *Intelligent Learning Infrastructures in Knowledge Intensive Organizations: A Semantic Web Perspective.* Idea Group, Hershey, PA, pp. 302-324.

Sicilia, M.A. and García-Barriocanal, E., 2005, On the convergence of formal ontologies and standardized e-learning. *Journal of Distance Education Technologies,* **3**(2): 12-28

Sicilia, M.A. and Lytras, M., 2005, The semantic learning organization. *The learning organization,* **12**(5): 402-410.

Sicilia, M.A. (ed.), 2006. *Competencies in organizational e-learning. Concepts and Tools.* Idea Group publishing, Hershey, PA.

Chapter 8

DEVELOPING COURSE MANAGEMENT SYSTEMS USING THE SEMANTIC WEB

Jorge Cardoso
Department of Mathematics and Engineering, University of Madeira, Funchal, Portugal –
jcardoso@uma.pt

1. INTRODUCTION

Many researchers believe that a new Web will emerge in the next few years based on the ongoing large-scale research and developments on the semantic Web. Nevertheless, the industry and its main players are adopting a "wait-and-see" approach to see how real-world applications can benefit from semantic Web technologies (Cardoso, Miller et al. 2005). The success of the semantic Web vision (Berners-Lee, Hendler et al. 2001) is dependant on the development of practical and useful semantic Web-based applications.

While the semantic Web has reached considerable stability from the technological point of view, with the development of languages to represent knowledge (such as OWL (OWL 2004)), to query knowledge bases (RQL (Karvounarakis, Alexaki et al. 2002) and RDQL (RDQL 2005)), SPARQL, and to describe business rules (such as SWRL (Ian Horrocks, Peter F. Patel-Schneider et al. 2003)), the industry is still skeptical about its potential. For the semantic Web to gain considerable acceptance from the industry it is indispensable to develop real-world semantic Web-based applications to validate and explore the full potential of the semantic Web (Lassila and McGuinness 2001). The success of the semantic Web depends on its capability to support applications in commercial settings (Cardoso, Miller et al. 2005).

In several fields, the technologies associated with the semantic Web have been implemented with a considerable degree of success. Examples include semantic Web services (OWL-S 2004), tourism information systems (Cardoso 2004), semantic digital libraries, (Shum, Motta et al. 2000), semantic Grid (Roure, Jennings et al. 2001), semantic Web search (Swoogle 2005), and bioinformatics (Kumar and Smith 2004).

To take the development and widespread character of semantic Web applications a step further, we have developed a Course Management System (CMS) (Mandal, Sinha et al. 2004) based on an infrastructure entirely designed using the technologies made available by the semantic Web, namely OWL, RQL, RDQL, SPARQL, Bossom (Bossom 2005), and SWRL.

CMSs are becoming increasingly popular. Well-known CMSs include Blackboard.com and WebCT.com whose focus has centered on distance education opportunities. Typically, a CMS includes a variety of functionalities, such as class project management, registration tools for students, examinations, enrolment management, test administration, assessment tools, and online discussion boards (Meinel, Sack et al. 2002).

The system that we have developed is part of the Strawberry project and explores the use of semantic Web technologies to develop an innovative Semantic Course Management System (S-CMS). The S-CMS provides a complete information and management solution for students and faculty members. Our focus and main objective is to automate the different procedures involved when students enroll or register for class projects. Managing a large course and its class projects is a complex undertaking. Many factors may contribute to this complexity, such as a large number of students, the variety of rules that allow students to register for a particular project, students' background, and students' grades.

2.   S-CMS ARCHITECTURE

The architecture of our system is composed of seven distinct layers (Figure 8-1): source layer, connection layer, instance layer, query layer, inference layer, application layer, and presentation layer. The layers are articulated in the following way. The source layer includes all the data and information needed by our semantic course management system. It typically includes data stored in relational databases (other types of data source are also supported). At this level, we can find information which describes which faculty members teach which courses, which students are enrolled for a particular course, which students are enrolled in a degree, personal information about students and teachers, etc. The next layer, the connection layer, is responsible for connecting to the data sources, using a variety of protocols.

The instance layer is the first layer that uses semantic Web technologies. It is responsible for managing ontologies describing university domain information such as courses, students, projects, and teachers. It is also in charge of transforming the data and information extracted from the data sources into a set of ontology instances. Essentially, this layer creates a knowledge-base that will be used by the upper layers. It gets the local schema of heterogeneous data sources under consideration and creates a unique and virtual global scheme (i.e., an ontology). Since all data sources refer to the same ontology, theoretically there are not syntactic neither semantic conflicts.

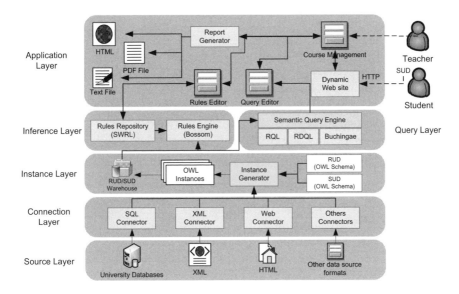

Figure 8-1. S-CMS architecture

The query layer supplies an interface that allows querying the knowledge-base. The inference layer allows carrying out inference using semantic rules on the knowledge-base. For example, it is possible to inquire if all the students enrolled in a project have all passed on the Knowledge Engineering course. The application layer provides the Course Management System *per se* to teachers and students. Teachers are able to create projects associated with courses and define semantic enrolment rules. Students are able to specify that they wish to enroll for a specific project. Additionally this layer gathers the knowledge inferred from applying the semantic rules to the semantic knowledge-base and formats it into a suitable presentation medium (such as PDF or HTML). In the next section we will describe each of the layers of our architecture in detail.

2.1   Source layer

Course management systems need to access a variety of data sources to access data and information about students, teachers, degrees, physical resources (such as class rooms and computing facilities), courses, and grades. To develop robust course information management applications it is important to develop an architecture that can access and integrate unstructured, semi-structured, and structured data. We will see that the use of an ontology will allow us to integrate data with different structures, resolving the structural heterogeneity of data sources.

Data sources are uniquely identifiable collections of stored data, called data sets for which there exist programmatic access and for which it is possible to retrieve or infer a description of the structure of the data, i.e. its schema. We have recognized various data sources that need to be considered when integrating university management systems: flat files, HTML Web pages, XML, and relational databases.

At the University of Madeira we have identified two main types of data sources that needed to be accessed in order to retrieve relevant information about courses and projects: HTML and databases data sources. Therefore, we have developed two Eclipse plug ins to access these types of sources (see next section).

HTML. Most, if not all, the Universities have Web sites for storing and advertising the description of their course, degrees, and projects. Course management systems require integrating Web-based data sources in an automated way for querying, in a uniform way, across multiple heterogeneous Web sites, containing university related information.

Databases. In universities, it is almost unavoidable to use databases to produce, store, and search for critical data. Yet, it is only by combining the information from various database systems that course management systems can take a competitive advantage from the value of data. Different university departments use distinct data sources. To develop course management systems, the most common form of data integration is achieved using special-purpose applications that access data sources of interest directly and combine the data retrieved with the application itself. While this approach always works, it is expensive in terms of both time and skills, fragile due to the changes to the underlying sources, and hard to extend since new data sources require new fragments of code to be written. In our architecture, the use of semantics and ontologies to construct a global view makes the integration process automatic, and there is no need for a human integrator. The University of Madeira database that we have used had around 200 tables, 600 views, a diversity of data types and a large dataset. The number of students is in the range of 13 000. One main problem that we found is that there was no documentation available describing the tables, attributes, and views.

2.2   Connection layer

The connection layer maintains a pool of connections to several data sources (in our implementation we use relational databases and HTML online Web pages). We use a connection layer to achieve two goals: abstraction and efficiency. On the one hand, the connection layer adds a level of abstraction over the data sources and it is responsible for presenting a single interface to the underlying data sources. On the other hand, the connection layer provides connection pooling to considerably increase application processing. When the instance layer requires data from the connection layer, connections to the data sources must be established, managed, and then freed when the access is complete. These actions are time and resource consuming. The use of a connection layer minimizes the opening and closing time associated with making or breaking data source connections. For the S-CMS application, we have developed three Eclipse plug ins. Two of the plug ins are customized to access MySQL and Microsoft SQLServer 2000 databases, while the third plug in is dedicated to retrieve information from HTML Web pages.

At this state the major difficulty that we had was to obtain a copy of the University database from the administrative department with real data. The authorization to use the database has taken more than 3 months to arrive. Furthermore, the copy of the database that was given to us had the data fields with sensitive information altered. Examples these fields included students' PIN and phone numbers.

2.3   Instance layer

Data integration is a challenge for course management systems since they need to query across multiple heterogeneous, autonomous, and distributed (HAD) university data sources produced independently by multiple organizations units. Integrating HAD data sources involves combining the concepts and knowledge in the individual university data sources into an integrated view of the data. The construction of an integrated view is complicated because organizations store different types of data, in varying formats, with different meanings, and referenced using different names (Lawrence and Barker 2001).

We have identified four types of information heterogeneity (Sheth 1998; Ouskel and Sheth 1999) that may arise when we try to integrated HAD university data sources:

1. **System heterogeneity**: Applications and data may reside in different hardware platforms and operating systems.
2. **Syntactic heterogeneity**: Information sources may use different representations and encodings for data. Syntactic interoperability can be achieved when compatible forms of encoding and access protocols are used to allow information systems to communicate.
3. **Structural heterogeneity**: Different information systems store their data in different document layouts and formats, data models, data structures and schemas.
4. **Semantic heterogeneity**: The meaning of the data can be expressed in different ways leading to heterogeneity. Semantic heterogeneity considers the content of an information item and its intended meaning.

Approaches to the problems of semantic heterogeneity should equip heterogeneous, autonomous, and distributed software systems with the ability to share and exchange information in a semantically consistent way (Sheth 1999).

To allow the seamless integration of HAD university data sources rely on the use of semantics. Semantic integration requires knowledge of the meaning of data within the university data sources, including integrity rules and the relationships across sources. Semantic technologies are designed to extend the capabilities of data sources allowing to unbind the representation of data and the data itself and to give context to data. The integration of university data sources requires thinking not of the data itself but rather the structure of those data: schemas, data types, relational database constructs, file formats, etc.

As a solution to the problem of integrating heterogeneous data sources we provide a uniform access to data. To resolve syntactic and structural heterogeneity we map the local data sources schema into a global conceptual schema. Since semantic problems can remain, we use ontologies to overcome semantic heterogeneity. An ontology is an agreed vocabulary that provides a set of well-founded constructs to build meaningful higher level knowledge for specifying the semantics of terminology systems in a well defined and unambiguous manner. Ontologies can be used to increase communication either between humans and computers. The three major uses of ontologies (Jasper and Uschold 1999) are:

1. To assist in communication between humans.

2. To achieve interoperability and communication among software systems.
3. To improve the design and the quality of software systems.

The main component of the instance layer is the Instance Generator. The data extracted by the connection layer is formatted and represented using two different ontologies, the RUD (University Resource Descriptor) and SUD (Student University Descriptor). In the following sections we describe the two ontologies and their instances.

2.3.1 Ontology creation

To deploy our ontologies we have adopted the most prominent ontology language, OWL (OWL 2004). The development of an ontology-driven application typically starts with the creation of an ontology schema. Our ontology schemas contain the definition of the various classes, attributes, and relationships that encapsulate the business objects that model a university domain. After conducting an analysis of ontology editors, we have selected Protégé (Knublauch, Fergerson et al. 2004) to construct our ontologies.

Since the objective of S-CMS application was to develop a system which provided the ability to a student enroll in a course projects, the inference over OWL documents (RUD and SUD) needed to answer to questions which included:

*   Who are the teachers and students?
*   What courses are offered by a department?
*   Which courses are assigned for a specific teacher?
*   For which courses a student is enrolled?
*   Which projects are assigned to a course?
*   What are the students' grades of taken courses?

The RUD and SUD ontologies have the following characteristics.

RUD (University Resource Descriptor). A University Resource Descriptor is a semantic knowledge-base that integrates information coming from several external data sources spread throughout the University of Madeira. As we have seen in section 2.1, data describing important resources to our S-CMS application were stored in relational databases or HTML Web pages. Our RUD integrated information about the physical recourses of the university, classes, courses and degrees offered, faculty members, students enrolled at the university, etc. All the information is represented in OWL. The RUD schema has much more information than the one that comes from the various data sources since it establishes hundreds of relationships between concepts. The relationships are fundamental and will be used by the inference layer to infer new knowledge.

SUD (Student University Descriptor). A Student University Descriptor is a resource that describes a university student. Each student of the university has a SUD. A SUD includes information such as the student's name, ID, courses taken, courses enrolled, degree, telephone number, age, etc. In our architecture, each SUD is represented in OWL.

Students can make available their SUD using two alternatives. They can simply put their SUD in their university home page or they can rely on the SUD management system to manage and advertise their SUD. The idea of SUDs was inspired by the concept of RSS (RSS 2005) (Really Simple Syndication). The technology of RSS allows Internet users to subscribe to websites that have provided RSS feeds; these are typically sites that change or add content regularly. Unlike RSS subscriptions, SUD do not include information about news but about students. Figure 8-2 illustrates part of the SUD schema for students.

```
( . . . )
<owl:Class rdf:ID="Student">
    <rdfs:subClassOf>
      <owl:Restriction>
        <owl:cardinality rdf:datatype=

"http://www.w3.org/2001/XMLSchema#int">1
        </owl:cardinality>
        <owl:onProperty>
          <owl:DatatypeProperty
rdf:ID="AverageScore"/>
        </owl:onProperty>
      </owl:Restriction>
    </rdfs:subClassOf>
    <rdfs:subClassOf>
      <owl:Class rdf:ID="Person"/>
    </rdfs:subClassOf>
    <rdfs:subClassOf>
      <owl:Restriction>
        <owl:onProperty>
          <owl:DatatypeProperty rdf:ID="StudentID"/>
        </owl:onProperty>
        <owl:cardinality rdf:datatype=
              "http://www.w3.org/2001/XMLSchema#int">1
        </owl:cardinality>
      </owl:Restriction>
    </rdfs:subClassOf>
  </owl:Class>
( . . . )
```

Figure 8-2. SUD schema represented in OWL

2.3.2 Ontology population

By ontology population we refer to a process, where the class structure of the RUD and SUD ontologies already exists and is extended with instance data (individuals). This can be done either by a computer or by a human editor. In our case, the RUD and SUD instances are created automatically by the instance generator. Figure 8-3 illustrates the SUD instance created for the student Lee Hall.

```
<Student rdf:ID="LeeHall2041999">
(...)
  <StudentID rdf:datatype=

"http://www.w3.org/2001/XMLSchema#nonNegativeInteger">
    2041999
  </StudentID>
  <StudentName>Lee Hall</StudentName>
  <Degree>Computer Science </Degree>
  <StudentEmail>lhall@mail.pt</StudentEmail>
  </StudentEmail>
  <Studies>
    <Subject rdf:ID="Semantic_Web">
      <SubjectName>Semantic Web</SubjectName>
(...)
    </Subject>
  </Studies>
(...)
</Student>
```

Figure 8-3. A SUD instance represented in OWL

2.3.3 Difficulties in creating and populating the ontology

During the process of creating the RUD and SUD ontology and generating the instance to populate the ontologies schema we have found the following difficulties:

- Since the University database has 200 tables and there was no documentation available it was difficult to identify and decide the relevant classes, subclasses and properties.
- There was a considerable amount of duplicate values in the database. Selecting the most appropriate values involved also a considerable ffort.
- There was no direct mapping between OWL classes and the corresponding database tables. The same happen with the HTML Web pages.

- Make use OWL expressiveness, namely with the especial properties such as transitivity, symmetry, inverse, functional, inverse functional.
- The examples of OWL documents that we have found in the Internet were few and simple and did not represent the true complexity of OWL documents.
- To take advantage of the expressive capabilities of OWL we had to increase the complexity of representation which was difficult to manage.
- As the classes and properties are connected in a recursive fashion we could not simply create all instances of a certain class because other might need to already have been defined.
- The tool that we have used to create ontologies, Protégé, although being very intuitive in its usage had an error when translating OWL documents.
- The Jena API (Jena 2005), used to programmatically manipulate OWL ontology models, did not load the models after a change.
- The generator of instances developed was not generic. It specific to this particular RUD and SUD schema, this brings some disadvantages in further enhancements because any change in the schema can led to modification at the programmatic level.

2.4   Query layer

The query layer provides a query interface to the knowledge-base formed with all the RUD and SUD ontology instances automatically generated. The query interface understands four distinct semantic query languages: RQL (RDF Query Language), RDQL (RDF Data Query Language), Buchingae, SPARQL. These languages allow querying ontology classes, navigating to its subclasses, and discovering the resources which are directly classified under them. Our initial objective was to make available to users a language that would enable us to query the native representation of our knowledge-base, i.e. OWL, but no suitable query language of this type exists yet.

Using this layer, teachers are able to query student and university information. For example, the following query expressed in RDQL allows selecting the students that have a GPA greater than 4.0 marks.

```
SELECT ?x,?c,?z
WHERE
    (?x <http://apus.uma.pt/RUD.owl#HasGPA> ?y),
    (?x <http://apus.uma.pt/RUD.owl#Studies> ?c),
    (?y <http://apus.uma.pt/RUD.owl#Value> ?z)
    AND ?z>4.0
```

As another example, the following query expressed in Buchingae allows a teacher to inquire about the students that are enrolled in a specific course,

```
query qu is p:Studies(?st, ?course) and
            p:Teaches(?prof, ?course);
```

These queries are not meant to be designed by the end users of the system. Such as with SQL queries, they are developed for users by the system administrator.

2.5   Inference layer

We have implemented a rule management system to extract and isolate course management logic from procedural code. Since the rules associated with the enrollment of students for class projects may change quite often, these changes cannot be handled efficiently by representing rules embedded in the source code of the application logic. The option to detach enrolment rules from the source code gives administrators an effective way of creating the rule base and of building and changing rules. The following list considers some advantages of separating enrolment rules from the application logic:

1. Student enrolment rule reuse across other course management systems.
2. A better understanding of enrolment rules through separate business rules.
3. Documentation of enrolment decisions through rules.
4. Lower application maintenance costs.
5. Ease of changing enrolment rules by using visual tools.

In S-CMS, the rules are defined in SWRL (Semantic Web Rule Language) or Buchingae. They correspond to axioms about classes (concept) or their properties of the instance stored in the OWL knowledge-base. By applying these rules to the set of facts it is possible to infer new facts.

SWRL was designed to be the rule language of the semantic Web enabling rule interoperation on the Web. SWRL is based on a combination of the OWL DL and OWL Lite. It provides the ability to write Horn-like rules expressed in terms of OWL for reasoning about OWL individuals.

Since SWRL rules are fairly well-known, we give an example of a Buchingae rule. The rule states that only students that have taken the course Knowledge Engineering (CS6100) and Logic Programming (CS6550) are eligible to enroll for a the class project of the course Introduction to Semantic Web (CS8050),

```
prefix builtin =
        http://www.etri.re.kr/2003/10/bossam-builtin#;
prefix RUD = http://apus.uma.pt/RUD.owl#;
namespace is http://www.etri.re.kr/samples#;

rulebase rb01
{
    (...)
    rule R01 is
      if
        classTaken(?x, RUD:CS6100) and
        classTaken(?x, RUD:CS6550)
          then
              eligible(?x, RUD:CS8050)
}
```

A large number of rule engines are available as open source software. Some of the most popular engines include Jess, Algernon, SweetRules, and Bossam. We chose Bossam (Bossom 2005), a forward-chaining rule engine, as the first rule engine candidate for our semantic course management system since it supports OWL inferencing, it works seamlessly with Java, is well documented, and is very easy to use and configure.

2.6   Application layer

The application layer is composed of two applications: the S-CMS manager and the dynamic enrolment Web site.

S-CMS Manager. We have developed an integrated class project management environment using Eclipse SDK 3.1.1 (Eclipse 2005). Eclipse is an open source framework focused on providing an extensible development platform and application frameworks for building software.

When a teacher interacts with the system, a list of all the courses that he is currently teaching is displayed. This information is retrieved from the RUD knowledge-base. The teacher is then able to create and delete class projects associated with a given course. Figure 8-4 shows the main screen of the S-CMS application.

For each class project created, the teacher is responsible for creating and managing the semantic enrolment rules. The integrated class project management environment has a SWRL and Buchingae rule editor available for this purpose. Semantic enrolment rules can be defined for specific projects (project enrolment rules), for a specific course (course enrolment rules), or for all the projects independently of the course (global enrolment rules). As explained previously, a teacher can define a project enrolment rule for the project Merging Ontologies Semi-Automatically of the course Semantic Web (CS8050) which states that only students that have taken the Knowledge Engineering course (CS6100) and Logic Programming (CS6550) can enrol.

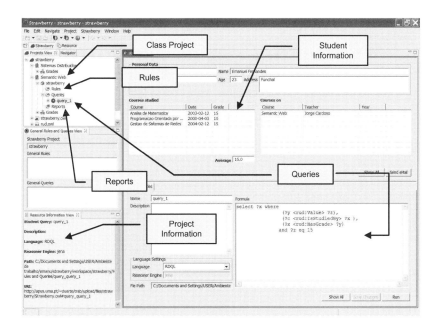

Figure 8-4. Strawberry main application

Dynamic Enrolment Web site. The Enrolment Web site is one of the interfaces for the Strawberry project. It has two main functions. First, it. allows for students to enroll into projects proposed by their lecturers and second, it allows the teacher to post reports and other relevant information so that students can easily access it, better enabling the communication process between teachers and students.

A student can enroll in a class project using the S-CMS as a single portal via HTTP/HTML. The S-CMS provides an overview Web page for each class project in which the student can enroll. The Web pages are automatically generated from the S-CMS manager.

Students can be added to a class project either by a bulk upload from the information stored in the RUD, or individually. In the latter case, the student has to indicate the URL of its SUD. The SUD will be read by the S-CMS and matched against a student instance in the RUD. All the information of a student relevant to enrolling for a class project will be retrieved automatically from the RUD. If a student may decide to drop out of a class project he only needs to resend his SUD to the system indicating that he wishes to drop out of a given project.

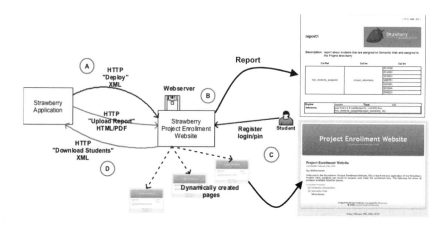

Figure 8-5. General structure of the Dynamic Enrollment Web site

Figure 8-5 illustrates the general structure of the Dynamic Enrollment Web site. The Web site reflects the current state of the S-CMS manager. The interaction with the S-CMS manager is the following:

a) Using the S-CMS manager, professors can dynamically deploy a Web site for students' enrollment. Professors do not have do deal with Web pages in any way, all the process is automatic. When a professor selects the deploy option, an HTTP connection is established with the Web server and an XML configuration file is uploaded. This file contains a listing of all the courses and project that should be shown in the Web site. Each course has an id, a name, a lecturer and a set of projects. Each project has an id, a name, a description, a last update date and a color.

b) The Web site automatically and dynamically creates a set of Web pages to enable students to register for projects. The module that carry out these tasks was build in PHP because it does not require any other software other than a simple HTTP Server with PHP, it allows to create pages physically dynamically, and made possible the use of XML to exchange data with the S-CMS manager.

c) Students register for projects

d) The list of students that have registered for a particular project is downloaded to the S-CMS manager using XML.

Report Generator. Once students have enrolled for class projects, it is helpful for teachers to have a tool to automatically generate a report indicating which students are in fact allowed to be part of a class project for which they want to enroll. Not all the students that send their SUD to enroll in a class project can indeed carry out the project. The decision that determines if a student can actually carry out a specific project is based on the semantic enrolment rules.

At the presentation layer, the teacher is able to generate enrolment reports that indicate which students are allowed to carry out a project and which are not. We support several formats for the reports. We use the Formatting Objects Processor (FOP 2005) to convert the results from applying enrolment rules to PDF, TXT, and HTML. The Formatting Objects Processor (FOP) is an open source Java API that can convert XML data into reports in PDF format, as well as other relevant formats such as TXT, SVG, AWT, MIF, and PS.

The Grading Ontology and its Plug-In. The grading plug-in is a feature of the Strawberry project on which a Grading Ontology is used to enable grading of students that attend a course. The plug-in enables users to define a grading policy to calculate the final grade. This plug-in allows teachers to create new evaluation items such as exams and calculate students' final grades based on weights. The use of ontologies in modeling a grading domain certainly adds a new degree of flexibility and reuse. The way the ontology can be plugged with exiting ones makes it easier to migrate it to adapt to different universities or schools. Any teacher has its own way to grade students. Different forms of evaluation exist even within one course. This implies that an automatic tool which calculates the grades is difficult to make, because there is no single way to calculate the final grade. For example, if a student does not make assignment n°1 than the final grade will be the grade of the final exam, otherwise the final grade will de 60% of the final exam and 40% of assignment n°1. A vast number of formulas for calculating grade can be applied.

3.   EVALUATION

To validate S-CMS we have carried out a benchmark in order to assess the scalability and performance of our architecture under system load. The application was installed at the Department of Mathematics and Engineering, University of Madeira. Our empirical experimentation has involved two machines: a server managing SQL Server 2000 and a client running S-CMS. Both machines had the same configuration. They were each equipped with

Intel P4 3.0 GHz processors, 512 MB main memory, 40GB 7,800 RPM IDE disks, and Microsoft Windows XP home. The computers were connected by a 100Mbit/s Ethernet LAN.

The server was managing the University database that had a size of 123 Mbytes with 200 tables and 600 views. The database included the description of approximately 13 000 students.

The client was running our S-CMS application. Loading the ontologies from the databases toke approximately 7 minutes and 32 seconds. The number of instances created was equal to the number of students in the database, i.e., approximately 13 000 instances. The ontology had a small footprint since we only need to import a subset of the data present in the database. (+-6 mega)

The results obtained are encouraging since loading an ontology from a database is inherently a heavy task. The system performance benchmarking exercise revealed that the proposed solution was able to scale to meet desired throughput and latency requirements.

4.   RELATED WORK

There are many tools dealing with course management which have been introduced into universities to redesign teaching in many aspects. These tools include support for teachers (e.g. course delivery and administration) and students (e.g. submissions and involvement). One limitation of the tools available is that they were not developed around the concepts and technologies associated with the semantic Web. As a result, they tend to be static repositories of information for which semantic querying and inferencing on students' data is not possible. Furthermore, they do not tackle the problem of integrating disparate university data sources. For example, MIT OpenCourseWare (OCW) (OCW 2006), WebCT (one of the most widespread commercial course management systems) (WebCT 2006), AIMS (AIMS 2006), Moodle (MOODLE 2006), and BSCW (Basic Support for Collaborative Work) (Klöckner 2000) are educational resource addressing faculty and students. They offer courseware such as syllabi, readings, and quizzes. The information available is mainly static and does not provide features to support querying, inferecing, and data source integration.

Semantics and ontologies have been employed as a common basis for information integration. Ontologies allow for the modeling of the semantic structure of individual information sources, as well describing models of a domain that are independent of any particular information source. Several systems have been developed using this approach. Projects include Carnot (Woelk, Cannata et al. 1993), InfoSleuth (Bayardo, Bohrer et al. 1997),

OBSERVER (Mena, Kashyap et al. 1996; Kashyap and Sheth 1998), and COIN (Bressan, Fynn et al. 1997). These projects differ from our work since they do not target a specific domain (i.e. University modeling) and they do not provide solutions to carry out inference on the ontologies created.

5. CONCLUSION

The development of the semantic Web has the potential to revolutionize the World Wide Web and its use. One fundamental aspect that will have a significant impact on the success of the semantic Web will be the ability of the research community to demonstrate the added value of using semantic Web technologies to develop better systems and applications. For the time being, the industry has adopted a "wait-and-see" approach to see how real-world applications can benefit from the semantic Web.

As a contribution to increasing the widespread use of these new technologies, we have developed a real-world application, a Semantic Course Management System (S-CMS), based entirely on semantic Web technologies. S-CMS can semantically integrate and extract heterogeneous data describing university resources, courses, degrees, and students, answer to complex semantic queries, and it is able to carry out reasoning using explicit semantic rules. The system supplies an integrated environment where teachers and students can easily manage class projects. The application presented has been employed successfully to manage student enrolment to class projects at the University of Madeira. Since S-CMS deals with heavily on semantics, the system was used to manage projects from the "Semantic Web" course taught at the Department of Mathematics and Engineering. We believe that S-CMS is also appropriate to support course projects from other departments and that it represents a good step towards the development of real-world semantic applications.

6. QUESTIONS FOR DISCUSSION

Beginner:
1. What typical data sources need to be integrated when developing a CMS?
2. What is a RUD?
3. What is a SUD?

Intermediate:
1. What types of information heterogeneity may arise when integrating data sources?
2. What difficulties have been found when in creating and populating the ontology described in this chapter?

Advanced:
1. Make an ontology for representing people of your business or organizations.
2. Build a Buchingae rule that states that only staff members that work on internal and external projects are eligible for travel funding.
3. Write an RDQL that selects the staff members that work in the research department.

7.   SUGGESTED ADDITIONAL READING

- Antoniou, G. and van Harmelen, F. *A semantic Web primer.* Cambridge, MA: MIT Press, 2004. 238 pp.: This book is a good introduction to Semantic Web languages.
- Davies, J., Studer, R., and Warren, P. *Semantic Web Technologies: Trends and Research in Ontology-based Systems.* John Wiley & Sons, 2006, 326 pp.: This book provides a comprehensive overview of key semantic technologies. It includes the description of concepts such as knowledge management, ontology generation, and metadata extraction.
- Berners-Lee. T., Fensel, D., Hendler, J., Lieberman, H., Wahlster, W. *Spinning the Semantic Web: Bringing the World Wide Web to Its Full Potential.* The MIT Press, 2005. 503 pp.: This book covers topics such as software agents, markup languages, and knowledge systems that enable machines to read Web pages and determine their reliability.

8.   REFERENCES

This work was partially funded by FCT, POCTI-219, and FEDER.

9.   REFERENCES

AIMS (2006). AIMS: Adaptive Information System for Management of Learning Content. http://www.win.tue.nl/~laroyo/AIMS/.

Bayardo, R. J., W. Bohrer, et al. (1997). InfoSleuth: Agent-Based Semantic Integration of Information in Open and Dynamic Environments. Proceedings of the ACM SIGMOD International Conference on Management of Data, ACM Press, New York.

Berners-Lee, T., J. Hendler, et al. (2001). The Semantic Web. Scientific American. **May 2001**.

Bossom (2005). Bossom engine for the semantic Web, http://projects.semwebcentral.org/projects/bossam/.

Bressan, S., K. Fynn, et al. (1997). The COntext INterchange Mediator Prototype. ACM SIGMOD International Conference on Management of Data, Tucson, Arizona.

Cardoso, J. (2004). Issues of Dynamic Travel Packaging using Web Process Technology. International Conference e-Commerce 2004, Lisbon, Portugal.

Cardoso, J., J. Miller, et al. (2005). Academic and Industrial Research: Do their Approaches Differ in Adding Semantics to Web Services. Semantic Web Process: powering next generation of processes with Semantics and Web services. J. Cardoso and S. Amit. Heidelberg, Germany, Springer-Verlag. **3387**: 14-21.

Eclipse (2005). Eclipse open source community, http://www.eclipse.org/.

FOP (2005). FOP (Formatting Objects Processor), http://xmlgraphics.apache.org/fop/. **2005**.

Ian Horrocks, Peter F. Patel-Schneider, et al. (2003). SWRL: A Semantic Web Rule Language Combining OWL and RuleML, http://www.daml.org/2003/11/swrl/.

Jasper, R. and M. Uschold (1999). A framework for understanding and classifying ontology applications. IJCAI99 Workshop on Ontologies and Problem-Solving Methods.

Jena (2005). Jena - A Semantic Web Framework for Java, http://jena.sourceforge.net/,.

Karvounarakis, G., S. Alexaki, et al. (2002). RQL: a declarative query language for RDF. Eleventh International World Wide Web Conference, Honolulu, Hawaii, USA.

Kashyap, V. and A. Sheth (1998). Semantic Heterogeneity in Global Information Systems: The Role of Metadata, Context and Ontologies, Academic Press.

Klöckner, K. (2000). BSCW - Educational Servers and Services on the WWW, Adelaide.

Knublauch, H., R. W. Fergerson, et al. (2004). The Protégé OWL Plugin: An Open Development Environment for Semantic Web Applications. Third International Semantic Web Conference (ISWC 2004), Hiroshima, Japan.

Kumar, A. and B. Smith (2004). On Controlled Vocabularies in Bioinformatics: A Case Study in Gene Ontology. Drug Discovery Today: BIOSILICO. **2**: 246-252.

Lassila, O. and D. McGuinness (2001). "The Role of Frame-Based Representation on the Semantic Web." Linköping Electronic Articles in Computer and Information Science **6**(5).

Lawrence, R. and K. Barker (2001). Integrating Data Sources Using a Standardized Global Dictionary. Knowledge Discovery for Business Information Systems. J. M. Zurada, Kluwer Academic Publishers: 153-172.

Mandal, C., V. L. Sinha, et al. (2004). "Web-based Course management and Web Services." Electronic Journal of e-Learning **2**(1): 135-144.

Meinel, C., H. Sack, et al. (2002). Course management in the twinkle of an eye - LCMS: a professional course management system. Proceedings of the 30th annual ACM SIGUCCS conference on User services, Providence, Rhode Island, USA, ACM Press.

Mena, E., V. Kashyap, et al. (1996). OBSERVER: An Approach for Query Processing in Global Information Systems based on Interoperation across Pre-existing Ontologies. Conference on Cooperative Information Systems, Brussels, Belgium, IEEE Computer Society Press.

MOODLE (2006). Modular Object-Oriented Dynamic Learning Environment (moodle), http://moodle.org/.

OCW (2006). OpenCourseWare. http://ocw.mit.edu/index.html, MIT.

Ouskel, A. M. and A. Sheth (1999). "Semantic Interoperability in Global Information Systems. A brief Introduction to the Research Area and the Special Section." SIGMOD Record **28**(1): 5-12.

OWL (2004). OWL Web Ontology Language Reference, W3C Recommendation, World Wide Web Consortium, http://www.w3.org/TR/owl-ref/. **2004**.

OWL-S (2004). OWL-based Web Service Ontology. **2004**.

RDQL (2005). Jena RDQL, http://jena.sourceforge.net/RDQL/.

Roure, D., N. Jennings, et al. (2001). Research Agenda for the Future Semantic Grid: A Future e-Science Infrastructure http://www.semanticgrid.org/v1.9/semgrid.pdf.

RSS (2005). RSS 2.0 Specification, http://blogs.law.harvard.edu/tech/rss.

Sheth, A. (1998). Changing Focus on Interoperability in Information Systems: From System, Syntax, Structure to Semantics. Interoperating Geographic Information Systems. M. F. Goodchild, M. J. Egenhofer, R. Fegeas and C. A. Kottman, Kluwer, Academic Publishers: 5-30.

Sheth, A. P. (1999). Changing Focus on Interoperability in Information Systems: From System, Syntax, Structure to Semantics. Interoperating Geographic Information Systems. C. A. Kottman, Kluwer Academic Publisher: 5-29.

Shum, S. B., E. Motta, et al. (2000). "ScholOnto: an ontology-based digital library server for research documents and discourse." International Journal on Digital Libraries **3**(3): 237-248.

Swoogle (2005). Search and Metadata for the Semantic Web - http://swoogle.umbc.edu/.

WebCT (2006). http://www.webct.com/.

Woelk, D., P. Cannata, et al. (1993). Using Carnot for enterprise information integration. Second International Conference on Parallel and Distributed Information Systems.

PART V – BUSINESS AND CUSTOMER MANAGEMENT

Chapter 9

INTEGRATION OF CUSTOMER INFORMATION USING THE SEMANTIC WEB
A Case Study

Jürgen Angele[1] and Michael Gesmann[2]
[1]*Ontoprise GmbH, Karlsruhe, Germany – angele@ontoprise.de*
[2]*Software AG, Darmstadt, Germany – michael.gesmann@softwareag.com*

1.   INTRODUCTION

Data that is essential for a company's successful businesses often resides in a variety of data sources. The reasons for this are manifold, e.g. load distribution or independent development of business processes. But data distribution can lead to inconsistent data which is a problem in the development of new businesses. Thus the consolidation of the spread data as well as giving applications a shared picture of all existing data is an important challenge. The integration of such distributed data is the task of Software AG's "crossvision Information Integrator" one of the components in the crossvision SOA suite (crossvision).

Information Integrator is based on ontologies. On one hand, data source ontologies can be generated from metadata of underlying data sources. Currently, SQL databases, Software AG's Adabas databases, and web services are supported types of data sources. On the other hand, more business oriented ontologies can be developed. These business ontologies make use of other business ontologies or can directly use data source ontologies. FLogic rules describe the information how objects in different ontologies are related to each other.

Using ontologies Information Integrator solves three major problems. First of all it provides all means to integrate different information systems. This means that comfortable tools are available to bring data from different systems together. This is partially already solved by systems like virtual or federated databases (Batini et al. 1986). Information Integrator is more powerful compared to most of these systems as it not only supports databases but additional sources like web services, applications etc. The second problem which is solved is that Information Integrator allows reinterpretation of the contents of the information sources in business terms and thus makes these contents understandable by ordinary end users and not only by database administrators. Finally this semantic description of the business domain and the powerful mapping means from the data sources to the business ontology solves the semantic integration problem which is seen as the major problem in information integration. It maps the different semantics within the information sources to the shared conceptualization in the business ontology. As an intended side effect, once such an integrated semantic description is in place, it might be used by other semantic applications which do understand these semantic descriptions.

Within the next section will explain the conceptual ideas behind the Information Integrator and explicate the already sketched layered architecture for applications. Thereafter, we shortly describe the Information Integrator product itself. First of all we will present the product architecture. Then, we illustrate the tool set that shall allow even inexperienced and occasional users to create and modify semantic models. Within Software AG Information Integrator was used for a first project Customer Information Gateway (CIG) whose mission was to integrate data that on one side resides in a support information system and on the other side is stored in a customer information system. Experiences we gained from that first project are presented in the last major section before we conclude with a summary section.

2.   CONCEPTUAL LAYERING

Conceptually Information Integrator arranges information and the access to information on four different layers (Figure 9-1):

- The bottom layer represents different data sources which contain or deliver the raw information which is semantically reinterpreted on an upper layer viz. ontologies. Currently relational databases, Adabas databases and web services are supported.
- The second layer assigns a so called "data-source ontology" to each of the data sources. These "data-source ontologies" reflect only database or WSDL schemas of the data sources in terms of ontologies and can be

created automatically. Thus they are not real ontologies as they do not represent a shared conceptualization of a domain.

- The third layer represents the business ontology using terminology relevant to business users. This ontology is a real ontology, i.e. it describes the shared conceptualization of the domain at hand. It is a reinterpretation of the data described in the data-source ontologies and thus gives these data a shared semantics. As a consequence a mental effort is necessary for this reengineering of the data source contents which cannot be done automatically.
- On a fourth layer views to the business ontologies are defined. Basically these views query the integration ontology for the needed information. Exposed as Web services they can be consumed by portals, composite applications, business processes or other SOA components.

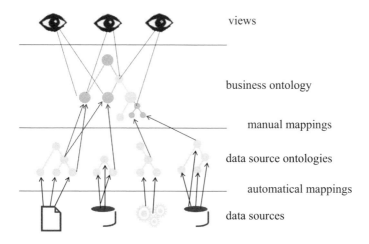

Figure 9-1. Conceptual layering of ontologies

The elements of the different layers are connected by so called mappings. The mappings between the data-sources and the source ontologies are created automatically, the mappings between the ontologies are manually engineered and the views are manually defined queries. Mappings define how source structures are mapped to destination structures. Thus mappings provide ways to restructure information, to rename information or to transform values. Up to now, we do not consider and do not plan to consider approaches which try to automatically derive such mappings (Rahm and Bernstein 2001).

This arrangement of information on different layers and the conceptual representation in ontologies and the mediation between the different models by mappings provide various advantages:

- The reengineered information in the business ontology is a value on its own. It represents a documentation of the contents of the data sources. The representation as an ontology is a medium to be discussed easily by non-IT experts. Thus aggregating data from multiple systems this business ontology provides a single view on relevant information in the user's terminology. More than one business ontology enables different perspectives into the same information.
- It is easy to integrate a new data source with a new data schema into the system. It is sufficient to create a mapping between the corresponding source ontology and the integration ontology and thus does not require any programming know-how; pure modelling is sufficient.
- The mediation of information between data sources and applications via ontologies clearly separate both. Thus changes in the data source schemas do not affect changes in the applications, but only affect changes in the mediation layer, i.e. in the mappings.
- This conceptual structure strongly increases business agility. It makes it very easy to restructure information and thus to react on changing requirements. Neither the data sources nor the applications have to be changed. Only the business ontology and the mappings have to be modified. Again no programming skills are required, all is done on a model level. Thus it minimizes the impact of change, eases maintenance and allows for rapid implementation of new strategies
- Ontologies have powerful means to represent additional knowledge on an abstract level (Friedland et.al 2004). So for instance by rules the business ontology may be extended by additional knowledge about the domain. Thus the business ontology is a reinterpretation of the data as well as a way to represent complex knowledge interrelating these data. So business rules are directly captured in the information model, they determine the optimal system access and bring every user to the same level of effectiveness and productivity.

3.   TOOL SUPPORT/ARCHITECTURE

The crossvision Information Integrator provides a full fledged tool environment for defining models, for mappings between these models and for running queries (Figure 9-2). IntegratorStudio is an ontology engineering environment based on OntoStudio™.

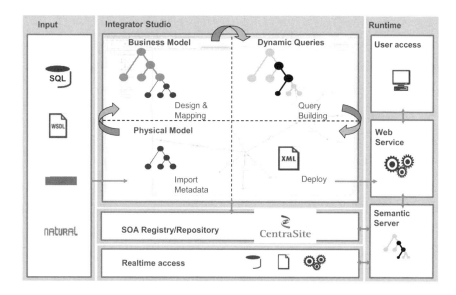

Figure 9-2. Architecture of the crossvision Information Integrator

It allows for defining classes with properties, instances of these classes and rules. Import capabilities generate "source ontologies" from underlying data sources. A powerful mapping tool allows user to interactively define mappings between ontologies by graphical and form based means (Figure 9-3). Besides defining correspondencies between the data source ontologies and the business ontology it allows to describe functional transformations like value transfromations. Rules may be defined with graphical diagrams (Figure 9-4). IntegratorStudio supports F-Logic, RDF(S), OWL for import and export. In practice the different information sources contain redundant ore even inconsistent information. We either use mentioned value transformations and/or additional rules to solve such problems. Queries which define the mentioned views can be generated and may be exported as web services.

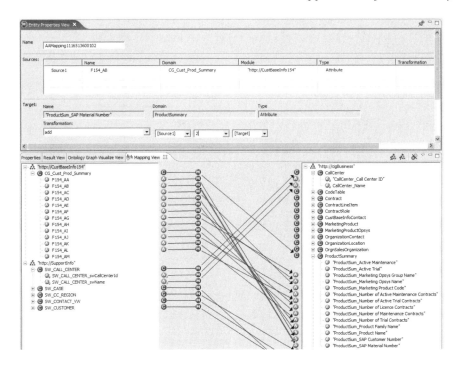

Figure 9-3. Mapping Tool in crossvision Information Integrator. The lower part defines the
mappings, while the upper part allows defining functional transformations

It allows for defining classes with properties, instances of these classes and
rules. Import capabilities generate "source ontologies" from underlying data
sources. A powerful mapping tool allows user to interactively define
mappings between ontologies by graphical and form based means (Figure 9-
3). Besides defining correspondencies between the data source ontologies
and the business ontology it allows to describe functional transformations
like value transfromations. Rules may be defined with graphical diagrams
(Figure 9-4). IntegratorStudio supports F-Logic, RDF(S), OWL for import
and export. In practice the different information sources contain redundant
ore even inconsistent information. We either use mentioned value
transformations and/or additional rules to solve such problems. Queries
which define the mentioned views can be generated and may be exported as
web services.

SemanticServer, the reasoning system, provides means for efficient
reasoning in F-Logic (Kifer, Lausen, and Wu 1995, ontoprise).
SemanticServer performs a mixture of forward and backward chaining based
on the dynamic filtering algorithm (Kifer and Lozinskii 1986) to compute
(the smallest possible) subset of the model for answering the query. During
forward chaining not only single tuples of variable instantiations but sets of

such tuples are processed. It is well-known that set-oriented evaluation strategies are much more efficient than tuple oriented ones. The semantics for a set of F-Logic statements is then defined by a transformation process of F-Logic into normal logic (Horn logic with negation) and the well-founded semantics (Van Gelder, Ross, and Schlipf 1991) for the resulting set of facts and rules and axioms in normal logic.

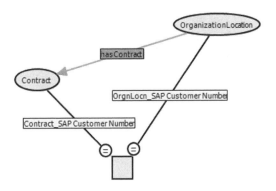

Figure 9-4. Graphical representation of a rule stating that if the customer number of an organization equals the contract number then this organization is owner of the contract

It is clear that our approach strongly relies on rules and reasoning about instance data. Compared to an approach using OWL + SWRL rules, F-Logic is the appropriate choice as reasoning over disjunctions and equalities as it is necessary in OWL + SWRL breaks down performance. Additionally OWL + SWRL relies on open world semantics while databases imply a closed world semantics. On the other hand OWL has its strengths in modelling ontologies. It provides more abstract modelling primitives, subsumption and constraint checking. So in future we additionally might provide a mixed approach, where OWL is mainly used for modelling ontologies and F-Logic for rules. It is clear that both semantics do not fit together and there must be some compromise to mix both approaches. For instance subsumption could be applied to reorganize the ontology and then this reorganized ontology is used in an F-Logic way, or cardinality restrictions could be reinterpreted as constraints to avoid equality reasoning.

Meta data like ontologies, their mappings, web service descriptions and meta information about data sources are stored in the CentraSite repository. Also, IntegratorStudio stores information about exported web services in CentraSite. During startup the inference engine SemanticServer which is based on OntoBroker[TM] loads the ontologies from the repository and then waits for queries from the exported web services. These queries are evaluated by SemanticServer and are online translated into calls to access connected data sources.

Thus SemanticServer represents the run-time engine, IntegratorStudio the modelling environment and CentraSite the meta data repository. SemanticServer is also integrated into IntegratorStudio thus enables immediate execution of queries to the ontologies.

4.   USE CASE: CUSTOMER INFORMATION GATEWAY

Within Software AG the Information Integrator was used for a first project whose mission was to integrate data that on one side resides in a support information system and on the other side is stored in a customer information system. The support information system maintains for example information about customers, their contact information and active or closed support requests. The customer information system stores information about clients, contracts etc. While the customer system stores its data in an Adabas database, the support system uses an SQL server. The integrated data view is exposed in a browser based application to various parties inside the company. For instance, instead of only seeing reported support requests support engineers shall get a more complete picture of a customer while talking with them.

For illustration purposes we first sketch a very simplified excerpt of imported data and the business ontology. Throughout the following examples we use FLogic syntax.

First of all there are two classes which have been generated by the mentioned automatic mapping from Adabas files:

```
FILE151_CONTRACT[FILE151_AA=>string;
                 FILE151_AE=>date]@Source151.
FILE152_CLIENT[FILE152_AA=>number;
               FILE152_AB=>string;
               FILE152_AC=>string]@Source152.
```

The cryptic names reflect the internal structure of Adabas files. The names "CONTRACT" and "CLIENT" have been specified by the user during the mapping process. Currently, it is application knowledge that FILE151_AA represents a contract number, FILE151_AE contract end dates, FILE152_AA is a customer id, FILE152_AB a customer name and FILE152_AC the customer address.

In our example we also consider two tables from the SQL database. Table "CUSTOMER" contains columns "id", "name" and "addr". Table "CASE" stores support requests with columns "caseId", "status", "customerId" and a foreign key "forCustomer". The resulting classes are:

```
CUSTOMER[id=>number;
            name=>string;
            addr=>string]@SourceSQL.
CASE[caseId=>number;
        status=>string;
        customerId=>string;
        forCustomer=>CUSTOMER]@SourceSQL.
```

The business ontology shall contain three classes:

```
Customer[name=>string;
            address=>string;
            supportRequests=>>SupportRequest]@Business.
SupportRequest[id=>number;
                    status=>string;
                    issuedBy=>Customer]@Business.
Contract[contractId=>string;
            endOfContract=>date;
            endOfContractFormatted=>string]@Business.
```

In the sequel we present some examples on how we used rules within our ontologies and derive some requirements and use cases for rule languages to be used in such a project.

4.1   Data source import

The system needs to be open in a sense that it allows for extensions which provide access to external data sources. In Information Integrator so-called built-in predicates implement this. In the sequel we abstract from a concrete syntax of these built-in predicates. Instead we illustrate this by a generic predicate "accessToSource":

```
accessToSource(connectionInfo, "tablename", "rowid1", X, "rowid2", Y, ...)
```

where *connectionInfo* describes all parameters that are needed to call the data source, *tablename, rowid1, rowid2* are names of some database tables or table columns, respectively. *X, Y* are the name of a variables which are to be bound by the built-in predicate.

In our example there are four rules which import data from external data sources:

```
FORALL X,Y
c("FILE151",X):FILE151_CONTRACT[FILE151_AA->X;FILE151_AE->Y]
<- accessToSource(connectionInfo, "FILE151", "AA", X, "AE",Y)
@Source151.
```

```
FORALL X, Y, Z c("FILE152", X):FILE152_CLIENT
        [FILE152_AA->X; FILE152_AB->Y; FILE152_AC->Z]
<- accessToSource(connectionInfo,"FILE152","AA",X,"AB",Y,"AC", Z)
@Source152.
```

```
FORALL X, Y, Z
c("CUSTOMER", X):CUSTOMER[id->X; name->Y; addr->Z]
<- accessToSource(connectionInfo, "CUSTOMER",
                "id", X, "name", Y, "addr", Z) ]@SourceSQL.
```

```
FORALL X,Y,Z
c("CASE", X):CASE[caseId->X; status->Y; customerId -> Z]
<- accessToSource(connectionInfo, "CASE",
                "caseId", X, "status", Y; "customerId", Z) ]@SourceSQL.
```

Import from data sources is easy, as long as the order of single result objects and the order of property values within a row are not significant. This is valid for imports from SQL and mostly also for import from Adabas. For data sources like web services which expect and return XML documents this is no longer true. For chaining of web services, i.e. the result of one or more web services serves as input for another web service, it is necessary to maintain the structure of the original result documents. Preserving the structure leads to complex rules.

4.2   Object and property mapping

It is very easy to define that an object in one model representing the data source is also an object in another model representing the business model. For example a contract object in the customer information system is also a contract object in the business model:

```
FORALL X X:Contract@Business <- X:FILE151_CONTRACT@Source151.
```

Similar rules exist for FILE152_CLIENT and CASE. Like for objects it is also easily possible to specify that a property in one ontology maps to a property in another ontology and that all property values in a first ontology are also values of the mapped property in the second ontology.

```
FORALL X, Y, Z
    X:Contract[contractId->Y; endOfContract->Z]@Business
    <-X:FILE151_CONTRACT[FILE151_AA->Y;FILE151_AE->Z]@Source151.
```

If the underlying data from the external sources contains such information, it is also easily possible to describe that two objects are the same. For example a client in the customer information system and a customer in the support information system represent the same object, if these have the same name and address. Please note, in both systems clients and customers, respectively, have a surrogate values as unique keys. But typically these values are not a viable object identifier across independent data sources. Therefore, we need to identify new identifiers. The example in rule terms:

```
FORALL X, Y, Z
    c("Customer", Y,Z):Customer[name->Y;address->Z]@Business
    <- X:CUSTOMER[name->Y; addr->Z]@SourceSQL.
```

```
FORALL X, Y, Z
    c("Customer", Y, Z):Customer[name->Y; address->Z]@Business
    <- X:FILE152_CLIENT[FILE152_AB->Y; FILE152_AC->Z]@Source152.
```

These simple types of mapping are essential for specification of business ontologies on top of data source or other business ontologies. All of these mapping rules can be described in the Information Integrator with graphical means, i.e. developers do not need to see the FLogic syntax.

4.3   Property value mapping

Often similar data that is represented in one way in a first database can be represented in a different way in another database. For example:

- data that is encoded in a single column or field might be scattered across multiple attributes in another database (comma-separated name versus firstname and lastname; encoding of some numeric or boolean bits into a single bit array)

- data with different representation (time and date values as a number, as XML types, as SQL values)

In all these cases it is very helpful to have an extensibility which allows for adding functions that implement necessary transformations.
An example in rule terms:

FORALL X, Y Y[endOfContractFormatted->X]@Business
<-EXISTS Z (Y:Contract[endOfContract->Z]
@Business and date2string(Z, X)).

where date2string() is a predicate that transforms a date from one presentation into another one.

4.4   Object references and more metadata

Every functional model needs to describe relations between objects. Object properties are used to express these relationships in a model. Object identifiers are object property values which reference the object with the identifier. These properties and property values are similar to foreign keys in relational databases. The foreign key information that is provided with the schema description can be used during generation of the data source model.
An example with a foreign key between table "CUSTOMER" (see above) and table "CASE" in rule terms:

FORALL X, Y X[forCustomer->c("CUSTOMER", Y)]@SourceSQL
<- X:CASE[customerId->Y]@SourceSQL.

This has to be mapped to the business ontology:

FORALL X, Y, Z1, Z2
    X:SupportRequest[issuedBy->c("Customer", Z1, Z2)]@Business
    <- X:CASE[forCustomer->Y]@SourceSQL
       and c("CUSTOMER",Y)[name->Z1; addr->Z2]@SourceSQL.

Also, the inverse reference could be generated. But, while there is a name for the foreign key constraint in SQL databases which can be used for the generation, there is no inverse name in schemas. Therefore the creation of the inverse relation is currently postponed to application development:

FORALL X,Y X[supportRequests->>Y]@Business
    <- Y:SupportRequest[issuedBy->X]@Business.

Even N:M relationships, which need to be implemented in two 1:N foreign key relations, can be expressed directly.

4.5   Queries

The learning of new languages is always a substantial investment, in particular if this involves the learning of new programming paradigms. Having different languages for the modeling and for the querying of ontologies bears the potential for impedance mismatches and causes additional costs. Therefore, rule language and query language should at best be the same. The Information Integrator uses FLogic not only as a language for ontology definitions but also as a query language. Because most application developers in the database area are not very familiar with FLogic and other logic languages the Information Integrator provides a graphical tool to define basic queries.

Like queries in database applications, the queries in our project shall provide some result information. It was not the goal to find all explanations, why the returned results are valid results, nor was it a goal to find all variable bindings that lead to a result. Using FLogic as a query language leads to some typical database query language requirements, for example:

- User-defined projections on the query result should be possible. Object relationships should be contained in the result. E.g. for one customer having multiple contracts each having contract items, then the query result should contain the information which contract item belongs to which contract within a single result per customer.
- Aggregations over data should be possible (although not yet used within the project).

4.6   Performance

Because the integrated view is used an application where e.g. support engineers expect immediate or at least fast answers for even complex requests while talking to a customer, the performance of the rule and query processing is a very important requirement. If responsiveness of the system is not sufficient (e.g. response in less than 2 seconds, which actually is not acceptable in many cases), the whole functionality will not be accepted by its users. This means, systems like the described one can only accept rule languages that allow for efficient processing.

Not surprisingly, experience with the system has shown that efficient processing also to a great extent depends on an optimized rule execution order and caching of intermediate results. Problems that showed up here are very similar to many query optimization problems in database systems.

For example, the data source mapping rules we had shown above always addressed only a single table or file in a database. However, a system that implements access to external data sources only via such single-table access rules will definitely not achieve sufficient performance. The reason for this is that resulting access operations do not make use of the data source's query capabilities like join-operations. Therefore, during query processing it is important to consider which data is stored in which system and to make use of existing indexes, uniqueness of values, or of join capabilities etc.

The current implementation of Information Integrator answers queries all at once. Like in other data intensive applications, it would sometimes be more convenient to have a streaming or cursor result which delivers first results quick and further results on demand.

5.   LESSONS LEARNT AND KEY COMMENTS

In most real-world business applications data is an essential and valuable basis for all business operations. Because data is often spread around in disparate data sources, data integration is a fundamental task. Such an integration has to acknowledge the data's semantics. Similar to integration of information from the web is done by using semantic web technology such technology can also serve as a mediator between data sources. This approach has been tested in the CIG project as described above. There are some key observations made in the course of that project.

- **Hide data access:** It is not sufficient to solely describe the data structures and their relationships. For usage within applications there need to be means to access the already existing external data sources. It is a good idea, to hide this from the user. From the conceptual point of view this is achieved by the data source ontologies which can be generated automatically. From the runtime point of view this is achieved by the system's extension capabilities with built-in predicates. Thus, users do not even need to know these predicates which are completely kept under control of the system.
- **Extensibility**: The SemanticServer allows users to implement their own built-in predicates that can be used by queries and rules. Such implementations are not only needed for the aforementioned data access predicates but also for additional built-ins that were needed to normalize the representation of property values. This extensibility is a prerequisite to allow for the integration of additional types of data sources.

- **Tool support:** Once the data source ontologies have been generated most of the application development is "ontological work", in particular creation of the business ontologies and mapping between ontologies. The most important observation in this context is that F-Logic is capable to express all types of relationships, however for inexperienced and occasional users it is very difficult to write down correct rules because there are only syntax checks. Even simple typos make rules get not considered or not create the intended results. Therefore, appropriate tooling is essential. The mapping tool, the rule editor or the query tool as described earlier are examples. The crux is that tools initially tend to support only simple use cases. More complicated problems (that cannot be expressed by simple graphical means) require more complicated rules. However, such complicated rules are more error-prone and consequently would require for extended tool support. As a conclusion the tools mentioned above need to support wide ranges of application scenario. At the same time, there needs to be error-detection support when writing rules and debugging-support when testing rules in the context of queries.

- **Performance:** Like in database system query processing, naïve query evaluation strategies typically result in too frequent and too expensive read operations on the data sources. Thus, internal optimization techniques which exploit the query capabilities of the underlying data sources are vitally important. Here, the Information Integrator uses so-called rewriters. Once a query has been compiled into an executable internal operator-graph these rewriters can reorder and merge data access operators, can move for instance comparison operators into these operators, or can combine simple scan operations into complex join operations. In order to do this job, these rewriters need to have an understanding of the syntax and semantics of the data access operations. As a consequence, this does only work, if the data access operations are provided by the system not by the applications (see first point "Hide data access").

- **Query optimization:** As pointed out rewriting and optimizing operator-graphs is essential. This can follow different patterns. In the first stage we adopt simple heuristics for algebraic transformations from relational database query processing. In a next phase transformations based on a cost-model and cost-estimations are planned. While these approaches to some extent try to predict the processing characteristics at execution time and intend to create the most efficient plan before starting the execution, there is another type of optimizer which is called "genetic optimizer". In a learning phase the genetic optimizer just tries various execution plans and remember the execution times. Once the learning phase is finished the execution engine re-executes the most efficient plan in the future. Within the CIG project this procedure is not used, mainly because this has impact on the application development process where an intermediate learning-phase has to be incorporated into the test phase before bringing the ready-to-use application into a production environment.

Most of the observations described here are specific for the integration of large amounts of data. But as stated earlier, this is an elementary step for further exploitation of such integrated information. Thus, the project does not only exploit semantic technology but also demands for appropriate processing techniques.

6.   SUMMARY

A data model in Information Integrator consists of ontologies. Data source models describe the structure of data that resides in external data sources. Business ontologies provide a conceptualization of business entities. FLogic rules are used to specify mappings which assemble higher-value business ontologies from other ontologies. Rules are the first choice to express semantics that is not immediately available within the data. Rules within the ontologies allow to express semantics that otherwise had to be evaluated in queries or applications. In contrast to traditional data-structure centric data integration approaches we here shift semantic knowledge about the data from application programs into the integration ontologies.

Within our first project, the access to information in these data models is still typical data retrieval and not so much knowledge inference. Therefore, many requirements expressed here are typical requirements for querying in data intensive applications (cursor, performance, query functionality).

With an increasing number of web services where quite some of them simply expose data, we also expect the need to support data integration for such web services. Because web services expect and expose structured data, a rule language should directly support this.

The crossvision Information Integrator based on ontoprise OntoStudio™ and Ontobroker™ is the first step for Software AG in the field of semantic technologies. Recently we joined various EU research projects like NeOn (Lifecycle Support for Networked Ontologies) (NEON), "Business Register Interoperability Throughout Europe" and "SemanticGov: Services for Public Administration" (SemanticGov). All these projects address concrete business cases. With our participation in these projects we intend to achieve deeper understanding of needs for adequate tooling and runtime systems when using semantics technologies for data integration. On the other hand we will contribute our knowledge about data-intensive processing.

7. QUESTIONS FOR DISCUSSION

Beginner:
1. What is the advantage of using ontologies for information integration in contrast to conventional techniques like ETL, virtual databases etc.?
2. Why and how can an ontology help in integrating unstructured and structured data?
3. Why can (real) ontologies not be generated automatically out of a database schema?

Intermediate:
1. What is the difference between an IT concept like a database schema and an ontology?
2. Which modifications can easily be handled in an ontology, but provide a lot more effort if they must be done in a database?
3. Why are the modeling primitives of an ontology more powerful than the modeling primitives of a database?

Advanced:
1. Which challenges are still to be done for semantic information integration?
2. Which problems are solved by a semantic middleware between data sources and applications?

8. SUGGESTED ADDITIONAL READINGS

- Staab S., Studer R. (eds.) *Handbook on Ontologies. International Handbooks on Information Systems*, Springer Verlag, 2003: A good introduction to ontologies and ontology representation languages.
- Pollock, J. and Hodgson, R. Adaptive Information: Improving Business Through Semantic Interoperability, Grid Computing, and The Semantic Web and its Applications 31 *Enterprise Integration*, Wiley-Interscience, September 2004: Practitioners should find this book to be quite valuable companion.

- Vladimir Alexiev, Michael Breu, Jos de Bruijn, Dieter Fensel, Rubén Lara, Holger Lausen (ed.) *Information Integration with Ontologies*. John Wiley & Sons, 2005.

9.   REFERENCES

Batini C., Lenzerini M., Navathe S.B (1986). A Comparative Analysis of Methodologies for Database Schema Integration. ACM Computing Surveys Vol. 18(4):323-364, 1986

N.J. Belkin N.J. (1980). Anomalous states of knowledge as a basis for information retrieval. The Canadian Journal of Information Science, 5:133--143, 1980.

Crossvision. http://www.softwareag.com/crossvision

Friedland N., Allen P., Matthews G., Witbrock M., Baxter D., Curtis J., Shepard B., Miraglia P., Angele J., Staab S., Moench E., Oppermann H., Wenke D., Israel D., Chaudhri V., Porter B., Barker K., Fan J., Chaw S., Yeh P., Tecuci D., Clark P.. Project Halo: Towards a Digital Aristotle. In AI Magazine, vol. 25, no. 4, winter 2004, pp. 29-4

Kifer M., Lausen, and Wu (1995). Logical foundations of object-oriented and framebased languages. Journal of the ACM, 42; (1995) 741–843

Kifer and Lozinskii (1986). A framework for an efficient implementation of deductive databases. In Proceedings of the 6th Advanced Database Symposium, Tokyo, August (1986) 109–116

Jaro M. A. (1989). Advances in record-linkage methodology as applied to matching the 1985 census of Tampa, Florida. Journal of the American Statistical Association 84:414–420, 1989.

Jaro M. A. (1995). Probabilistic linkage of large public health data files (disc: P687-689). Statistics in Medicine 14:491–498, 1995.

NEON. http://www.neon-project.org

Ontoprise. How to write F–Logic programs – a tutorial for the language F–Logic, 2002.

Rahm E., Bernstein P. (2001). A survey of approaches to automatic schema matching, VLDB Journal 10(4):334-350, 2001

SemanticGov. http://www.semantic-gov.org

Chapter 10

BUSINESS PROCESS MANAGEMENT AND SEMANTIC TECHNOLOGIES

Christian Drumm, Jens Lemcke and Daniel Oberle
*SAP Research, CEC Karlsruhe, SAP AG, Germany – d.oberle@sap.com,
jens.lemcke@sap.com, christian.drumm@sap.com*

1. INTRODUCTION

The term *Business Process Management* (*BPM*) refers to activities performed by enterprises to optimize and adapt their business processes. A *Business Process* (*BP*) is an activity in a company that uses resources and can involve the activities of different departments. Although it can be said that organizations have always been using BPM, new impetus was brought by *Business Process Management Systems* (*BPMS*), i.e., software tools, allowing the direct execution of the business processes without a costly and time intensive development of the required software. Management of business processes involves their design, execution, and monitoring. *Business Process Design* encompasses the capture of existing processes with graphical editors to document the processes and repositories to store the process models. BPMS allow *Business Process Execution* by using a patchwork of interfacing software with human intervention required where certain process steps can only be accomplished with human intervention. Finally, *Business Process Monitoring* encompasses the tracking of individual processes so that information on their state can be easily seen.

Conventional BPMS are primarily designed for intra-enterprise process management, and they are hardly used to handle processes with tasks and data separated by enterprise boundaries, for reasons such as security or privacy. However, the nature of most business processes involves the cooperation of two or more roles to achieve a specific task. Hence, newer

BPMS are increasingly enhanced by corresponding functionality to manage also *Collaborative Business Processes* (*CBP*). New challenges arise with incorporating collaborative business process functionality. First, the hitherto manual design of collaborative business processes is a tedious task which increases with the complexity of the partners' processes. Second, the partners' data formats will differ in most cases, such that a mediation is required. Realizing this mediation usually is a one-off and manual endeavor.

In this chapter, we show how semantic technologies can be used to counter both challenges. For the *Design of Collaborative Business Processes*, we exploit the capabilities of Semantic Web Service composition engines. This rather effortless problem reduction prevents implementing a new, dedicated solution and, thus, saves development efforts. Our solution works semi-automatic, i.e., the initial composition result is a suggestion which can be changed by the user. For *the Execution of Collaborative Business Processes* we also propose a semi-automatic approach. Mediations between the partners' data structures are generated with the help of a common domain ontology. We claim that the ontology captures an agreed understanding of business data which is identical across partners. Thus, the ontology can be exploited to improve the mediation between the partners' data formats.

Our chapter is structured as follows. We first elaborate on the design and execution of the collaborative business processes on the general level in Sections 2 and 3, respectively. We then draw our attention to our prototype implementation in Section 4. We substantiate our claims by detailing a demo scenario and proof of concept implementation in a real-world SAP Research tool suite (Sections 5 and 16). Sections 7 to 9 close by concluding, questions, as well as suggestions for further reading.

2.   DESIGN OF COLLABORATIVE BUSINESS PROCESSES

The main task for the automatic design of a collaborative business process is the integration of two business processes which have been modeled by to partners. The effort for manually designing the CBP increases with the complexity of the partners' processes. Therefore, this section proposes to facilitate this task. We apply *Semantic Web service* (SWS) composition to semi-automatically design the CBP, because SWS composition solves a fairly similar problem. However, in order to apply a semantic Web service composition engine on business processes, we need to transform them to the format used by the composition engine. This step is called lifting. Consequently, we need to interpret the composition engine's output in terms of the original business processes. This is called lowering. The overall process is depicted in Figure 10-1. We first describe the task of the composition engine in Section 2.1. Sections 2.2 and 2.3 explain the lifting and lowering.

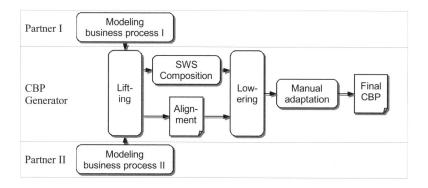

Figure 10-1. Design overview

2.1 Semantic Web service composition

A semantic Web service composition engine works on semantically enriched descriptions of Web services. We therefore introduce the concepts of Web services and semantic Web services in Sections 2.1.1 and 2.1.2, before we explain the functionality of the composition engine in Section 2.1.3.

2.1.1 Web service definition

Here, it is essential to understand that a Web service description in WSDL consists of the definition of independent, atomic (or: stateless) operations. A Web Services Description Language (WSDL 2001) definition of a Web service interface includes the specification of a set of operations, messages, parts and data types. The data types are described as XML Schemas (XSD 2001) building on top of one another. A message can be divided into parts. Each part is defined by a data type. A general WSDL operation consists of two messages: an input and an output message. We abstract from more detail of WSDL, since it is irrelevant to what we explain in the following. The interested reader may refer to the background material.

In an enterprise integration scenario, the potential business partners run their internal business processes. At certain points, these processes need to communicate to the processes of other partners. Such a communication point is modeled using a standardized WSDL definition to facilitate technical integration.

There exist a lot of techniques for the composition of (atomic) Web service operations to complex workflows. However, a successful invocation of a Web service operation could depend on the execution of other operations representing sequentially preceding steps of the internal business process. Without additional information on the behavioral semantics of a Web service's operations, a composition cannot create a correct collaborative business process in the general case. *Semantic Web service* technologies allow for the description of such additional information.

2.1.2 Semantic Web service definition

The components of a semantic Web service definition include a formal description of the Web service functionality, its inputs and outputs, and its behavioral requirements. The formal description of semantic Web services includes an annotation which is expressed by using an ontology (McIlraith, Son et al. 2001). An ontology is an explicit specification of a (shared) conceptionalization. Technically, an ontology consists of concepts, relations and axioms. A formal definition handy for our purposes will be given in Section 2.2.1.

There are two competing frameworks for the expression of semantic Web services: OWL-S (OWL-S 2004) and WSMO (WSMO 2004). The METEOR-S (METEOR-S 2004) project aims at the same target, but is restricted to the adaptation of existing languages, like WSDL-S. OWL-S and WSMO were developed completely from scratch to fully support the whole potential of semantic technologies. The explanations of this chapter build on the WSMO model.

We will now go briefly through the different components of a semantic Web service description in the WSMO model. Each semantic Web service description in WSMO contains a capability. The capability describes the Web service's functionality. It is used for the discovery and selection of appropriate services for a specific task specified as a WSMO goal. Inputs and outputs belong in WSMO to the interface of a Web service. They are represented by concepts of an ontology. This will be detailed within Section 2.2. Another part of the WSMO interface describes the behavioral requirements, called *choreography* in WSMO.[51] The choreography in

---

[51] Please note that the terminology in WSMO differs from the recommendation of the W3C. The W3C uses the term "choreography" for "linkages and usage patterns between Web services". In WSMO, "choreography" describes the behavioral requirements of one single Web service. In the context of WS-CDL, this notion is sometimes referred to as "behavioral interface". This chapter follows the WSMO terminology.

WSMO can be expressed by a slightly adapted form of *UML v2.0 activity diagrams.*

2.1.3 Functionality of semantic Web service composition

The semantic Web service descriptions of the participating business partners are the inputs for a semantic Web service composition engine. The composition engine compares the inputs and outputs that are defined as ontology concepts in the two choreographies and connects them where possible. For the decision whether a connection is possible, the composition engine expects semantically equivalent concepts to be expressed by the same ontological concept. Therefore, the composition engine just needs to look for equivalent concepts in the two behavior descriptions that it can connect.

After identifying matching concepts, the composition engine connects fitting input and output nodes by a transformation activity node as a placeholder. As an outlook, this placeholder will later be backed by a mapping service that executes a conversion which possibly needs to be performed in the real-time execution of the combined process. The result of the composition is a business process that contains the process steps of both parties, their interconnection via mapping activities, and those inputs and outputs that could not be interconnected. The composition is successful, when there are no inputs and outputs left that could not be connected to corresponding communications of the other party.

2.2   Lifting

As described at the beginning of this section we need to transform the process descriptions into a format used by the semantic Web service composition engine. This transformation is achieved by mapping the process descriptions to the elements of an ontology. The process that creates this mapping is called lifting and consists of two parts: i) the lifting of the in- and output messages described in the WSDLs and ii) the lifting of the process description. In order to understand the details of the lifting process we first need to introduce what an ontology is in our context (see Section 2.2.1). Next we describe in detail how WSDL messages are lifted in Section 2.2.2 and finally explain how process descriptions are lifted in Section 2.2.3.

Example Ontology:

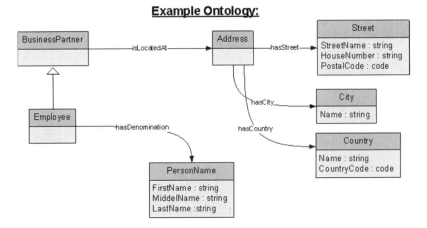

Figure 10-2. An excerpt of an ontology describing the domain of business partners. In this figure boxes represent the concepts C, $\rightarrow$ represent the relations R, arrows with a with triangle represent the concept hierarchy $\leq_C$ and the strings inside the boxes represent the attributes A with their associated data types T.

2.2.1 Ontology

The definition of ontology we are useing in this chapter is based on the definition presented in Stumme et al. (2004). We define the term ontology as follows:

Definition 1 (Ontology). An ontology O is a structure

$$O := (C, R, A, T, \leq_C, \leq_R, \leq_A, \leq_T, \sigma_R, \sigma_A)$$

where:

- C is a set of concepts aligned in a hierarchy $\leq_C$
- R is a set of relations aligned in a hierarchy $\leq_R$
- A is a set of attributes aligned in a hierarchy $\leq_A$
- T is a set of data types aligned in a hierarchy $\leq_T$
- $\sigma_R : R \rightarrow C \times C$ is the signature of R
- $\sigma_A : A \rightarrow C \times T$ is the signature of A.

In addition to that we define the domain of $r \in R$ as $dom(r) := \pi_1(\sigma_R(r))$ and the range as $range(r) := \pi_2(\sigma_R(r))$.

Figure 10-2 shows an example ontology. This ontology contains the concepts *BusinessPartner, Employee, Address, Street, City, Country* and *PersonName*, as well as the relations *isLocatedAt, hasStreet, hasCity, hasCountry* and *hasDenomination*.

2.2.2 Lifting WSDL messages

In this section we show how the lifting of the XML schemas, which describe the in- and output messages of the process steps, to the corresponding ontology concepts is performed. The result of this step is the alignment in Figure 10-1. This alignment is necessary in order to transform the descriptions of the input processes into a semantic Web service description that can be used by the composition engine. In addition, the alignment is necessary to transform the output of the composition engine into back to a description of a collaborative business process. Furthermore the alignment will later on be used to create the mappings that are necessary to execute the collaborative business process during runtime.

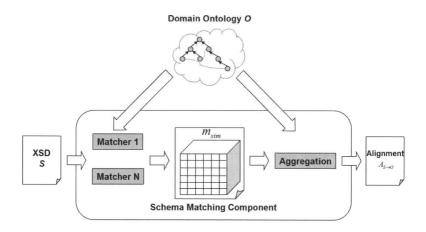

Figure 10-3. The architecture of the schema lifting component

Figure 10-3 shows the architecture of the schema lifting component that creates the alignment between am XML schema and the ontology. This architecture is based on the architecture of the COMA system (Do and Rahm 2002). The component takes as input an XML schema *S* and the domain ontology *O* and yields an alignment $A_{S \to O}$ between S and O.

In order to create the resulting alignment first N independent matchers are executed. Each of these matchers exploits different properties of the XML schema and the domain ontology entities in order to calculate a similarity $sim: [0,1]$ between a given element in the XML schema and a certain concept, relation or attribute in the ontology. A detailed explanation of these matchers is given in Section 2.2.2.1. The result of the execution of the matchers is a three dimensional similarity matrix m_{sim} of dimension $i \times j \times k$ where i is the number of elements and attributes in the XML schema, j the number of concepts, relations and attributes in the ontology and k the number of executed matching algorithms.

The resulting alignment is created by the aggregation step. In this step the three dimensional similarity matrix m_{sim} is aggregated into the two dimensional matrix m'_{sim} containing one similarity value for each pair of XML schema and ontology entity. The matrix m'_{sim} is calculated based on the following formula:

$$m'_{sim,i,j} = \frac{1}{k} \sum_{k} w(m_{sim,i,j,k})$$

where w is a weighting function. In our system a sigmoid weighting function ($w_{sig}(x) = \frac{1}{1 + e^{k(-x+0.5)}}$) is used for aggregating the similarity matrix. The advantage of a sigmoid weighting function is that low similarity values are further decreased where high similarity values are further emphasized (Ehrig and Sure 2004). The resulting alignment is then calculated based on m'_{sim}. A detailed explanation of the algorithm used for calculating the resulting alignment is given in Section 2.2.2.2.

2.2.2.1   Matchers

The goal of the matchers is to identify which elements of the XML schema correspond to which entities in the ontology. In order to identify these correspondences correctly it is necessary to exploit different information contained in the XML schema and the ontology. Consider for example a XML element named *Seller* and an ontology concept named *Vendor*. A simple comparison of the name of the two entities will yield a similarity of 0 but if a dictionary is used to compare the names, *Seller* and *Vendor* can easily be identified as synonyms. Therefore the resulting similarity should be very high. This simple example already shows that it is necessary to implement different matchers exploiting different information to identify the correspondences correctly. Consequently we implemented a set of five matchers using different algorithms to calculate the similarty between XML schema and ontology entities in our system. In this subsection we describe each of the matchers in more detail.

Edit distance matcher: The edit distance matcher computes the similarity $sim_{ed}(e_1, e_2)$ of two entities based on the edit distance $ed(\sigma_1, \sigma_2)$ of the entities names σ_1 and σ_2. The resulting similarity is normalized using the minimum length of the two input strings. This matcher achieves good results in situation where the names of ontology and schema entities are very similar.

$$sim_{ed}(e_1, e_2) = \max(0, \frac{\min(|\sigma_1|, |\sigma_2|) - ed(\sigma_1, \sigma_2)}{\min(|\sigma_1|, |\sigma_2|)})$$

Wordnet synonym matcher: The wordnet matcher uses Wordnet[52] in order to calculate the similarity $sim_{wn}(e_1, e_2)$ of two entities. Based on the configuration of the matcher, either the entity names or the optional entity documentation is used as a starting point. First the input strings are tokenized and white space as well as punctuation marks are removed, resulting in two token sets T_1 and T_2. Using the Wordnet thesaurus the number of synonym tokens $syn(T_1, T_2)$ in the two sets is calculated. The overall similarity sim_{wn} of the two token sets is then computed using the dice coefficient.

$$sim_{wn}(e_1, e_2) = \frac{2 * syn(T_1, T_2)}{|T_1| + |T_2|}$$

Data type matcher: The data type matcher uses a predefined similarity matrix for XML schema data types in order to calculate the similarity of two entities. As XML schema data types are only define for leave node in the XML schema and data type properties in the ontology this matcher will only generate positive similarity values for those entities.

SoftTFIDF matcher: The SoftTFIDF matcher is an additional linguistic matcher. It uses the SoftTFIDF matching algorithm developed by Cohen et al. (2003) to calculate the similarity $sim_{stfidf}(e_1, e_2)$ of two entities. Similar to the wordnet matcher the input strings are first tokenized into two sets T_1 and T_2. In the next step the term frequency *TF* and the inverse document frequency *IDF* for the tokens are calculated based on the formulas presented

[52] http://wordnet.princeton.edu

in Cohen et al. (2003). Note that the SoftTFIDF matcher uses a constituent matcher which can be any of the matching algorithms described above to calculate the similarity of the tokens.

Related entities matcher: The related entities matcher is a hybrid matching algorithm that calculates the similarity $sim_{re}(e_1, e_2)$ of two entities using a recursive algorithm. First the similarity of leaves in the XML schema tree and ontology entities are calculated using an constituent matcher. After that the similarity of internal nodes in the XML schema tree and ontology entities is calculated as based on, the similarity of related entities. The similarity $sim_{re}(e_1, e_2)$ is defined as

$$sim_{re}(e_1, e_2) = sim_{con}(e_1, e_2) \quad \text{iff } e_1 \text{ is a leave in the XML schema tree}$$

or

$$sim_{re}(e_1, e_2) = \frac{2 \cdot matching(\theta, e_1, e_2)}{|children(e_1)| + |children(e_2)|} \quad \text{otherwise.}$$

Furthermore $children(e)$ is the set of direct children or directly related ontology entities (data type and object properties) of e and $matching(\theta, e_1, e_2)$ is the number of entities with $sim_{con}(e_1, e_2) \geq \theta$.

2.2.2.2   Aggregation

In the next step the lifting is calculated based on m'_{sim}. The ontology is exploited as an additional knowledge source during this step. The rational behind this approach is, to also exploit the domain knowledge during the final aggregation. Instead of simply selecting the pair of entities with the highest similarity as alignment candidates, the search for possible match candidates is restricted to entities in the ontology that are related to the previous matched ones. Algorithm 10-4 describes our aggregation algorithm in more detail.

The aggregation algorithm starts by first adding the seed node and the seed concept to the alignment and adds them to the lists of current ontology entities and current nodes. After this the algorithm iterates over the list of current ontology elements and always performs the following steps:

1.   The set of ontology entities in the neighborhood of the current ontology entity is calculates. The neighborhood is defined as all

entities in the ontology that have a distance θ_O to the current ontology entity.

2. The set of children nodes of the current node is calculated. Again a parameter θ_S is used to define the search depth.

3. For each element in the set of ontology entities the most similar node in the set of children nodes is searched.

4. If the similarity of n and $e \geq \tau$, n and e are added to the alignment and appended to the respective lists.

Input: The similarity matrix m'_{sim}, the domain ontology O, top-level schema node n_s, the seed concept c_s
Output: The resulting lifting $L_{S \to O}$

```
1  L_{S→O}.addLiftingElement(n_s,c_s);
2  currentOntoEntityList ← c_S;
3  currentNodeList ← n_s;
4  while currentOntoEntityList ≠ ∅ do
5      e ← currentOntoEntityList.removeFirstElement();
6      n ← currentNodeList.removeFirstElement();
7      el ← getAllOntoEntitiesInRange(e, θ_O);
8      nl ← getAllChildNodesInRange(n, θ_S);

9      forall n ∈ nl do
10         e ← findMostSimilarEntity(n, el);
11         if m'_{sim}(n, e) ≥ τ then
12             L_{S→O}.addLiftingElement(n,e);
13             currentOntoEntityList.append(e);
14             currentNodeList.append(n);
15         end
16     end
17 end
18 return lifting;
```

Figure 10-4. The aggregation algorithm

2.2.3 Lifting processes

In order to be able to use semantic Web service composition engine for the creation of a collaborative business process, we need to transform the existing information in the WSDL and process descriptions to a semantic Web service definition. Therefore, the information of one business partner results in one single semantic Web service definition. In the following, we explain how to obtain each necessary part of the semantic Web service definition.

*   Contractual offers of a business partner can be modeled in its service capability to enable later matchmaking between requests and service offers. Since the Web service capability will not be used in our approach, we leave this part of the semantic Web service description empty.

- Each WSDL operation of a business partner is represented by an input node and an output node connected via a sequential control edge in the choreography of this partner's semantic Web service definition. We refer to this construct as a *semantic Web service operation.*
- The data communicated by an input and output node is represented by ontology concepts that are obtained by the alignment step of the lifting from the corresponding WSDL operation's XML schema. This step is detailed in Sect. 2.2.2.
- The semantic Web service operations are connected by Activity Diagram constructs that resemble the workflow of the process of the partner.

2.3   Lowering

In order to complete the problem reduction of creating a collaborative business process via semantic Web service composition, we need to give a mapping how to interpret the result of the composition engine as a collaborative business process. A collaborative business process is defined as the process steps of the respective partners, plus their appropriate interconnections. Providing the mapping is straight-forward, because the composition did not alter the original process structure of the business partners. Therefore, each process step of the composed semantic Web service can be interpreted as a process step of the original business processes. Each newly created communication link between two different semantic Web services can be interpreted as part of the thus created collaborative business process.

In the case of an unsuccessful composition, the partly connected collaborative business process can be treated as a first suggestion of an incomplete collaborative business process for manual adaptation by the business partners.

3.   EXECUTION OF THE COLLABORATIVE BUSINESS PROCESS

In the previous section we described how a Collaborative Business Process is generated in our system. First the syntactical process descriptions are lifted, next we execute the semantic Web service composition engine and finally lower the result to the syntax level again. This steps yield an intermediate Collaborate Business Process which is presented to the user for manual adaptation. After the manual adaptation step the final CBP is available. The final CBP and the alignments generated in the lifting step (see

Figure 10-3) during the generation of the CBP are the input data necessary in order to create an execute CBP. The steps necessary to create an executable CBP will be described in this section.

In order to understand the following sections we first need to introduce the concepts mediation and mediator. In general a mediator is responsible for coping with heterogeneity in open systems. This task is usually called mediation. The concept of a mediator has first been introduced by Wiederhold (1992). In the context of Web services, we refer to mediation as the task of translating between the different input and output message formats used by independently developed services. This translation requires the availability of *transformations* describing how message instances corresponding to a source message schema are translated into message instances corresponding to a target message schema. Developing these translations is currently done manually using either some graphical tool or general purpose programming languages. Especially with the large, complex message schemas common in B2B communication, this development process is very tedious and error prone. In order to facilitate this tedious process we create the necessary mappings semi-automatically by exploiting semantic technologies.

The steps necessary to create an executable CBP are depicted in Figure 10-5. The required inputs are the final CBP create in the previous step as well as the alignment created in the lifting step. The alignment is used by the *mapping extraction* step which generates intermediate transformations. After a manual adaptation by the user the final transformations and CBP are deployed. The CBP is deployed to the two business execution environments of the partners whereas the transformations are deployed to a *mediator*. The following subsections describe each step in more detail.

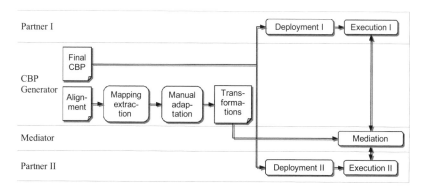

Figure 10-5. Overview of the process steps necessary to create an execution CBP

3.1   Mapping extraction

In order to enable the execution of the collaborative business process during runtime, it is necessary to create transformations between the in- and output messages of the services connected to the process steps. These transformations are generated based on the alignments created beforehand (see Section 2.2.2). The creation of the transformations is done in two steps. First related elements in the two source schemas are identified based on the alignment. Second, executable mapping rules are created. The following subsections explain each of the steps in more.

3.1.1 Location of related entities

The first step in the creation of the transformations is the identification of related entities in the source and the target XML schemas associated with corresponding service operations. As these schemas were most likely developed independently, the identification is not straight forward. As an example consider the two schemas and the ontology depicted in Figure 10-6.

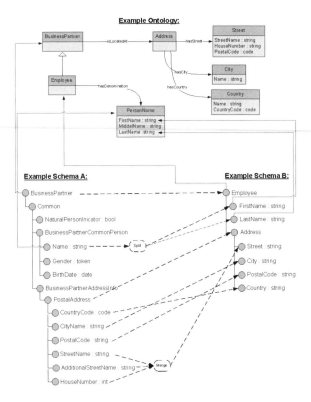

Figure 10-6. Example showing the mapping extraction

The element *BusinessPartner* in schema A is lifted to the concept *BusinessPartner* of the ontology, whereas the element *Employee* of schema B is lifted to the concept *Employee* of the ontology which is a sub-concept of the concept *BusinessPartner*. However, in order to create the correct transformation (shown by the dashed arrows) we need to identify that the elements BusinessPartner and Employee are related. A second example is the relation between the *Name* element in schema A and the elements *FirstName* and *LastName* in schema B. In order to create the correct transformation we need to identify the relation between these three elements.

The location of related entities in the source and the target schema is performed by the algorithm described in Algorithm 10-7. The algorithm starts by iterating through the list of all entities of the target schema. For each entity of the target schema we use the alignment $A_{T \to O}$ to identify the ontology entity it is lifted to. If a lifting of the current entity to an ontology entity is found, this ontology entity is used as a basis to find related source schema entities. If not the next target schema entity is used.

Input: The lifting of the source schema $L_{S_S \to O}$, the lifting of the target schema $L_{S_T \to O}$, the domain ontology O, the range parameter ρ.
Output: List $relatedEntitiesList$ of related schema entities.

```
1   targetSchemaEntityList ← S_T;
2   while targetSchemaEntityList ≠ ∅ do
3       e_T ← targetSchemaEntityList.removeFirstElement();
4       if L_{S_T→O}.containsLifting(e_T) then
5           e_O ← L_{S_T→O}.liftingTarget(e_T);
6           if L_{S_S→O}.containsLiftingTo(e_O) then
7               relatedEntitiesList.add(e_T, L_{S_S→O}.liftingSource(e_O));
8           end
9           else
10              if L_{S_S→O}.containsLiftingToSuperEntity(e_O, ρ) then
11                  relatedEntitiesList.addAll(e_T, L_{S_S→O}.superEntityLiftingSources(e_O, ρ));
12              end
13              if L_{S_S→O}.containsLiftingToSubEntity(e_O, ρ) then
14                  relatedEntitiesList.addAll(e_T, L_{S_S→O}.subEntityLiftingSources(e_O, ρ));
15              end
16              if L_{S_S→O}.containsLiftingToProperty(e_O, ρ) then
17                  relatedEntitiesList.addAll(e_T, L_{S_S→O}.propertyLiftingSources(e_O, ρ));
18              end
19          end
20      end
21  end
22  return relatedEntitiesList;
```

Figure 10-7. The algorithm for identifying related schema elements

In order to find related source schema entities the alignment of the source schema, $A_{S \to O}$ is first checked for a schema entity that is lifted to the current ontology entity. If such a schema entity is found, the source and the target schema entity are added to the related entities list. If no such schema entity is found, it is checked if a lifting of a source schema entity to the super- and sub-entities of the current ontology entity is found. All these are added to the related entities list. Note that the check of super and sub-entities of the ontology is only performed within a certain range ρ of the current ontology entity.

3.1.2 Mapping rule creation

In general it is not possible to automatically create the mapping rules expression relating two entities. As an example consider the split operation applied to the *Name* element of schema A in Figure 10-2. We might be able to identify, that in the given situation a split is necessary but we do not know if the Name element in schema B contains a string of the form "*Firstname Lastname*" or of the form "*Lastname, Firstname*". Therefore, we cannot know what character indicates the separation of the two name elements and therefore cannot provide a complete specification of the split operation.

For this reason we define a set of abstract mapping operations. These operations enable us to create abstract mapping rules and present them to the user. The user needs to complete some of the abstract operations in order create an executable mapping. The abstract mapping operations available in our system are:

- **move:** The move operation is used for direct (1:1) mappings between entities of the source and target schema.
- **join:** The join operation maps the contents of several source elements into one target element (m:1). Note that the join operation preserves the individual values of the source elements (e.g. concatenation of 2 strings).
- **merge:** Similar to the join operation, the merge operation maps several source elements onto one target element. However, the merge operation does not preserve the individual values of the source elements (e.g. adding the values of two integers).
- **split:** The split operation maps the value of one element in several target elements (1:n). The original value is not preserved by this operation (e.g. splitting a string at spaces).
- **replicate:** The replicate operation maps the value of one element in several target elements (1:n). In contrast to the split operation, the original values are preserved (e.g. copying a string onto several targets).

In order to create abstract mapping rules based on the list of related entities identified in the previous step we apply a pattern based approach. The patterns describe which relations between elements of two schemas lead to the creation of which abstract mapping rules. Figure 10-8 shows some examples of the patterns we have identified. If, for example, an element of schema A is lifted to the same ontology entity as one element of schema B (example (a) in Figure 10-8), we create an abstract move operation between them. A more complex situation is shown in example (d) in the figure. Here an element of schema A is lifted to a ontology entity which consist of two parts. To each of these parts elements from schema B are lifted. In this case we apply the abstract split operation.

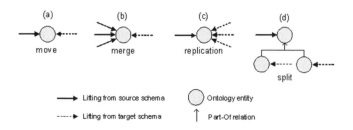

Figure 10-8. Example patterns for the creation of abstract mapping rules

Using the approach described above mapping rules for all related schema elements identified in the previous step are generated. Finally, the resulting mapping rules are presented to the user for manual adaptation and finalization.

3.2 Deployment and execution of the partner processes

After the transformations have been generated, all data necessary to execute the CBP is available. Therefore the next step is to deploy the information on the respective business process execution engines. The necessary deployment steps depend mainly on the setup of the execution engines. In our context two variants of an execution environment are possible. Either there is one central instance of an execution engine available that controls the execution of the CBP by invoking web services of the partners or each partner has its own execution environment controlling only the execution of his part of the CBP. As we assume that each partner already has a business process execution engine available in order to execute internal business processes, the second option is more suitable in our context. As a result, the deployment step will only deploy the parts of the CBP related to one partner to the respective execution engine.

3.3   Mediation

During runtime, the two business process execution environments of the partners execute the CBP by invoking either local or remote Web services. In case of remote Web service invocations the execution of a transformation might be necessary in order to cope with heterogeneous message formats. These transformations can be executed using different approaches. Either the message transformations can be executed locally on the execution environments of each partner or the execution of the transformation can be implemented as a service. As the first approach requires a modification of the execution environments, we chose the second approach for the execution of the mediation. However, execution the transformations as an external service still leaves the following implementation options:

- Implementing n services, each one only executing one transformation
- Implementing m service, each on executing a set of related transformations
- Implementing only one service executing all transformations.

Each of these options has different advantages and disadvantages. The first approach fits nicely to the idea of service oriented architectures. Each service implements exactly on transformation. The problem of creating message transformations can be reduced to the problem of locating appropriate transformation services and in addition to that failing service can be replaced by similar ones. However, the problem with this approach is that currently no transformation services are available on the net. Furthermore, we mediate between message formats that are not standardized. Therefore it is unlikely to find the appropriate services anyway. The result is the need to develop and manage n service leading to a significant management effort. The same arguments are true for the second option as it is similar to the first one except that each service is capable of executing multiple transformations.

The third option is disadvantaged because it is a centralized solution resulting in the creation of a single point of failure. However, it simplifies the deployment and execution of CBP significantly. Only one general purpose mediator with a repository of available transformations needs to be developed. Each transformation generated in the previous step is deployed to this mediator. During runtime each invocation of a Web service is always routed through the mediator. If a transformation between the source and the target message format is available in the repository it is executed, otherwise the message is simply forwarded to the partner process.

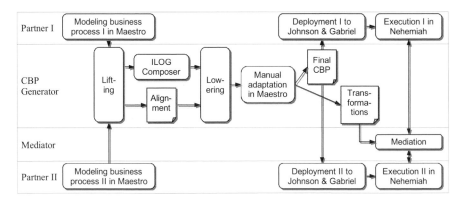

Figure 10-9. Overall procedure

4. IMPLEMENTATION

In the Sections 2 and 3 above, we have discussed the design and execution of collaborative business processes. This section presents an implementation of the concepts described and evaluates our efforts in an example scenario from the logistics domain. Figure 10-9 shows the steps of the overall procedure consisting of the design and the execution of a collaborative business process. In contrast to the overview graphics in Figure 10-1 and Figure 10-5, we denote the tools used for executing the single steps. The Sections 4.1 and 4.2 detail the concrete implementation of the design and execution phase. For a detailed description of the SAP Research tool suite used, we refer to the background reading (Born 2006; Greiner, Lippe et al. 2006; Schulz, Sadiq et al. 2005).

4.1 Design

The existence of a model of each partner's business process denoted by the "modeling business process" tasks in Figure 10-1 is a prerequisite for the automatic design of a collaborative business process. For these modeling tasks, we rely on the Maestro tool in our implementation which is part of a SAP Research business process management tool suite. Using Maestro, each business partner creates a model of its business process. Such a process can be exported, discussed and interconnected with a business partner's process in a *coalition view* containing all involved parties' business processes. In the coalition view, the control flow of the actual collaborative business process can be defined by manually interconnecting the process steps of the partner processes via arrows denoting control flow.

At this point, we deviate from the standard sequence of actions in Maestro modeling. Instead of manually defining a collaborative business process involving the different parties, we export the public process descriptions to the file system. The public process descriptions are now input to our CBP generator. Inputs to this step are the public process descriptions; output is the collaborative business process proposal. The proposal is to be checked by the business expert as denoted by the "manual adaptation" task in Figure 10-1. Therefore, we import the output of the collaborative business process generator back to the Maestro tool.

The generation of the collaborative business process occurs in three steps as denoted in Figure 10-1. The central "semantic Web service composition" step is implemented by the existing semantic Web service composition engine from ILOG, called "ILOG composer" (Albert, Binder et al. 2005a; Albert, de Sainte Marie et al. 2006; Albert, Henocque et al. 2005b,c). The ILOG composer works on the basis of semantic process descriptions similar to UML v2.0 activity diagrams. Message exchanges are abstractly expressed by the evolution of an instance of an ontology. It creates a composed workflow called *orchestration* conforming to Section 2.1. In order to use the ILOG composer, the collaborative business process generator performs a lifting and a lowering. During lifting, two things happen. First, an alignment is created as described in Section 2.2.2. Second, semantic Web service descriptions are generated which are fed to the ILOG composer as explained in Section 2.2.3. The orchestration and the alignment are fed to the lowering engine. During lowering, the semantic Web service orchestration is related back to the process model of Maestro (see Section 2.3).

The result of the design phase of a collaborative business process is a automatically proposed and manually adapted collaborative business process as well as a proposed and checked set of message transformations. In the following, we focus on our implementation of the execution of the just created collaborative business process.

4.2   Execution

As a prerequisite for the execution of a collaborative business process, we expect that each business partner has abstracted from its internal IT landscape by defining access points via WSDL operations. For the hosting of the WSDL descriptions, we rely on the Johnson tool which is part of the SAP Research tool suite. A WSDL description contains the actual address of the respective real, executable Web service. Such a Web service will usually be hosted on some application server accessible via a network. Through the interface of Johnson, single Web service operations, called *operation endpoints*, can be accessed by other components of the tool suite such as Gabriel. Gabriel can be used to define *tasks*. Such a task can either be a manual task or be backed by a Johnson operation endpoint. Further detail on the operation of Johnson and Gabriel can be obtained from the background material.

On top of Johnson and Gabriel sits the Nehemiah tool. It is able to execute collaborative business process created in Maestro directly in order to test them. Via a Web interface, the coalition view of the collaborative business process can be accessed. By clicking on a process step, the connected task will be executed. In case the current task is defined by an operation endpoint in Gabriel, the respective Web service operation will be called as defined in Johnson. After the execution of the current task, Nehemiah updates the process graphics of the collaborative business process to communicate the progress of the test run. An example and a screenshot is given in Section 5.

Before the CBP which was created during the design phase can actually be executed using Nehemiah two more steps need to be performed: firstly the CBP has to be finalized and deployed to the runtime environment of the partners and secondly the necessary mediators need to be created and deployed. In the following subsections we describe each of these steps in more detail.

4.2.1 Finalization and deployment of the CBP

After the design of the CBP is finished it cannot immediately be deployed onto the execution environment. Instead it has to be finalized first. This step is specific to the chosen system environment and will therefore not be further detailed.

The next step after the CBP has been finalized is the actual deployment onto the runtime environment. During this deployment the finalized collaborative business processes of the partners are deployed on the respective runtime environments. In addition, the runtime environments are configured during deployment to invoke the mediator service when necessary. Details on the mediator service is given in the next subsection.

4.2.2 Mediator service

In our implementation the mediator is a general purpose mediation Web service which is called *mediator service* in the following. It consists of a repository storing the deployed transformations and an execution engine that is capable of executing the transformations. In our implementation the transformations are XSLT scripts (XSLT 1999) and the execution engine is an XSLT processor. The mediator service has two operations: i) deploying a new transformation and ii) executing a transformation. The first operation is used to deploy a new transformation to the transformation repository. The second operation is the one invoked by the different partners during the execution of the CBP. It takes as arguments the source and the target service URI, the source and target service operation and the payload. The service URI and operation information is used to determine which transformation has to be executed. This transformation is then retrieved from the repository and executed on the payload. The result of the execution is then sent to the target service.

In order to integrate the generic mediator service with the runtime environment the Nehemiah engine has to be configured to route the communication between the two partners in the CBP through the mediator service. This configuration is performed when the finalized CBP is deployed onto the runtime environment.

5.   DEMO SCENARIO

In order to prove the applicability of our approach, we applied the implementation described in the preceding section to the frequently occurring, real-world *carrier-shipper* business process supported by SAP. The *carrier-shipper* process is an instance of the standard SAP *order-to-cash* process in the logistics domain.

5.1   Carrier-shipper process

The carrier-shipper process involves three parties: a customer, a shipper, and a carrier. As illustrated in Figure 10-10, the customer first places a sales order with the shipper, who enters it in its local SAP system. After that, the appropriate steps for delivery and picking and packing are taken. After sending the shipping information to the *express shipping interface* (XSI), the goods are labeled and the manifest is sent to the carrier. This is the trigger for the actual shipping by the carrier which is tracked by the shipping process step in the SAP system of the shipper. The last activity is the execution of the billing process. Sometimes, carriers change their conditions of service. In this case, they need to notify the shipper of those updates. Also, for a new contractual cooperation between a shipper and a carrier, the new conditions need to be input into the shipper's system.

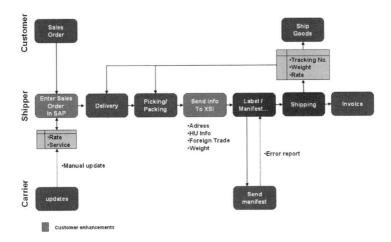

Figure 10-10. Carrier-shipper process

The fulfillment of the prerequisites discussed in Section 4 above is straight forward for the shipper party. As announced in 2004, SAP currently develops *enterprise SOA* which provides access to SAP business processes via Web service interfaces. Valid process models can be obtained from standard SAP documentation and modeled in Maestro. Figure 10-11 shows the SAP shipper business process.

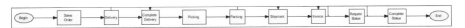

Figure 10-11. Public shipper process in Maestro

In contrast, carriers usually provide their functionality via proprietary Web service interfaces advertised on their Internet pages. However, no process information is available for the carrier Web services we examined. That means the Web services of the carriers are designed in a way that they can be accessed in a stateless manner. In terms of our approach, this means that the carrier Web services just require following a trivial public process for their successful accession. Such a trivial process consists of a fork-and-merge construct containing every single process step relating to the respective Web service operation. The carrier process modeled in Maestro is shown in Figure 10-12.

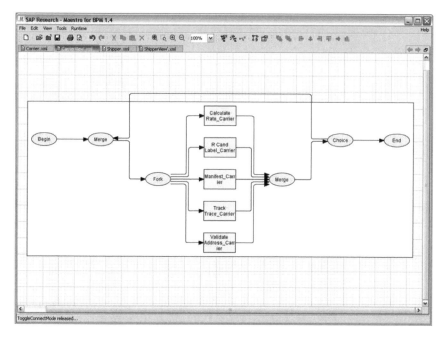

Figure 10-12. Public carrier process in Maestro

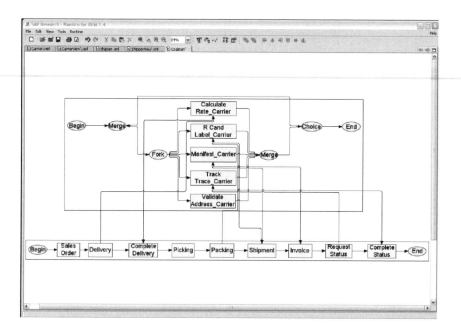

Figure 10-13. Suggested collaborative carrier-shipper business process in Maestro

Following our approach, we export the modeled processes from Maestro and successfully apply our tool generating an automatic suggestion for a collaborative business process. Importing the result back into Maestro yields the collaborative business process shown in Figure 10-13. The various Web services of the carrier and the shipper are correctly invoked during execution by the Nehemiah tool. Messages passed between the parties are correctly mediated and thus can be understood by the respective communication partner.

5.2 Benefits of our approach

By successfully implementing the carrier-shipper process, we have proved our concepts to work as intended. However, the benefits of our solution require some modeling efforts. We summarize and compare both in the following.

In contrast to current practice, our solution allows the suggestion of a collaborative business process *without* requiring either participating business party to change their own operation signatures, business processes or message structures. In a traditional setting, business partners willing to cooperate would establish their cooperation through a lot of meetings. First, understanding the partner's business vocabulary is a prerequisite for the further steps. Second, the partners need to agree on conceptually matching operation signatures to align the granularity of their operations. Third, they have to align their business processes. This is sometimes done by the larger partner dictating its proprietary process to be followed by its suppliers. And fourth, all partners need to develop transformations that convert the other partner's messages to their own internal representation.

Of course, standards exist for most of the named artifacts in many domains. This does however not solve the problem due to at least two reasons. First, many *different* standards exist and thus still must be transformed into each other. Second, companies do not necessarily adopt the specifications in the standards to define their internal business processes and message formats. Thus, a transformation still needs to be implemented manually.

For our solution to work, the business partners need to rely on a domain ontology that covers the business domains of all parties involved. The building of an ontology is a costly process that has to be executed by a knowledge engineer in cooperation with experts of the domains tackled. In addition, our solution requires the checking of the proposed collaborative business process and the transformations, because an automatically generated mapping cannot always be correct.

The comparison of costs and benefits when applying semantic technologies to the design and execution of collaborative business processes summarized in Table 10-1 is difficult to measure and depends on many subjective factors.

Table 10-1. Cost-benefit comparison

Feature	Additional effort	Saved effort
Agreement on common *business terms*	Modeling *domain ontology*	Long-term learning process of partner's business *vocabulary*
Coping with heterogeneous *operation signatures*	Same as above	Adapting own software to partner's or standard *operation signatures*
Design CBPs using heterogeneous *business processes*	Potential manual adaptation of suggested *collaborative business process*	Adapting own business process to match partner's or standard *process requirements*
Executing CBPs using heterogeneous *message formats*	Potential manual adaptation of suggested *transformations*	Manual design of message *transformations*

However, two major correlations can be observed. First, the value of our solution strongly depends on the complexity of the business processes involved. Of course, in a small demonstrating example, the modeling efforts easily outweigh the savings. However, it is a matter of fact that business processes become more complex in the future and more companies start to model and formalize their so far ad-hoc processes to participate in e-Business. The more companies participate in e-Business, the more important it will be to flexibly adapt to market changes. That is, the simplification of changing from one carrier to another is equally important for carriers and shippers. Shippers are enabled to integrate and choose the most appropriate carriers more easily. Carriers are enabled to deliver more innovative services by adapting their processes without spending too much integration work with the existing or thus newly acquired shipping customers. Second, the value of our solution also strongly depends on the quality of the proposed collaborative business process and the suggested message transformations. In our semi-automatic approach, the user still has to examine the suggested solution. This becomes easier the better the proposal is. The quality of the collaborative business process and the message mappings, again, strongly depends on the quality of the domain ontology. Therefore, the effort spent in modeling can reduce the effort needed for checking the proposal and manual remodeling the collaborative business process. The optimum of this well-known trade-off between early modeling and late hard-coding lies somewhere in the middle between both extremes.

6.   RELATED WORK

Activities from the two areas of business process design and execution are related to our work. We give an overview over research performed in both areas in this section.

6.1   Design

Different strategies are proposed in research for facilitating the design of collaborative business processes. Besides utilizing patterns (Benatallah, Dumas et al. 2002), templates (Karastoyanova and Buchmann 2004) and knowledge from existing processes via recombination (Bernstein, Klein et al. 1999), the workflow composition approach is very dominant. Work using this approach mainly falls into two categories (Rao and Su 2004). Members of the one category are concerned with a planning-like composition of atomic elements to a workflow. Examples for this are e-workflow (Cardoso and Sheth 2003), the ASG composer (Meyer, Overdick et al. 2005), and others (Doshi, Goodwin et al. 2004; Kim, Spraragen et al. 2004; Mayer, McGough et al. 2003). Members of the second category take procedural constraints of the single elements into account. We strictly differentiate between both categories as only the second is related to our work. In this chapter, we used the ILOG composer (Albert, Binder et al. 2005a; Albert, de Sainte Marie et al. 2006; Albert, Henocque et al. 2005b,c) which is a result of the DIP project.[53] The composer Ws-Gen of the ASTRO project can in addition cope with Boolean variables and multiple fallback goals (Pistore, Marconi et al. 2005). Other work, though using atomic tasks, adds rules or preconditions and effects to express certain dependencies between the single tasks (Chun, Atluri et al. 2002; Laukkanen and Helin 2003).

6.2   Execution

With respect to the automatic creation of message mappings mainly research in two areas is related to our approach, namely database and XML schema matching and ontology alignment. The surveys of Rahm and Bernstein (2001) and Shvaiko and Euzenat (2005) present a nice overview of these two research areas. Besides some previous work exists in the area of lifting XML

---

[53] http://dip.semanticweb.org/

schemas to ontologies (Battle 2004; Bohring and Auer 2005; Ferdinand, Zirpins et al. 2004; Volz, Handschuh et al. 2004). However, all existing approaches focus on the creation of "ad hoc" ontologies whereas our approach lifts schemas to existing ontologies.

7. CONCLUSION

In this chapter we showed how to counter the two fundamental challenges of designing and executing collaborative business. We have seen that semantic technologies are very helpful here, as substantiated by our proof of concept in a real-world SAP Research tool suite. In contrast to current practice, our solution allows the suggestion of a CBP without requiring either participating business party to change their own operation signatures, business processes or message structures. The comparison of costs and benefits when applying semantic technologies is difficult to measure and depends on many subjective factors. However, the benefits outweigh the costs with the increasing complexity of the business processes.

8. QUESTIONS FOR DISCUSSION

Beginner:
1. Which steps does Business Process Management involve? List.
2. What is a Business Process Management System? Explain.
3. What is the difference between Business Processes and Collaborative Business Processes?
4. Why are Collaborative Business Processes much more complex to implement than company-internal Business Processes?

Intermediate:
1. What are the advantages and disadvantages of reusing an existing reasoner as the basis for composition instead of implementing a custom composition algorithm? Discuss.
2. Can the creation of collaborative business processes be a completely automatic process? Explain.
3. Why are semantic technologies especially helpful in combining heterogeneous businesses?
4. Why is a lifting and lowering step necessary when utilizing Semantic Web technologies for process integration?

5. Why is it necessary to use different matching algorithms in the lifting step?
6. What is the rational behind the exploitation of the domain ontology during the aggregation of matcher results?

Advance:
1. What considerations are key when integrating the business processes of two multiple companies?
2. List common properties of use cases in which the additional semantic modeling pays out.

Practical exercises:
1. Find two XML schemas describing a purchase order and compare them. Identify related elements and possible mapping functions.
2. Group exercise: Find a partner. One of you models individually a book purchasing process and the other a book selling process. Try to connect your two processes.

9.   SUGGESTED ADDITIONAL READING

- Staab, S. and Studer, R., editors. *Handbook on Ontologies*. International Handbooks on Information Systems. Springer, 2004. ISBN 3-540-40834-7: This book gives a good introduction to the basics of ontologies.
- Bussler, C. *B2B Integration - Concepts and Architecture*. Springer, 2003: The book covers concepts for the whole spectrum of business integration from the exchange of business events to business process integration.
- Kashyap, V. and Sheth, A. *Information Brokering Across Heterogeneous Digital Media - A Metadata-based Approach*. Number 20 in The Kluwer international series on advances in database systems. Kluwer Academic Publishers, 2000: This book especially deals with information integration.

10.   REFERENCES

Albert, P., W. Binder, et al. (2005a). D4.12 – Goal-oriented sws composition module specification. Technical report, EU-project DIP. http://dip.semanticweb.org/documents/D4a12.pdf.

Albert, P., C. de Sainte Marie, et al. (2006). D4.15 – Goal-oriented sws composition prototype. Technical report, EU-project DIP. http://dip.semanticweb.org/documents/D4.15CompositionModulePrototype.pdf.

Albert, P., L. Henocque, et al. (2005b). Configuration-based workflow composition. In DBL (2005), pages 285–292.

Albert, P., L. Henocque, et al. (2005c). A constrained object model for configuration based workflow composition. In Bussler and Haller (2006), pages 102–115.

Battle, S. (2004). Round-tripping between xml and rdf. In International Semantic Web Conference(ISWC). Springer.

Benatallah, B., M. Dumas, et al. (2002). Towards patterns of web services composition. URL citeseer.ist.psu.edu/benatallah02towards.html.

Bernstein, A., M. Klein, et al. (1999). The process recombinator: a tool for generating new business process ideas. In ICIS, pages 178–192. URL citeseer.ist.psu.edu/bernstein99proces.html.

Bohring, H. and S. Auer (2005). Mapping xml to owl ontologies. In Proceedings of 13. Leipziger Informatik-Tage (LIT 2005).

Born, M. (2006). Service enabling of business process management tools. Diploma Thesis, Albstadt-Sigmaringen University, Germany.

Cardoso, J. and A. Sheth (2003). Semantic e-workflow composition. J. Intell. Inf. Syst., 21(3):191–225. ISSN 0925-9902. doi:http://dx.doi.org/10.1023/A:1025542915514.

Chun, S. A., V. Atluri, et al. (2002). Domain knowledge-based automatic workflow generation. In Database and Expert Systems Applications : 13th International Conference, DEXA 2002 Aix-en-Provence, France, September 2-6, 2002. Proceedings, page 81ff. http://www.springerlink.com/content/55ra4dhu04wfxnq1.

Cohen, W. W., P. Ravikumar, et al. (2003). A comparison of string distance metrics for name-matching tasks. In Proceedings of the IJCAI 2003.

Do, H.-H. and E. Rahm (2002). COMA - a system for flexible combination of schema matching approaches. In Proc. 28th VLDB Conference.

Doshi, P., R. Goodwin, et al. (2004). Dynamic workflow composition using markov decision processes. In ICWS '04: Proceedings of the IEEE International Conference on Web Services (ICWS'04), page 576.

Ehrig, M. and Y. Sure (2004). Ontology mapping - an integrated approach. In 1st European Semantic Web Symposium. URL http://www.aifb.uni-karlsruhe.de/WBS/ysu/publications/2004_esws_mapping.pdf.

Ferdinand, M., C. Zirpins, et al. (2004). Lifting xml schema to owl. In Web Engineering - 4th International Conference, ICWE 2004.

Greiner, U., S. Lippe, et al. (2006). Designing and implementing crossorganizational business processes -description and application of a modeling framework. In Interoperability for Enterprise Software and Applications Conference I-ESA.

Karastoyanova, D. and A. P. Buchmann (2004). Automating the development of web service compositions using templates. In GI Jahrestagung (2), pages 517–523.

Kim, J., M. Spraragen, et al. (2004). An intelligent assistant for interactive workflow composition. In IUI'04: Proceedings of the 9th international conference on Intelligent user interface, pages 125–131. ACMPress, New York, NY, USA. ISBN 1-58113-815-6. doi:http://doi.acm.org/10.1145/964442.964466.

Laukkanen, M. and H. Helin (2003). Composing workflows of semantic web services. In Proceedings of the Workshop on Web-Services and Agent-based Engineering. URL http://jmvidal.cse.sc.edu/library/laukkanen03a.pdf.

Mayer, A., S. McGough, et al. (2003). Iceni dataflow and workflow: Composition and scheduling in space and time. URL citeseer.ist.psu.edu/mayer03iceni.html.

McIlraith, S. A., T. C. Son, et al. (2001). Semantic web services. IEEE Intelligent Systems, 16(2):46–53. ISSN 1541-1672. doi:http://dx.doi.org/10.1109/5254.920599.

METEOR-S (2004). METEOR-S: Semantic Web Services and Processes. Online. http://lsdis.cs.uga.edu/projects/meteor-s/

Meyer, H., H. Overdick, et al. (2005). Plngine: A system for automated service composition and process enactment. In Proceedings of the WWW Service Composition with Semantic Web Services (wscomps05), pages 3–12. University of Technology of Compiegne, Compiegne, France. ISBN 2-913923-18-6.

OWL-S (2004). The OWL Services Coalition. OWL-S: Semantic markup for web services. Online, 2004

Pistore, M., A. Marconi, et al. (2005). Automated composition of web services by planning at the knowledge level. In IJCAI, pages 1252–1259.

Rahm, E. and P. A. Bernstein (2001). A survey of approaches to automatic schema matching. VLDB Journal: Very Large Data Bases, 10(4):334–350.

Rao, J. and X. Su (2004). A survey of automated web service composition methods. In SWSWPC, pages 43–54.

Schulz, K., W. Sadiq, et al. (2005). Research into greater interoperability. SAP Info. Http://www.sap.info.

Shvaiko, P. and J. Euzenat (2005). A survey of schema-based matching approaches. Technical report, Informatica e Telecomunicazioni, University of Trento.

Stumme, G., M. Ehrig, et al. (2004). The karlsruhe view on ontologies. Technical report, University of Karlsruhe, Institute AIFB.

Volz, R., S. Handschuh, et al. (2004). Ontolift demonstrator. Deliverable 12, WonderWeb: Ontology Infrastructure for the Semantic Web. URL http://wonderweb.semanticweb.org/deliverables/D12.shtml.

Wiederhold, G. (1992). Mediators in the architecture of future information systems. In M. N. Huhns and M. P. Singh, editors, Readings in Agents, pages 185–196. Morgan Kaufmann, San Francisco, CA, USA. URL citeseer.ist.psu.edu/wiederhold92mediators.html.

WSDL (2001). Web services description language. Online. Http://www.w3.org/TR/wsdl.

WSMO (2004). Digital Enterprise Research Institute (DERI). Web service modeling ontology. online, 2004. http://www.wsmo.org

XSD (2001). W3C XML schema definition. Online. Http://www.w3.org/XML/Schema.

XSLT (1999). W3C XSL Transformations. Online. Http://www.w3.org/TR/xslt.

PART VI – ENTERPRISE MANAGEMENT AND SECURITY

Chapter 11

ONTOLOGY-BASED KNOWLEDGE MANAGEMENT IN THE STEEL INDUSTRY
Arcelor's use cases

José Arancón[1], Luis Polo[2], Diego Berrueta[2], François-Marie Lesaffre[3], Nicolás de Abajo[1] and Antonio Campos[2]

[1]*Arcelor Research Knowledge Innovation Center (KIN), ArcelorMittal, Avilés, Spain – jose.arancon@arcelor.com, nicolas.abajo@arcelor.com*
[2]*CTIC Foundation, Gijón, Spain – luis.polo@fundacionctic.org, diego.berrueta@fundacionctic.org, antonio.campos@fundacionctic.org*
[3] *ArcelorMittal, Fos, France – fm.lesaffre@arcelor.com*

1. INTRODUCTION

ArcelorMittal is the world's number one steel company, with 330,000 employees in more than 60 countries. The company is the product of the union of two of the world's leading steel companies, Mittal Steel and Arcelor. With industrial activity in 27 countries across Europe, the Americas, Asia and Africa, ArcelorMittal has a balanced geographic diversity within all the key steel markets. Leading R&D and technology, ArcelorMittal must face the challenges of such an international group.

In this scenario, Arcelor Research Knowledge Innovation (KiN) Centre, aims to classify, model and put into service the knowledge of this Group. Everyone in the Group has to make decisions in their job. Investment, allocation, line piloting, etc. All these activities need at the time of decision-making the right information and the right knowledge. These knowledge intensive tasks steer, in a certain way, the business processes. As well as the important efforts made in R&D in products and processes, the Group devotes a real effort to make the most of information techniques applied to the steel business.

KiN innovates where knowledge intensive tasks steer critical business processes. These areas include Business Optimisation (Supply Chain, Sales, Purchasing, and Marketing), ArcelorMittal Customer Solutions based on knowledge, Industrial Processes support (Factory-wide, line piloting, process models) and transversal services assistance. KiN provides solutions based on the advanced technologies of Artificial Intelligence and information treatment such as data mining, knowledge-based systems, simulations or optimization techniques.

In the domain of Semantic Web, KiN is collaborating with the Semantic Web Researcher Group of the CTIC Foundation which specializes in semantic technologies for industry, e-government and e-business. The CTIC Foundation houses the W3C Spanish Office, and is also participating in working groups of the W3C Semantic Web Activity. Both ArcelorMittal and the CTIC foundation groups have collaborated in the analysis of the necessities and opportunities identified in the steel sector for Semantic Web technologies. The results are presented in this chapter.

The chapter is organized as follows: first, the motivation and use cases for applying semantics in the industry environment are discussed. Then practical experiences in ArcelorMittal group are presented. We conclude summarizing remaining open issues in the Semantic Web and our future work.

2. MOTIVATIONS AND USE CASES

This section begins with a discussion of motivations for applying Ontologies technologies in the industry. In particular, the advantages of ontologies as knowledge representation artifacts are emphasized. Some use cases are identified within the company: knowledge capitalization tools, a unified data description layer and supply chain management.

In many industrial fields object oriented programming, logic programming, relational databases and many artificial intelligence applications are currently in use. Ontologies are formal mechanisms to represent knowledge (Gruber 1995), which is not a new concept in computer science and artificial intelligence. However, only ontologies are capable of integrating all aspects listed below:

- **Structural clarity**: ontologies provide hierarchical organization of elements with principles similar to those of object oriented programming and object oriented databases. The resulting structured information base makes it possible to represent relationships between domain objects in a more natural way than relational databases. Furthermore, it allows us to represent hierarchical relations that are hard to formalize in relational algebra. As a result, the final structure is much clearer than that obtained using a classical relational database.

- **Human understanding**: ontologies provide a semantic approach in order to enrich these domain objects, making them closer to human understanding.
- **Maintainability**: the hierarchical organization of domain concepts as classes with roles and instances provides simple extension of the knowledge base. This maintainability advantage of ontologies contrasts with one of the weaknesses of traditional relational databases, which have a specific fixed schema, often only understandable by its creators or qualified developers.
- **Reasonability**: another important feature of ontologies, depending on the language used, is that they may have formal semantics. They include mechanisms to add logical or operational rules among the concepts of the ontology. Therefore, it is possible to infer new knowledge and check consistency of the ontology.
- **Flexibility**: the flexible nature of this technology motivates its use as a common representation layer for many heterogeneous applications or information sources, from legacy databases to semantic web services.
- **Interoperability**: over the last two decades, there have been some powerful ontology languages, such as KIF, DAML, Frame Logic or Conceptual Graphs by Sowa. Not until now has a wide consensus been reached about the underlying logical formalism, namely Description Logics (Baader and Nutt 2002), a decidable fragment of First Order Logics. In addition, W3C is currently promoting standardization policies to develop an interoperable language allowing the interchange of ontologies as part of the Semantic Web initiative (Berners-Lee, Hendler et al. 2001). The result of this effort is the OWL family of languages (McGuinness and Van Harmelen 2004).

In summary, ontology technology is a powerful tool for knowledge management, information retrieval and extraction, information exchange in agent-based systems as well as dialogue systems. In the rest of this section, some fields of applicability of ontologies in the steel industry will be introduced.

2.1 Knowledge capitalization tools

"Knowledge capitalization" covers a group of applications devoted to manage content, documents and information, structured so that users can easily access the knowledge and add or modify data. Currently, different solutions are available in the market for these purposes, under categories such as Content Management Systems (CMS), Document Management Systems (DMS), wikis, dynamic web portals, search engines, etc.

Ontologies can play a significant role to develop projects previously approached with this kind of legacy information management technologies. In order to fulfill this vision, two components will be required: ontologies and a software platform to exploit them.

In this chapter, we identify different projects in which this approach is implemented.

2.1.1 Semantic search

Searching in large sets of documents has become a common task for information systems, and one of the most profitable services in the web. However, the simplest search techniques based on string-matching the query and the documents (Baeza-Yates and Ribeiro-Neto 1999), are often limited. This is particularly true for internal information portals, where the domain is more constrained and the documents are less heterogeneous than in the web.

Over the last decades, the research centers of ArcelorMittal have authored thousands of documents. Nowadays, an industry-leader information retrieval product enables ArcelorMittal researchers to query this document set through an internal website. It combines string-based searching with algorithms to detect language of sources, expansion of queries with topic sets assigned to words (translations, synonyms), exploitation of existing metadata information and classification of documents in taxonomies defined with boolean combinations of topic sets queries and statistical scoring.

The company conducted a project to improve the quality of the results by using semantics. Based on this project, and the CTIC Foundation's experience in semantic search in legal documents, some ways of introducing semantics in the search process were identified:

- Lemmatization (or stemming) and other language-dependent, domain-independent techniques can improve the recall of the retrieval by isolating the meaning of each individual word from the actual spelling of the word.
- Thesauri of synonyms, broader terms and narrower terms are language-dependent, domain-dependent techniques that can be applied to the documents and the queries in order to improve the recall. They require a vocabulary expressed in a proper format, such as WordNet. However, each domain has its own vocabulary, and therefore the development of an expensive custom vocabulary for each domain is often required. We hope that the availability of SKOS (Miles and Brickley 2005), a

common framework for vocabulary exchange, will promote vocabulary re-use.

- Metadata is probably the most straightforward approach to semantic searching. The RDF framework (Manola and Miller 2004) excels as the framework with which to represent metadata about resources. There are two kinds of metadata: content-dependent and content-independent. The first describes properties such as author, date, language or format, and is relatively inexpensive to create. The second describes the actual content of the document: topics, keywords, etc., and is more complicated to create.

- Ontologies provide precisely-defined vocabularies for the metadata, and can be used to classify documents.

One drawback of metadata-based search engines is their high complexity in terms of user interface. Users are often presented non-trivial search forms to enter their queries. While this may be acceptable for experts, it should be avoided for inexperienced users. Common strategies to overcome this problem are: a) hiding the metadata from the user; b) applying semantics (vocabularies, ontologies) to offer suggestions to filter the results (when there are too many), or to rewrite the query (when there are no results); c) using faceted browsing to help users to create their own complex queries without having to understand the complexity of the process.

2.1.2 Human resources and networking

The importance of human resource management in multinational companies is greater than ever. Departments within the company need to exchange professional information: contacts, employees' profiles, documentation, etc. In addition, this kind of information usually resides in individual hard drives and personal files, and most of it is lost when the employee leaves the company. Generally, the field of Human Resources (HR) is a generic domain into which a great deal of effort in terms of knowledge management tends to be placed. Furthermore, a company like Arcelor is organized into groups which work on certain tasks. These working groups are frequently scattered geographically and their activity needs central planning and information sharing.

It seems justified to apply efforts to centralize and share Human Resources information. There are some traditional solutions, such as Human Resource Management Systems (HRMS), which are usually one of the modules of the Enterprise Resource Planning (ERP) softwares. A typical ERP integrates all the data and processes of an organization. These systems are based on unified databases to store and integrate data from all aspects of the enterprise. Nevertheless, an HRMS could be an insufficient answer to ArcelorMittal's needs. ERPs are used and designed for administrative purposes and for planning-aid. Semantic Web technology could bring together Human Resources Management, networking and Internet scenarios, like e-Recruitment (Mochol, Oldakowski et al. 2004).

Ontologies provide an interoperability framework to build semantic web platforms. Activities like personnel recruitment or human resources management handle the same objects: people, qualifications, skills, etc. Socially-oriented ontologies relate people with documents, plans or activities in the enterprise. In these potential applications it would be possible to reuse the impressive body of domain knowledge available in the form of classifications and taxonomies (ISCO 1988). A semantic web platform could exploit this information in three ways:

1. **Hierarchy:** by means of ontologies, complete formal descriptions of organizations could be provided (OKAR Working Group 2005). Ontologies hierarchically organize the key concepts of the enterprise, necessary for many human resources relationships: departments, projects, activities, working groups, etc. In this structure, an element of an organization is not isolated from the organization itself. However, the distinction between the temporal relations that are perdurable and those that are not should also be present. This distinction, which is not so evident, is becoming more and more relevant considering the dramatic change of organizational structures that companies are suffering. In some cases they are moving towards a decentralized model or even without an apparently formalized hierarchy (i.e. Linux development communities) (Malone, Thomas W. et al. 2004). For instance, the current hierarchical position of an employee in a company is a variable attribute. Furthermore, the same employee can play different roles at the same time: the leader of one project may occasionally work as a consultant for another project (Masolo, Vieu et al. 2004). Nevertheless, the experience gained by this employee in the different roles is a perdurable characteristic that should be considered in a different manner. HR departments need to manage these skills and orientate the necessities following continuous organizational changes. The question that arises here is if the formalization of a perdurable hierarchical structure of a company (i.e. in the form of an ontology) could be stable and commonly shared by different business models. Ontology technology provides powerful means to achieve this objective due to its capabilities for conceptualization and maintenance. At the same time, it is also clear that the modeling phase is the most critical part of a system designed for HR management and is not always so evident.

2. **E-Recruitment:** nowadays, job postings are written in the form of plain text. Semantic annotation of job postings using concepts from an ontology results in language independent descriptions that are processable by machines. Although many businesses still rely on newspaper advertisements to recruit personnel, online job exchange services and online personnel marketing is increasingly used. Internet has demonstrated to be an effective communication medium for recruitment. Nevertheless, due to the vast amount of suppliers, services and channels in the Web, visibility is rather limited. Semantic Web technology can improve recruitment procedures, facilitating the job search and simplifying the organization's viewpoint. In the case of ArcelorMittal, internal mobility is common and has similar principles to a recruitment process. Posts frequently need to be filled with the Human Resources existing in the Group. There are three main phases in a typical recruitment process in which semantic annotations could help to automate the pre-selection of potential candidates: describing the requirements of the job position, publishing the job position and decision making (discovery and evaluation of candidates).

3. **Experts Assignment:** a semantic-based platform can use techniques similar to those of e-Recruitment, to help in the discovery and assignment of "the appropriate employee". In a big company, technical experts are geographically scattered around the world. Sometimes working groups for a certain task must be organized in a short time period. If the personnel were semantically described in such a way that it could be used by machines, the platform would search and associate employee profiles (skills, qualifications, experience, abilities, etc.) to specific job positions. An ontology describes not only the people in the organization, but also the job requirements. The system would exploit this information to infer suitable candidates.

2.2   Unified data description layer

In a huge company scattered all over the globe and built by a continuous merging of smaller companies, information systems are heterogeneous, disperse and often redundant. There are all kinds of software components, from knowledge management to simulation, from on-line process control to Enterprise Resource Planning (ERP). At the same time, productivity greatly depends on the ability to inter-communicate these internal systems, and also to interface with third-parties (providers, customers, etc.).

XML has emerged as the syntactical solution for inter-application data communication, replacing ad-hoc data serialization formats (Bray, Paoli et al. 2006). In this context, XML is an extraordinary tool. It allows data to be transferred across any kind of technological boundary, such as different architectures, in-memory data representation conventions, character encodings, software vendors, etc. In addition, it promotes software re-use (i.e. XML parsers). XML instances can be checked for syntactical correctness against grammars (XML Schema), queried (XQuery, XPath) and transformed (XSL). Furthermore, applications can set up dialogues wrapping XML documents using commodity protocols (web services).

However, XML documents are meaningless. They contain data, but the meaning of the data must be externally agreed by the users of the document. Note that simply defining a XML Schema does not add enough semantics to the XML document, as an XML Schema is just a grammar that is used to check which vocabulary constructions are valid. The importance of this hindrance is easily underestimated, but it has a large impact in the long-term. Actually, it destroys almost all hope of achieving a fully automated communication (i.e. without human participation) among software systems. In other words: there are two major alternatives to set up a communication between different applications:

1. The applications agree to use a common XML vocabulary which is a standard in the industry. This is the case, for example, of web servers and web browsers, where the common vocabulary is XHTML. However, there is no such thing as a widely accepted industrial standard XML vocabulary for any purpose.
2. Some human mediation adapts the vocabulary understood by each agent in the communication, for instance, through XSL transformations. Of course, this is possible only if precise, human-readable descriptions of the vocabularies are available.

This remark can also be applied for other exchange formats between applications.

Ontologies have the potential to fix this situation by providing precise, machine-readable semantic descriptions of the data. Let us examine some use cases in the industry:

- Legacy relational databases can be wrapped with semantic interfaces that describe the meaning of the stored data. This is probably the only feasible approach to introduce semantics in databases in the short-term. Whatever the benefits may be, companies will hardly migrate their huge, reliable relational databases to native ontology repositories. Fortunately, this vision of a smooth transition is shared by many others, so the mapping from relational databases to ontologies (known as R2O) is now the subject of active research.

- Steel producers use models and simulation tools to predict or control the impact of unexpected events on production (e.g. a delay of a raw material shipment, a plant breakdown or a strike), to obtain new methods to optimize productivity (e.g. machine tuning), or to predict several environment variables such as customer's demand. Industrial models or simulation tools are often integrated into large software applications or complex information systems. Although models are differently built depending on physical principles, data analysis, statistical techniques or simulation softwares, they all share a common set of input and output variables and a set of transformations applied to them. Thus, they would benefit from greater re-use if they could share a common vision of the domain variables. Coincidentally, this is almost the definition of ontology. In addition, they could be linked together, connecting their inputs and outputs. Once again, this reminds us to revise the applications of semantic web services which are based on similar premises.

- Distributed searches are being improved. As previously described, enterprise information is usually scattered throughout a myriad of data repositories. One immediate consequence is that searching for a particular piece of information is extremely difficult. In fact, the user must start by determining which repository may contain the information and then querying that repository. If the search gives no results, the user will probably move into another repository and try again. Modern software products for corporate search can index multiple data repositories, effectively allowing a cross-search to be conducted through a common interface. Nevertheless, without proper semantics, this search process is practically a "no-brainer", particularly in multilingual environments. One of the promises of the semantic web is that adding explicit semantics to the information (and the repositories) will enhance our ability to recover it. The results so far look promising (Barrero, Moreno et al. 2005).

2.3   Supply chain management

Supply chain is a coordinated system of organizations, people, processes and resources involved in moving a product or service from suppliers to customers. The management of this system, known as Supply Chain Management (SCM), is rather complex: coordinating groups of independent business units and companies to temporarily work together as one unit to plan, design, produce, and deliver a product to satisfy an immediate or projected market demand at the highest possible performance level. In addition, irregularities such as delays in a production process are the result of variances in processing times and processing quality. The orders are often related. In this way, the order of a set of final coils involves different suborders (raw materials, transportation services, intermediate products, etc.).

When modeling a supply chain, different heterogeneous processes must be abstracted in the form of models. Simulation is an effective support tool despite this complexity of supply chain modeling. On one hand, the supply chain environment is highly dynamic. Thus, if the knowledge used to run simulation models is not synchronized, the accuracy of these models' outputs cannot be assured. On the other hand, multinational enterprises use different information technologies to store and manipulate data which vary in scale, usage and level of technology. In fact, most of the supply chain data resides in these heterogeneous systems, distributed throughout the supply chain network. The efficiency of these systems is focused on their internal processes. They can become islands of automation, isolated from the rest of the components of the supply chain. It is necessary to identify a means to access all these systems remotely and a mechanism to extract the information from their data schema, in order to build a global model.

One hypothesis at ArcelorMittal Research is that ontology engineering could become an effective technology for supporting supply chain modeling (Fayez, Rabelo et al. 2005). Ontologies built for this purpose have to handle the following issues: identify the knowledge and data required for a specific model, and develop mechanisms to extract it; populate the ontology with the required knowledge; build simulation models and implant a generic procedure to fill the necessary input values.

2.3.1 A business processes abstraction: The SCOR model

Integration between companies is the main challenge of supply chains. Ontologies could provide a unified view of the business rules of the different partners involved in the common supply chain process. At the same time, they could help partners to manage their own business rules without changing their own technologies. In this way, ontology technology permits a unified dynamic view of the business rule logic, no matter what the original form of the rules might be.

Modeling the supply chain means formalizing different views: the supplier, the costumer, the life cycle of the product, etc. One possible approach is to design a business activities framework based on existing supply chain standardized abstractions, such as the SCOR model (Supply Chain Council 2003). This provides a common, shared vocabulary of supply chain concepts. The Supply Chain Operations Reference (SCOR) model was developed by the Supply Chain Council. This model is an abstraction of a reference business process, and generically describes any supply chain to any degree of detail. The SCOR model is one of the shared, broadly accepted conceptualizations and knowledge base within the supply chain community. Our future plans in this field are based on the following points:

1. First of all, to design a metamodel for supply chain applications: the ontology based upon the SCOR model. This ontology will enable the integration of all the key information for the simulators or applications in each part of the supply chain network in a coherent representation. The SCOR model is structured around five supply chain processes: Plan, Source, Make, Deliver and Return. Moreover, these processes are decomposable. As the SCOR model does not provide an explicit view of the process, material or information flow, the ontology has to take into account the main categories of the supply knowledge: *product* (product design, product cost, material information), *process* (process cost, process quality), *resource* (capacity of resource), *inventory* (control policy), *order* (demand or order quantity, due dates) and *planning* (forecasting methods, order schedule).

2. Secondly, the idea is to create an ontology-based platform to gather knowledge distributed over the whole supply chain and run the global simulation experiments. The ontology-based platform will be able to integrate each simulator's model: inputs, outputs, considered parameters, etc. Moreover, our supply chain ontology could help in future systems designs: guidelines, templates and structured vocabularies provided by the ontology based on the SCOR model could be reused.

2.3.2 Modeled factory and metallurgical routes

This section analyses the potential application of ontology design and semantic web standards for the description of metallurgical routes in the steel industry. A metallurgical route involves a set of processes from order-to-production that must be represented before developing applications to deal with them. Past experience in ArcelorMittal has shown the following common drawbacks when developing systems that manage metallurgical routes:

- Lack of modularity: the systems that deal with metallurgical routes are usually difficult to maintain. The processes involved in such routes are in continuous evolution. Implementing new constraints, changing or adding new process steps are often complex and time consuming tasks.
- Lack of standardization: Rule based systems usually lack of standardization either in the language or in the methodology to define rule flows. In fact, these systems usually depend on commercial

software. The knowledge implemented in these softwares is not reusable, difficult to migrate to new systems or to extend to other production facilities.

- Lack of integration between business models and production rules: Some of the current existing platforms to develop rule base systems cover this aspect with a certain success and robustness. They allow certain level of integration between the static representation of the business domain (Business concepts and relations) and the logic and production rules that work on the top of it. Even some of them provide assisted environments to maintain rules. Unfortunately, they also count with the drawback previously explained.

To overcome these shortcomings we will determine whether the usage of ontologies and semantic web technology can improve the architecture of such systems.

The idea is to make a formal description of the concepts that occur in the metallurgical routes. All concepts would be formalized as ontology classes. These would include the different installations, the final products and the intermediate products. These concepts or 'blue prints' should be agreed on by the different plants. They would represent a common understanding of production lines and products.

For instance, the concept *HotRollingMill* refers to different rolling mills in different plants of the company. This concept has certain properties:

- Minimum/maximum entrance width
- Minimum/maximum exit width
- Productivity
- Thickness reduction capacity
- Input material is of type *Slab*
- Output material is of type *HotRoll*

The facilities in the different factories are represented by instances of the *HotRollingMill* concept. These instances are given actual values that apply for each specific facility.

Using a common ontology would provide a common vocabulary to exchange information. By sharing a common "blue print", the data would be assured to have the same meaning. Moreover, using a semantic web standard to implement the ontology, it would be guaranteed to have a common, shared language for exchanging the information.

Semantic web technology opens several possibilities. From an architectural point of view, data could be stored in a decentralized way. Every factory could store data specifying the state of its facilities as it suits them best. The only thing they would have to do is to expose a web service. Thus the instances representing their facilities could be queried. The services would be responsible for translating the plant specific representation of the data to the common ontology representation.

The web services might be more powerful than pure data providers. Behind the web services, models could be implemented and maintained in a decentralized way by the plants.

Going back to our example, *HotRollingMill* would be available via a web service to the applications that need its information details.

In this scenario the complexity of the maintenance is reduced by increasing the modularity and decentralization. The internal behaviour of the objects is not exposed. Moreover, they would be maintained by local teams close to the lines, thus assuring that the state of the instances in the system truly reflect the physical state of the facility.

Adding new installations becomes very straightforward; a web service needs to be imposed that provides access to the installation information (or the installation model).

Using a modular – web service component based – and decentralized design, allow us to expand the functionality of the applications to other processes of a metallurgical route.

In the case that the systems in this domain require reasoning through business rules, there are some questions that arise from the usage of the semantic web technology: how the rules can be implemented to enable the backward search; and whether the semantic web technology can be used to express certain business rules.

Obviously, the more intelligence is encapsulated in the web services, the fewer rules are needed. The most coherent choice would be to express the business rules in the same environment as the ontologies. If an ontology is modified, it is undesirable to change the business rules in a different system. A weak link between the ontology and the business rules increases the risk of inconsistencies when one of the two is changed.

If rules can not be expressed in the same language as ontologies, another appropriate reasoning engine and rules language is required. However the question still remains: is it worth using the ontology language purely for standardization and data exchange? If so, synchronizing ontology data models and data models in rule based systems would require a great deal of effort. A brief example on ArcelorMittal experience with industrial processes modeling and meta modeling will be described in the paragraph 3 of this chapter. Finally, it will be concluded with further information on open issues regarding semantic services and combination of ontologies and rules.

2.4   Use cases summary

To sum up, key information about Arcelor's use cases is captured in the table (Table 11-1).

Table 11-1. Use cases summary

Use Case	Semantic Technologies	Practical Solutions
Semantic Search	Ontologies, metadata, thesauri and taxonomies.	ARIADNE Project
H.R. and Networking	Ontologies, international classification and rules.	Under development
Unified Data Description Layer	Ontologies and data mediation	Under development
Expert Knowledge and Industry process modeling	Ontologies and rules	Under development
Supply Chain Management	Ontologies, SCOR model, semantic web services and rules	Under development
Modeled Factory	Ontologies and rules	Metallurgical routes descriptions and Visonto

3.   PRACTICAL EXPERIENCES

Ontologies are powerful formalisms to capture knowledge. In the industrial domain, knowledge is a key factor in productivity, and it is obvious that experienced workers are more productive that novice ones. Capturing knowledge is merely a step towards achieving the real objective: sharing knowledge among the employees who execute similar tasks. In order to raise overall productivity, the company facilitates the transfer of knowledge from its experienced employees to the inexperienced ones. However, increased productivity is not the only benefit of this: experienced employees are less likely to have industrial accidents. Thus, larger companies spend considerable amounts of money to improve the skills of their employees.

As the company grows, it becomes common to have different teams of people in different countries, speaking different languages, essentially performing the same tasks (for example, at several steel mills throughout the world). Unfortunately, these teams will probably never speak to each other, so they will never share their knowledge in the company's benefit.

Even in the same location, there is a natural renewal of staff. With a staff of thousands, older experienced employees retire everyday and the company loses their knowledge. To replace them, young, inexperienced workers are taken on and the company must spend money on their training. Therefore, there is a strong motivation to aid knowledge transfer and sharing. In this context, ontologies are valuable because of their closeness to the human mind.

3.1   Expert Knowledge and Industry Processes Modeling

There is much to comprehend about metalworking and factory modeling: how to manage bottlenecks, solve inventory and work-in-process problems like line stoppages and material defects, optimize production rates, determine plant capacity, etc. Ontology technology is becoming a powerful tool to develop reusable formal models of particular domains. The goal is to build a shared abstraction of metalworking concepts and to use it as an interoperable framework in production lines modeling and product life cycle management.

In ArcelorMittal an ontology which focuses on the process, equipments, problematic and best practices of the continuous annealing line has been developed. The continuous annealing is a good example as it is a critical phase in the steel production. The annealing restores steel's plasticity which is lost during the previous cold-rolling process which was needed to obtain certain thickness in the steel strip. Problems of fold and strip displacement can appear during annealing. In the same way, other processes follow the continuous annealing such as tempering, coating, etc. All processes can have problems and defaults in final products; these can be accumulated and appear latter in other processes with the same or a different form. So, all the lines have in common certain elements or concepts. They all have a physical structure of tools and equipments, perform a process and supply a product. Figure 11-1 illustrates the main upper concepts involved in a production line.

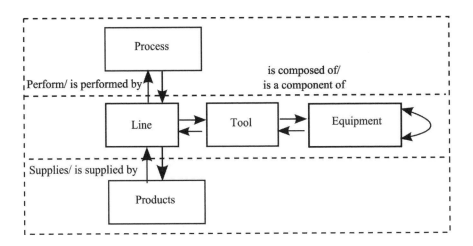

Figure 11-1. Representation of a generic production line

The main building blocks of an ontology are *concepts* representing sets of objects, *properties* representing relationships between objects, *individuals* representing specific objects, and *attributes* representing characteristics of individuals. The usual objects of generic continuous annealing lines have been identified and organized to build the model of this process, linking it later with other processes.

- **Production line**: A production line involves a set of sequential operations or processes established in a factory whereby materials (e.g. steel strips) are put through an industrial process (e.g. annealing) to produce an end-product (e.g. packaging steels), suitable for market-selling under quality requirements. The production line is also made up of machines and equipment that participate in product manufacturing. Figure 11-1 illustrates a sequence of production processes.

- **Tools/Equipment**: From a physical point of view, a production line is just a configuration of machines, devices and tools. These must also be taken into account to develop a conceptual model. For example, in the rolling process, metal is passed through pairs of rollers. Information about these kinds of objects helps in factory management (equipment purchase, maintenance, etc.). This information also improves production line simulation and helps us to understand how workflow is affected by the physical configuration of the production line (e.g., stoppages take place at a particular roll of the line, defaults in strip appear due to degradation of rolls…).

- **Industrial process**: A process is a particular course of action intended to achieve a result. An industrial process is a particular technique involving thermodynamic, chemical or mechanical steps to manufacture a product. A technique is actually a practical method to obtain material modification (manufacturing). The technique sequences the industrial process in ordered tasks. Therefore, the tasks are targets which must be fulfilled by specific action to complete the whole process. The fulfillment of these targets is controlled in the line via on-line signals of measure devices (process parameters). To manage this knowledge in continuous change, it would be needed to use temporal relations such as temporal causality, precedence or temporal overlapping (coincidence).

- **Product**: the goal of a production line is to fabricate an end-product; raw material is transformed into finished goods for sale. There have been created ontologies to describe products and their information about steel properties (level of hardness, thickness, mechanical properties, etc.) in each step of the whole process could contribute to product life cycle management.

In summary, our annealing production line ontology is based upon three major categories: elements of products, processes and structure of production lines (including tools/equipment) with certain relations between them. It results on the description of what is produced, how and with which means. These elements describe the business model of each line. From these upper classes, the Ontology grows in a hierarchy of classes and relations that achieve enough detail to solve specific use cases (fold risk management, frame to extend to other lines, processes and use cases). Some of them, for instance industrial process and product, take part of models already formalized such as the SCOR model. The aim is also to reuse the formal abstraction developed for the Continuous Annealing Line in other factories. However, some interoperability needs have been detected.

3.1.1 Enhancing ontology reuse and interoperability

As different models are developed for different production lines which share many concepts, the need for interoperability and reusability arises. The solution that has been adopted involves the development of a meta-modelling framework that specifies how to build the ontology for each particular domain. This framework comprises three major components:

1. **Ontology language.** Until now, we have used Protégé (Protégé 2006) native format: Open Knowledge Base Connectivity (OKBC), a format based on Frames paradigm. However, we are translating our ontologies to OWL-DL language (McGuinness and Van Harmelen 2004). OWL is the W3C recommendation for building ontologies in the Semantic Web. Furthermore, OWL has been designed to provide an interoperable language for semantic descriptions due to its underlying semantic model (RDF) and its XML syntax (also known as RDF/XML). We focus mainly on the OWL-DL variant because of its correspondence with an expressive description logic, *SHOIN(D)*, a decidable and tractable fragment of First Order Logic (Baader and Nutt 2002). One of the major advantages of OWL-DL is that it supports maximum expressiveness while retaining computational completeness and decidability.
2. **Common semantics.** To build a semantic framework we need not only the same language, but also similar semantics: we have to share vocabulary and points of view. A standard upper ontology like SUMO (Niles and Pease 2001) or DOLCE (Masolo, Borgo et al. 2003) gives us a core of properties, axioms and theorems flexible enough to be used for every domain representation. Moreover, we need to share the same vocabulary for knowledge interchange (Hepp 2006; Leukel, Schmitz et al. 2002). Various organizations are attempting to define standards for

specific domains. Existing taxonomies like "Process Specification Language" (PSL 2006) for industrial processes, and Common Procurement Vocabulary (CPV 2002) or United Nations Standard Products and Services Code (UNSPSC 2006) for products and services are some examples.

3. **Meta-modeling.** The ontology approach to meta-modeling that has been undertaken consists of multilayering the conceptualization: the first, highest level describes the more general concepts, as in every steel factory ontology (production line, process, tool, etc.); the lower level is specific for each line, it describes the line, what tools it uses and for what processes, and so forth; an intermediate layer facilitates reuse of common parts, since some processes, equipment and concepts belong to several process lines; this intermediate layer consists of libraries of shared components that can be instantiated in any of the particular models. Figure 11-2 shows a graph that explains the relationships between these layers.

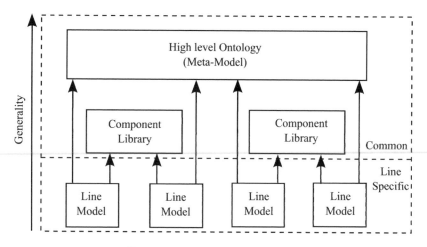

Figure 11-2. Graph of model relations

While this graph has been kept simple for the sake of clarity, the relationships can be much more tangled; besides deriving from the meta-model, each production line model can make use of several component libraries (Cuenca, Parsia et al. 2005; Rector 2003). Furthermore, the component libraries can be related among each other, each drawing not only from the meta-model but also from components in other libraries. For instance, one component library might define a *Cylinder*, and another component library a *TemperMill*, taking the definition of the *Cylinder* from the former; the production line model would refer to the meta-model for the general layout, to the second component library for the *TemperMill*, and to the first component library for the spare cylinders.

The greatest challenge in this scheme is the deployment procedure. Care must be taken to properly separate the layers at the right level, so that the evolution of the common ontology does not force major rebuilding of the specific models. Also, this level of separation is dynamic; for instance, a given piece of equipment might be considered specific at first, but afterwards moves to a component library if modeling of additional production lines also requires it. Since the process line models are defined according to the higher level ontology, the transfer is quite straightforward, but interactions between levels should be checked for.

In order to follow this dynamic evolution, a set of knowledge bases is being built. Each of these describe one of the blocks in the diagram (i.e. there is one for the higher level ontology, one for each component library and one for each line model) and tracks all the changes throughout its version history.

3.1.2 Annotation properties, expert knowledge and networking

Our production line ontology not only implies industrial equipment to perform steel fabrication tasks, but also company staff to maintain devices, control the process, test product quality, etc. These employees are technical experts, such as welders or engineers. As we mentioned before, our goal is to capture this knowledge and manage it in a collaborative framework. The formal definition of concepts in the ontology gives us a shared abstraction of the continuous line technique. However, this is not sufficient. We would like to provide experts with flexible mechanisms to document the ontology. The Semantic Web technology and, to an even greater extent, the RDF model allow us to treat production line knowledge as information about a set of web resources. In the RDF model, anything can be a web resource due to its URIRef usage. Moreover, OWL language has a special kind of property (annotation property), to add metadata information to any resource of an ontology (concepts, individuals or properties).

There are some predefined annotation properties in OWL (*rdfs:comment* or *rdfs:seeAlso*). Of course, OWL is open to create new properties if ontology developers need them. These can be used by experts to add documentation to the ontology, so they can link ontology resources (process of annealing, rolls, packaging steels) with specific information objects (CAD designs, technical manuals, instruction manual, technical terms, observations of experts, pictures, etc.). Gathering this kind of knowledge is the first step towards a collaborative ontology-based platform and networking. Although documentation resources could be dispersed among different working teams, projects, or even different databases, OWL can easily access them. An OWL ontology can manage resources from different distributed sources due to its RDF roots and its XML syntax.

In addition, as was mentioned above, applying a social network enhances the utility of the factory ontology. Technical experts take part in the product manufacturing process; they work in the production line and they are members of working teams, so they are part of the hierarchy of the organization. Acquaintance relationships, working associations and employee profiles should be introduced in the referred ontology. This knowledge helps to organize the factory staff, describing each job position and knowing which workers are in charge of each step of the production line. We can combine this information with ontology documentation enhancing our approach with vocabularies such as Dublin Core (DCMI 2006). In summary, we think our production line ontology will be a helpful tool for knowledge capitalization and networking. Experts share the same model of the whole process and they can interchange information and documents by means of the ontology.

3.2   Visonto: a tool for ontology visualization

The market offers a range of tools for ontology authoring, but this is just the first step towards knowledge transference. In addition, there is a remarkable lack of generic, easy to use applications to visualize the knowledge captured in the ontologies. We can find specialized tools for particular ontologies and generic tools with a cryptic interface for users untrained on Description Logics or RDF.

Arcelor identified this lack and launched a project with the CTIC Foundation aiming to develop Visonto, a generic ontology visualization platform that could be customized for each domain. At the moment of this publication the project is still under development, but the main lines have already been defined and early prototypes are being tested.

One of the main points of Visonto is the balance between flexibility and customization. Undoubtedly more flexibility means higher development costs, but also greater opportunities for reuse. A key decision was made to embed the customization rules in the ontology itself, effectively allowing authors to customize the way the ontology should be displayed. Therefore, no additional tools or skills are required to write presentation rules in a separate language.

These presentation rules select the information and its organization by means of some presentational abstractions such as "point of view" or "filter". In addition, they also specify the information layout, grouping and formatting. This is achieved through presentational abstractions similar to the visual widgets in desktop applications and web pages (labels, text fields, lists, links, images, etc.).

Another relevant decision was the choice of Description Logic abstractions (concepts, instances, roles) as the basis of the knowledge model. Once again this is a balance between adding support for additional formalisms (for instance, rules) and keeping the model as simple as possible. However there are plans to explore paths to increase the expressivity of the model without a significant increase of the complexity perceived by users. In particular, domain rules are desirable as there are vast amounts of industrial knowledge in this format.

3.2.1 Views

Once customized for a particular domain Visonto offers a set of "views" of the information that are similar to those of authoring tools like Protégé or Swoop: a concept list, a tree showing the concept hierarchy and tabbed views with details. The information is heavily linked, so users can browse the knowledge base as they do with web pages (in fact, they can even bookmark the concepts). At the present stage users are not allowed to modify the knowledge base. However, they can post comments about the concepts. These comments are shared among all the users, effectively creating a forum for discussion, increasing or maybe pointing out mistakes in the knowledge base. Future developments will make it possible to make small modifications to the ontology, such as creating new instances or changing property values.

Multilinguism is a must for a world-wide company. Therefore, Visonto supports multilingual ontologies. Almost all the information in an ontology is language-agnostic. However, annotation properties (such as labels and descriptions) and user's comments are language-dependent. Visonto scans the availability of localized information for each concept and includes it in the view. There are other subtle and easily managed differences regarding the proper way to display the information, but without effect on the ontology, for example, units of measurements (meters/feet, Celsius/Fahrenheit, etc.) or number and date formatting.

Searching is a fundamental feature of any information system. Consequently, Visonto exhibits two different approaches to query the knowledge base.

- First, the built-in string-based search feature enables the user to quickly find a concept by its name, description or even the comments attached by users. This feature mimics the behavior of the simple search interfaces provided by almost every web site on the Internet, and it is particularly useful to "auto-complete" as you type.

- Second, a more elaborate query engine is available, exposing a subset of the powerful SPARQL query algebra (Prud'hommeaux and Seaborne 2006). Of course, users are not expected to write a single token in SPARQL, and the underlying algebra is, to some extent, hidden from them. Furthermore, Visonto tries to hide even the ontology structure (in contrast with traditional database querying, where users must have some knowledge about the tables and the cardinality of the relationships). This is accomplished by means of a user friendly interface, based on the query-by-example (QbE) paradigm, where variables are replaced by the spatial layout of the sentences. Unfortunately, there is an obvious loss in the expressivity of the queries, but in return, there is a great advantage in terms of ease of use for untrained users.

Another remarkable feature of Visonto is the ability to group and filter the information through "points of view" and "filters". The former are alternative, synthetic roots for the concept tree, defined by the ontology author. They provide a different view of the hierarchy and enable faceted browsing of the knowledge base. The latter are also defined by the ontology author, and provide the ability to trim down the contents of the knowledge base. They work by creating a temporary subset of the concepts with a certain criterion, for example, "show me just this machine and all the machines by the same provider". A careful design of the criteria may provide a better insight of the knowledge and reduce the need to execute queries to find the desired information.

3.2.2 Visonto architecture

At the beginning of the project, it became clear that Visonto would be a web application, in order to satisfy some of its objectives:

- Easy deployment, without any additional software to be installed by the client.
- Knowledge sharing and collaborative environment. A common pool of ontologies and comments.

A web application makes it possible for several users to access the same knowledge base from different places, in the same way as a wiki.

It was also decided that Visonto would be incrementally built, starting with a small prototype with the core features to build upon. This model has made it possible to create a customer-driven application, and to exploit the feedback of early versions in order to develop a more valuable product for the user. Therefore, at the moment of this publication, Visonto is still an unfinished product lacking some features, but with a solid foundation and excellent expectations.

The iterative development has, to some extent, constrained its architecture. For example, Visonto currently allows users to attach their comments to the concepts of the ontologies, but so far does not provide ontology-editing capabilities. This means that comments are stored outside the ontologies, in a separated database.

Not surprisingly for a web application, the architecture exhibits three layers, as seen in Figure 11-3. The business and data-access tiers contain several highly decoupled components with small interfaces. For each component, one or more alternative implementations are available, each of them linked to a particular technology or framework. For example, the ontology repository component is currently implemented as a WebDAV client, but it may be easily replaced by an alternative implementation that stores the ontologies in a semantic database. The whole application is assembled by a lightweight dependency-injection framework.

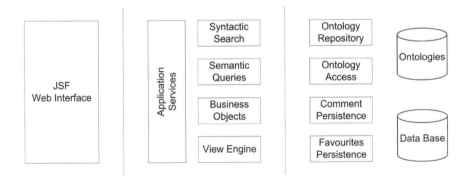

Figure 11-3. Architecture of the Visonto application

This highly modular architecture is the key to another desirable feature: the support for several ontology languages. Nowadays, the web ontology language (OWL) is the recommendation of the W3C. As Visonto basic abstractions are rooted in the Description Logic, it shows an excellent support for the OWL-DL variant. However, there are more ontology languages than just OWL. In particular, it is planned to add support for WSML-DL (De Brujin 2005) and RDF-Schema to Visonto in the near future. The former seems straightforward, as the logical foundation of WSML-DL is also Description Logics. The latter is expected to be more complicated because of some advanced features of RDF and RDF Schema such as meta modeling, that are beyond the expressivity of Description Logics.

In the more distant future, Visonto might be extended to add support to completely different knowledge formalisms, especially rules, given its extraordinary importance in industrial applications. This will obviously require significant changes to the architecture and the user interface of Visonto. Other long-term proposed extensions involve interfacing with external software components, such as reasoners, (semantic) web services and simulators.

3.3   ARIADNE: enrichment of syntactic search

Ariadne is an internal project at ArcelorMittal that has demonstrated the benefits of improving a commercial string-based search engine with linguistic and semantic techniques. Using the Verity/Autonomy K2 product, a private web site was set up in order to allow members of the research staff to retrieve documents authored by the internal R&D centers of the company. The indexation spider was instructed to examine documents in different formats and repositories. A customized J2EE web user interface was built on top of the search engine API. The result is a powerful knowledge capitalization tool focused on information retrieval that has a clear benefit in research productivity and knowledge re-use.

However the string-based matching process is sometimes limited. The most complex part is related with multilinguism. The document corpus contains information in several languages used within the company, such as Dutch, English, French, German and Spanish. Therefore, a simple query such as "steel products" must produce matches in all these languages. In this case the string search has to be enriched with enough detail and accuracy avoiding "noise" in results.

The same issue is present in generic web searching on the Internet. In an unrestricted context, such as the whole web, solving this issue seems unapproachable at the moment. However, in a restricted context such as research on the steel industry, we can envision some solutions. The Ariadne project opted for applying combined linguistic and semantic techniques to improve the retrieval and maintenance of the raw string-based search tool.

- The linguistic techniques included: a) algorithms to detect the language of the source documents, chiefly based on n-grams; b) stop-word lists customized for each language; c) stemming functions to remove morphological variants of the terms.
- As for the semantics, several options were considered, from a simple thesaurus expressed in RDF to more complex OWL ontologies. In the

end, a choice was made for a thesaurus built with RDF that has some resemblance to the SKOS framework. The thesaurus contains concepts linked with properties such as "generic", "specific", "synonym", "translation" and "instantiation", and is used to expand the initial query.

In addition to the web interface for the search system, a graphical user interface was developed in Java, exploiting the Jena framework. The purpose of this GUI was twofold: to ease the creation of the thesaurus by replacing the mark-up with forms, and to provide visual assistance for debugging the query expansion process.

The result of this effort is an improved information retrieval system that makes it possible to retrieve all the relevant documents for a query in one single step, no matter what the document language is.

4. CONCLUSIONS

ArcelorMittal is a vast testbed for technologies (including information technologies), that may contribute to enhancing productivity or reducing operation costs. But regardless of how promising a technology may seem at the research stage, it must show its value prior to its adoption in the production environment. Over the last years, the developments of semantic web technologies have been closely followed by the research department at ArcelorMittal. As a result, their strengths and weakness have been identified, at least in the context of their applicability in the domain of the company, and these first projects are still ongoing.

4.1 Open issues

4.1.1 Development of large ontologies

Given that technology allows to organize and use in the proper way various ontologies, the process to develop them by various engineers in a consistent way is not yet in our mind precisely defined. There is clearly a call to the Ontology Engineering on the model of the Software Engineering to provide methods, tools and processes to ensure the quality of the product and the efficiency of the projects. There have been made strong efforts in developing methodologies to model ontologies (e.g. Gruning), reasoners to check consistency of the ontology models and tools to make semiautomatic mapping or merging. Despite all these achievements, there is room for improvement with challenging opportunities as completely automatic merging of large ontologies.

4.1.2 Semantic Web services

Along with knowledge representation, Semantic Web Services (SWS) are probably the most interesting application of the semantic web in the business domain. Web services are usually thought of as mechanisms for retrieving data and firing actions remotely across the Internet. Any company has a number of suppliers and customers, and web services may be applied to communication with these third party agents. However, for a huge company, linking the internal applications is not a minor problem. Therefore, semantic web services can be applied in both scopes.

Unfortunately, at present our opinion is that SWS have not yet reached the maturity level required for large-scale deployment in the industry. Currently there is remarkable research activity on this area that will, no doubt produce key technology for tomorrow's electronic business. Some of the currently open issues are:

- There is no standard for SWS. Different research groups have concurrently created several proposals, which is positive in the long-term, because it guarantees the quality of the result. However, it is a source of uncertainty in the short-term. Companies are not inclined to invest in non-standard technology because of the important risk of vendor-lock.
- There is not a complete software tool-set to run SWS. Their execution requires the support of software environments that are still unfinished. There are, however, more mature applications to create the required semantic descriptions of the web services.

Does this mean that companies should wait until SWS are ready for business? Certainly not. Even if they cannot benefit from SWS now, they can start preparing themselves to adopt SWS as soon as possible.

4.1.3 Combining ontologies and rules

Description Logics (and the ontology languages that are built on them) are powerful tools to capture static knowledge (the static relationships between the concepts in a domain). However, we often find that there is also a dynamic part of the knowledge that deals with processes, conditions and complex relationships between concepts. This second part is outside the scope of Description Logics, and consequently, cannot be represented with ontology languages such as OWL-DL or WSML-DL.

Rules are the most extended formalism to represent the dynamic part of the world. In fact, the industry has been using rules for years, and it is common to find large knowledge bases expressed as sets of rules and managed by a rule engine (forward-chaining, backward-chaining, logic programming, etc.).

The unification of ontologies and rules under a common (inter-operable) model may be the next big leap in knowledge representation. Such a model would allow developers to choose the best representation for each type of knowledge in the same base. Static knowledge would be captured into ontologies, which are easier to maintain, check and extend. Dynamic knowledge would enrich the static model to add behavior and evolution, allowing complex inferences to be run.

Unfortunately, it is hard to integrate both aspects without losing some valuable features. The main issue is to achieve a delicate balance between expressivity and computability. In knowledge representation, increased expressivity means harder computability and higher complexity of algorithms. This was, for example, motivation for the specification of three different flavors of OWL. Of course, the balance is driven by the underlying logical formalism. While there is some consensus around one formalism (Description Logics) for ontologies, the same is not true for rules. In fact, an ongoing effort at W3C is an attempt to define a common Rule Interchange Format (RIF), so they can be shared across diverse rule engine technologies. Due to the wide range of available options, this interchange format will be designed as a core with optional extensions. A practical integration between ontologies and rules will not be possible in the foreseeable future unless the rules community agrees on this set of core features for rule systems.

4.2   Future lines of work

We have discussed the application of the semantic web technology within a large company. Actually, we are only scratching the surface of this promising technology, and we are confident that more applications will arise as the tools become more mature. Some of our present and future lines of work are:

- Develop ontologies. The sub-domains in the steel industry are almost endless, so are the ontologies to be modeled. However, the resources required to create new ontologies are limited. We must find techniques to predict the effectiveness of a new ontology in terms of the relationship between its development cost and its value for the company.

- Increase the value of each ontology by promoting re-use. Some of the strategies to accomplish this objective are: a) using parts of an existing ontology in the definition of a new one to reduce development cost; b) finding more applications for each ontology. The former drives us to high-level ontologies and patterns that are immediately re-usable. The latter is realized by designing ontologies that can be applied to several areas: unified data layer, semantic search, knowledge transference, semantic web services, etc.
- Promote the usages of semantic web services for data interchange and process communication, both inside the boundaries of the company and also in the interaction with third-parties. We aim to reduce maintenance costs and increase the flexibility and re-use of software components.
- Develop software tools to cover those knowledge-capitalization demands that are not fulfilled by current products.

5. QUESTIONS FOR DISCUSSION

Beginner:
1. Why are the needs of traditional sectors (such as steel production) different from Internet companies?
2. Why are ontologies useful outside the web?

Intermediate:
1. What kind of knowledge cannot be represented using OWL? What is the usual approach to capture this knowledge?
2. How can ontologies facilitate knowledge sharing in a multilingual environment?
3. What are the main objectives of an ontology visualization tool?

Advanced:
1. Why are dynamic processes a challenge for ontologies based on Description Logics?
2. How would you calculate the (economic) value of an ontology?

Practical exercises:
1. Choose a traditional production industry and design a small ontology for it.
2. Create an ontology model of the logical sequence of an industrial process and its participants.

6.   SUGGESTED ADDITIONAL READING

- Geroimenko, V., and C. Chen (eds.) *Visualizing the Semantic Web. XML-Based Internet and Information Visualization.* Springer. 2006. 248 pp. This book presents several developments in the field of ontology visualization.
- Fensel, D., *Ontologies: a Silver Bullet for Knowledge Management and Electronic Commerce.* Springer. 2004. 162 pp. This book is a good introduction for tools and applications of ontologies in the context of the Semantic Web technology.

7.   REFERENCES

Baader, F. and W. Nutt (2002). Basic Description Logics. <u>Description Logic Handbook</u>. F. Baader, D. Calvanese, D. L. McGuinness, D. Nardi and P.F. Patel-Schneider, Cambridge University Press: 47-100.

Baeza-Yates, R. and B. Ribeiro-Neto (1999). <u>Modern Information Retrieval</u>. Addison Wesley.

Barrero, D. F., M. R. Moreno, et al. (2005). <u>SEARCHY: A Metasearch Engine for Heterogeneus Sources in Distributed Environments</u>. International Conference on Dublin Core and Metadata Applications. Madrid, Spain.

Berners-Lee, T., J. Hendler, et al. (2001). "The Semantic Web". <u>Scientific American</u>. **May 2001**: 34-43.

Bray, T., J. Paoli et al. (2006). Extensible Markup Language (XML) 1.0 (Fourth Edition). W3C Recommendation. <u>http://www.w3.org/TR/2006/REC-xml-20060816/</u>.

CPV(2002). Common Procurement Vocabulary. <u>http://simap.eu.int/shared/docs/simap/nomenclature/l_34020021216en00010562.pdf</u>.

Cuenca, B., B. Parsia et al (2005). "Combining OWL Ontologies using E-Connections". <u>Elsevier's Journal of Web Semantics</u>, vol. 4(1): 40-59.

DCMI (2006). Dublin Core Metadata Initiative. <u>http://dublincore.org/</u>.

De Bruijn, J., editor (2005). The Web Service Modeling Language WSML. ESSI WSML working group. <u>http://www.wsmo.org/TR/d16/d16.1/v0.21/</u>

Fayez, M., L. Rabelo and et al. (2005). <u>Ontologies for Supply Chain Simulation Modeling</u>. 2005 Winter Simulation Conference, Orlando, FL, USA.

Fellbaum, C., editor (1998). <u>WordNet: an electronic lexical database</u>. MIT Press.

Gruber, T.R. (1995). "Toward Principles for the Design of Ontologies Used for Knowledge Sharing". <u>Int. Journal of Human-Computer Studies</u>, Vol. 43:907-928.

Hepp, M. (2006) <u>The True Complexity of Product Representation in the Semantic Web</u>. 14th European Conference on Information System, Gothenburg, Sweden.

ISCO (1988). International Standard Classification of Occupations. Eurostat.

Leukel, J., V. Schmitz, et al. (2002). <u>A Modeling Approach for Product Classification Systems.</u> 13th International Workshop on Database and Expert Systems Applications, Aix-en-Provence, France: 868-874.

Malone, T.W. et al. (2004). "The future of work". <u>Harvard Business School Press</u>.41-54.

Manola, F., and E. Miller (2004). RDF Primer, W3C Recommendation, http://www.w3.org/TR/rdf-primer/.

Masolo, C., L. Vieu, et al. (2004). Social roles and their descriptions. 9th International Conference of Principles of Knowledge Representation and Reasoning. Whistler, Canada: 267-277.

Masolo, C., S. Borgo, et al. (2003). Wonderweb deliverable d18: the wonderweb library of foundational ontologies. Technical Report. LOA-CNR. http://wonderweb.semanticweb.org/deliverables/documents/D18.pdf.

McGuinness, D., F. Van Harmelen (2004). OWL Web Ontology Language Overview, W3C Recommendation, http://www.w3.org/TR/owl-features/.

Miles, A. and D. Brickley (2005). SKOS Core Guide, W3C Working Draft, http://www.w3.org/TR/2005/WD-swbp-skos-core-guide-20051102/.

Mochol M., R. Oldakowski, et al. (2004). Ontology Based Recruitment Process; Workshop: Semantische Technologien für Informationsportale, at INFORMATIK, Ulm, Germany, September 2004: 198-202.

Niles, I., and A. Pease (2001). Towards a standard upper ontology. 2nd International Conference on Formal Ontology in Information Systems, Ogunquit, Maine, USA.

OKAR Working Group (2005). Ontology for Knowledge Activity Resources Guide. Fujitsu Laboratories and Ricoh Company. http://www.ricoh.com/src/rd/img2/ds_okar_draft_20050204_en.pdf.

Protégé (2006). Protégé Ontology Editor. http://protege.stanford.edu/.

Prud'hommeaux, E., and A. Seaborne (2006). SPARQL Query Language for RDF. W3C Working Draft. http://www.w3.org/TR/rdf-sparql-query/.

PSL (2006). Process Specification Language. http://www.mel.nist.gov/psl/ontology.html.

Rector, A.L. (2003) Modularisation of domain ontologies implemented in Description Logics and related formalisms including OWL. 2nd International Conference on Knowledge Capture, Sanibel Islandm, FL, USA: 121-128.

Supply Chain Council (2003). Supply Chain Operations Reference (SCOR) Model V.6.0.

UNSPSC (2006). United Nations Standard Products and Services Code. http://www.unspsc.org/.

Chapter 12

BRINGING SEMANTIC SECURITY TO SEMANTIC WEB SERVICES

Richard Scott Patterson[1], John A. Miller[1], Jorge Cardoso[2] and Mike Davis[3]
[1] *Knowledge Integrity Inc., Silver Springs, MD, USA*
[2]*Department of Mathematics and Engineering, University of Madeira, Funchal, Portugal –*
jcardoso@uma.pt
[3]*U.S. Department of Veterans Affairs& Chair HL7 Security Committee*

1. INTRODUCTION

Currently, the World Wide Web is primarily composed of documents written in HTML (Hyper Text Markup Language), a language that is useful for visual presentation. HTML is a set of "markup" symbols contained in a Web page intended for display on a Web browser. Most of the information on the Web is designed only for human consumption. Humans can read Web pages and understand them, but their inherent meaning is not shown in a way that allows their interpretation by computers.

The information on the Web can be defined in such a way that it can be used by computers not only for display purposes, but also for interoperability and integration between systems and applications. One way to enable machine-to-machine exchange and automated processing is to provide the information in such a way that computers can understand it. This is precisely the objective of the semantic Web – to make possible the processing of Web information by computers. "The Semantic Web is not a separate Web but an extension of the current one, in which information is given well-defined meaning, better enabling computers and people to work in cooperation." (Berners-Lee, Hendler et al. 2001). The next generation of the Web will combine existing Web technologies with knowledge representation formalisms (Grau 2004).

Currently the Web is under evolution and different approaches are being sought in order to come up with the solutions to add semantics to Web resources. To give meaning to resources and links, new standards and languages are being investigated and developed. The rules and descriptive information made available by these languages allow the type of resources on the Web and the relationships between resources to be characterized individually and precisely.

To give meaning to Web resource and links, the research community has developed semantic standards such as the Resource Description Framework (RDF) (RDF 2002) and the Web Ontology Language (OWL) (OWL 2004). RDF and OWL standards enable the Web to be a global infrastructure for sharing both documents and data, which make searching and reusing information easier and more reliable as well. RDF is a standard for creating descriptions of information, especially information available on the World Wide Web. What XML is for syntax, RDF is for semantics. The latter provides a clear set of rules for providing simple descriptive information. OWL is an extension of RDF and provides a language for defining structured Web-based ontologies which allows a richer integration and interoperability of data among communities and domains.

1.1   Semantic Web Services

Many believe that a new Web will emerge in the next few years, based on the large-scale research and development ongoing on the semantic Web and Web services. The intersection of these two, semantic Web services, may prove to be even more significant. Academia has mainly approached this area from the Semantic Web side, while industry is beginning to consider its importance from the Web services side (Cardoso, Miller et al. 2005). Semantic Web services are the result of the evolution of the syntactic definition of Web services and the semantic Web as shown in Figure 12-1.

Several approaches have been developed to bring semantics to Web services, including WSDL-S (Akkiraju, Farrell et al. 2006), OWL-S (Martin, Paolucci et al. 2004; OWL-S 2004), and WSMO (WSMO 2004; Feier, Roman et al. 2005). The work presented in this chapter uses the first approach, WSDL-S. This approach to creating semantic Web services consists in mapping concepts in a Web service description (WSDL specification) to ontological concepts and it is described into more detail in the next section.

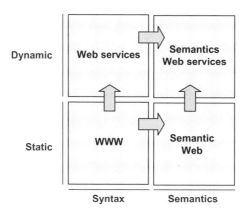

Figure 12-1. The nature of semantic Web services

1.2 Semantically annotated Web Services: WSDL-S

One solution to create semantic Web services is by mapping concepts in a Web service description to ontological concepts. Using this approach, users can explicitly define the semantics of a Web service for a given domain. With the help of ontologies, the semantics or the meaning of service data and functionality can be explained. As a result, integration can be accomplished in an automated way and with a higher degree of success.

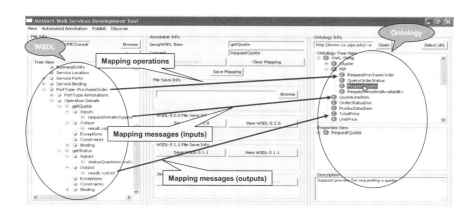

Figure 12-2. Annotating Web services with ontological concepts

WSDL-S (Patil, Oundhakar et al. 2004; Rajasekaran, Miller et al. 2004) establishes mapping between WSDL descriptions and ontological concepts.

The idea of establishing mappings between service, task, or activity descriptions and ontological concepts was first presented in (Cardoso and Sheth 2003). Figure 12-2 illustrates METEOR-S WSDL-S Annotator tool (Patil, Oundhakar et al. 2004) and the mapping that have been established between WSDL descriptions and ontological concepts.

Based on the analysis of WSDL descriptions, three types of elements can have their semantics increased by annotating them with ontological concepts: operations, messages, preconditions and effects. All the elements are explicitly declared in a WSDL description.

* **Operations**. Each WSDL description may have a number of operations with different functionalities. For example, a WSDL description can have operations for both booking and canceling flight tickets. In order to add semantics, the operations must be mapped to ontological concepts to describe their functionality.
* **Message**. Message parts, which are input and output parameters of operations, are defined in WSDL using the XML Schema. Ontologies – which are more expressive than the XML Schema – can be used to annotate WSDL message parts. Using ontologies not only brings user requirements and service advertisements to a common conceptual space, but also helps to use and apply reasoning mechanisms.
* **Preconditions and effects**. Each WSDL operation may have a number of preconditions and effects. The preconditions are usually logical conditions, which must be evaluated to true in order to execute a specific operation. Effects are changes in the world that occur after the execution of an operation. After annotating services' operations, inputs and outputs, preconditions and effects can also be annotated. The semantic annotation of preconditions and effects is important for Web services, since it is possible for a number of operations to have the same functionality, as well as the same inputs and outputs, but different effects.

```
<?xml version="1.0" encoding="UTF-8"?>
<definitions name = "StudentManagement" targetNamespace=
"http:.../StudentManagement.wsdl20"
  xmlns="http://www.w3.org/2004/03/wsdl"
  xmlns:tns="http.../StudentManagement.wsdl20"
  xmlns:sm="http:.../StudentMng.owl#"
  xmlns:mep=http:.../TR/wsdl20-patterns>
<interface name = "StudentManagementUMA">
  <operation name = "RegisterStudent" pattern = "mep:in-out" >
    <action element = "sm:RegisterStudent" />
```

```
        <input messageLabel = "student" element = "sm:StudentInfo" />
        <output messageLabel = "ID" element = "sm:StudentID" />
    </operation>
    <operation name = "StudentInformation" pattern = "mep:in-out" >
        <action element = "sm:StudentInformation" />
        <input messageLabel = "ID" element = "sm:StudentID" />
        <output messageLabel = "student" element = "sm:StudentInfo" />
    </operation>
    <operation name = "checkStatus" pattern="mep:in-out" >
...
    </operation>
</interface>
</definitions>
```

Figure 12-3. WSDL-S example

The WSDL-S specification from Figure 12-3 indicates that the Web service supplies two operations: 'RegisterStudent' and 'StudentInformation'. The first operation has an input named 'student', semantically described by the ontological concept "sm:StudentInfo", and an output named 'ID', semantically described by the concept "sm:StudentID". The operation 'RegisterStudent' is semantically annotated with the ontological concept "sm:RegisterStudent". The second operation, 'StudentInformation', uses similar ontological concepts to annotate the input, output, and action. The ontological concepts are expressed in the ontology http://dme.uma.pt/jcardoso/StudentMng.owl#, which is specified using OWL (OWL 2004).

To create, represent, and manipulate WSDL-S documents, WSDL4J (http://sourceforge.net/projects/wsdl4j/) can be used. WSDL4J provides JAVA API's for WSDL parsing and generation. WSDL4J supports extensibility elements providing an easy mechanism to add new extensions. This allows WSDL to represent a specific technology under various elements defined by WSDL.

2. WEB SERVICES SECURITY BACKGROUND

Web services can be used to expose inter-organizational components such as business critical data, business processes and internal workflows (Shivaram 2003). Organizations may expose some of these components in order to capitalize on the cost savings and reduced complexity that Web services can add to there SOA. Because the SOA is more dynamic, loosely defined, and ubiquitous, new security measures are needed to protect key business information. There are currently standards proposed or accepted regarding authentication, encryption, and identity management. These areas of Web service security use a combination of tried-and-true technologies such as keys, username token, and RSA encryption, along with newer technologies such as XML signature (XML-Signature 2002) and SAML (Security Assertion Markup Language) (SAML 2.0 2005).

In securing Web services, there are five fundamental areas to consider; Message Level Protection, Message Privacy, Parameter Checking, Authentication, and Authorization. When examining these areas it is important to stay within the context of Web services and not network security in general. This is because network security is at a different layer of the ISO model; Web service security is at the application layer. As we discuss these areas of security, observe the following. Some of solutions use the same or similar technologies to achieve vigilance. Not all of the technologies used were developed for Web services and may have been around for many years. Which of these areas could benefit from semantics? Four of the five areas have been addressed; however, authorization has not. Authorization aided by Semantics is not only important in Web services, but the Semantic Web as well.

As Web services continue to evolve into Semantic Web services for automated discovery and execution of business processes (Verma 2005), two questions become more prevalent. From the Service Providers perspective, how much information should be shared with an entity to which there is no previous relationship. From the Requesters perspective, how does the Requester know if they will have access to the information and resources they discover through automated discovery?

We will begin our discussion by reviewing the technologies currently in place to secure Web services. The following section take a look at an approach which uses semantics, along with current technologies, to aid Providers and Requesters in answering the questions posed above.

2.1   Message privacy

Message privacy deals with the confidentiality of a message. Here unauthorized entities should not be able to access the information within the message. It is important to remember here that a part of this information is the XML Signature and Token, found in the message header, which can be seen in Figure 12-4. To ensure confidentiality an encryption scheme must be implemented.

Since Web services can be chained together to form complex services, traditional point-to-point encryption schemes, such as SSL, do not suffice. Point-to-point schemes work at the Network layer of the ISO model.

Therefore, once the message has been received by an entity it is decrypted in its entirety. This entity may be an intermediary and not the provider of the service, Figure 12-4. Furthermore, a message may cross multiple trust domains due to routing caused by elaborate messaging communications (Web Services Architecture 2004). What is needed is an end-to-end encryption scheme.

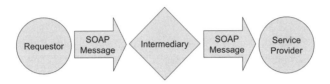

Figure 12-4. Soap message in transit

The XML Encryption standard provides the necessary framework for accomplishing this task. XML Encryption allows for the encryption of any combination of the message body, header, attachments, and sub-structures (XML-Encryption 2002).

When a message or part of a message is encrypted, the encryption information can be made available in the message header. This information is useful for complex services since each Web service in the chain will need to know how to decrypt the section of the message relevant to their service. This information should not be the actual key to decrypt the message.

An example will clarify. When a requester encrypts a message body and XML Signature information in the header, it may then specify in the header that it has used the providing service's public key. A public key allows for the encryption of data but only the private key may decrypt the data. Once the provider receives the message it sees that the message has been encrypted using its public key. The provider then decrypts the message using its private key.

XML Encryption allows multiple different keys to be used with in a message to encrypt different sections, elements, of the message. Each encrypted section is referenced in the message header and mapped to the key information if provided. This provides end-to-end encryption through intermediaries which may also be accessing the parts of the message.

Table 12-1 provides an overview of the algorithms specified in the XML-Signature and XML-Encryption standards. Required algorithms are the minimal to comply with the standard; while recommended is just that, recommended.

Table 12-1. XML Algorithms

Purpose	**Algorithm**	**Specified as**
Digest	SHA1	Required
Digest	SHA256	Recommended
Signature	DSAwithSHA1 (DSS)	Required
Signature	RSAwithSHA1	Recommended
Canonicalization	Canonical XML (omits comments)	Required
Canonicalization	XML with Comments	Recommended
Transform	XPath	Recommended
Transform	Enveloped Signature	Required

2.2   Message level protection

Message level protection has to do with message integrity. This means being able to detect when a SOAP message (message) has been modified from its original state and the ability to guarantee that the contents have not been modified (Web Services Architecture 2004). This is done by creating a message digest.

A message digest is an encoded message, a cryptographic checksum of an octet stream (WS-Security 2002), which is created using an algorithm. The SHA-1 algorithm (NIST 1993), in Table 12-1, is required in the XML Signature specification. The only parameter is the element to be signed. The provider of the Web service receives the message, the digest, and is told which algorithm has been used to create the digest. Using this information, the service provider is able to recreate the digest and compare it to the digest which it received from the requester.

When a message is passed from a Requester Web service to a provider Web service, the message body should be digitally signed using the XML Signature specification. There are several Token options for signing a message. These options fall under one of two categories; they can either be endorsed or unendorsed. An endorsed token is one which the claims of the Token can be validated by a trusted authority. An example of this kind of Token is a X.509 certificate. An unendorsed Token is one which the claims may not be validated by a trusted authority. However, there is such a thing as a proof-of–possession unendorsed Token. An example of this is a username-password Token.

When signing a message, the signature parameters consist of a security token and the message digest. It is worth noting that the second parameter can be an XPath node-set. The output is the message signature which will appear in the message header. Figure 12-5 (WS-Security 2002) shows the key or token used to sign the message (1), the message digest (2), the signature value (3), and the unencrypted message body (4).

The provider service must have a way to verify the contents of the message. In order to do so the provider must have the message, the digest, determine the algorithm used to create the digest, and access the key or token. Security elements in the header of the message contain information on the algorithm and Token.

The provider can use this information to compare the digest to the message. Any changes, even the addition of one white space to the original message can be detected. This clearly solves the problem of Message Level Protection.

2.3 Message validity

Message validity is ensuring that the contents of a message are appropriate to the service and that they are well formed. Checking the contents of a message can be subdivided into two categories, verifying data types and checking for malicious code. Verifying that the data types passed to an operation are those which the services are expecting is straight forward. Checking for malicious code within the message is not so straight forward.

```
      <?xml version="1.0" encoding="utf-8"?>
      <S:Envelope
         .....
        <S:Header>
          <m:path xmlns:m="http://schemas.xmlsoap.org/rp">
            .....
          </m:path>
        <wsse:Security>
(1)       <wsse:BinarySecurityToken ValueType="wsse:X509v3"
          EncodingType="wsse:Base64Binary" Id="X509Token">
            MIIEZzCCA9CgAwIBAgIQEmtJZc0rqrKh5i...
        </wsse:BinarySecurityToken>
        <ds:Signature>
          <ds:SignedInfo>
            <ds:CanonicalizationMethod Algorithm="http://....#"/>
```

```
      <ds:SignatureMethod Algorithm="http://...."/>
      <ds:Reference>
        <ds:Transforms>
          <ds:Transform Algorithm="http://...#RoutingTransform"/>
          <ds:Transform Algorithm="http://.....#"/>
        </ds:Transforms>
        <ds:DigestMethod Algorithm="http://...#sha1"/>
(2)       <ds:DigestValue>EULddytSo1...</ds:DigestValue>
        </ds:Reference> </ds:SignedInfo>
(3)   <ds:SignatureValue>
          BL8jdfToEb1l/vXcMZNNjPOV
      </ds:SignatureValue>
      <ds:KeyInfo>
        <wsse:SecurityTokenReference>
          <wsse:Reference URI="#X509Token"/>
        </wsse:SecurityTokenReference>
      </ds:KeyInfo>
      </ds:Signature>
    </wsse:Security>
  </S:Header>
  <S:Body>
(4) <tru:StockSymbol xmlns:tru="http://..../payloads">
      QQQ
    </tru:StockSymbol>
  </S:Body>
</S:Envelope>
```

Figure 12-5. Soap message with a XML-signature

Malicious code within a message can appear as part of the XML message or as parameters to be passed to operations. XML viruses and XML worms are commonly passed within the contents of any XML document or message (Lilly 2002). Because these are common in the Web environment there is software available to safely scan XML to determine if it contains either a virus or a worm.

Even after verifying that the parameters within a message are appropriate for the operation(s), their may be malicious code present. For example, it may be verified that a string is being passed to an operation which then queries a SQL database. SQL injection attacks are of the string data type. Therefore verifying that a string is being passed is not enough. Best practices for programming disallow and check for the presence of a ';' in any parameter which will be passed to a SQL database. The ';' in SQL allows for SQL commands to follow.

Ensuring that a message is well-formed is another step in Message Validity. Since the messages are in XML, it is possible that a message contains a circular-reference. A circular-reference may appear maliciously or through poor programming. Circular-references cause a system to encounter a run-out-of-memory error and shutdown (Lilly 2002). When done maliciously this is know as a denial-of-service attack. Proper parsing of a message will catch nested loops.

2.4 Authentication

Authentication can easily be described as verify to ones own level of certainty that an entity is who they claim to be. In its simplest form, authentication could be a username and password combination. However, this is only possible if there is already a relationship between the requester and provider.

Because of the distributed nature of Web services, a requester may be previously unknown to the provider. When an unknown requester authenticates it sends information about themselves to the provider. This information is known as credentials. It is up to the provider to verify this information. Now there are different degrees of verifying credentials and this can be directly affected by the type of credential that is sent. This is where the provider's own degree of scrutiny comes into play. In general, the more sensitive the information is which is being made available through a Web service, the higher the level of certainty must be. This certainty can be achieved through verification of the credentials. In the case of a previously unknown requester, the highest level of certainty can usually be achieved through a trusted authority. Trusted authorities issue certificates which can be used for authentication. A provider can evaluate the certificate and contact the trusted authority for verification.

However, their may be an intermediate service contacting the provider on behalf of the requester and once established the requester and provider will communicate. Assuming that the intermediary has authenticated the Requester and there is a trust relationship between the intermediary and the provider, the provider may take the 'word' of the intermediary and believe with a level of certainty that the requester is whom they claim to be. This can be done through the use of SAML or a certificate issued by the intermediary. Here the intermediary is providing the verification.

3.   AUTHORIZATION

In organizations, highly sensitive data and information must be protected with access control systems. These control systems allow defining and controlling which users are authorized to access specific applications and data but prohibit the access of unauthorized users.

Nowadays, organizations are built on heterogeneous IT infrastructure. As a result, a variety of systems with proprietary access control mechanisms, such as Unix, Windows, MAC, and mainframes exist and are incompatible. In proprietary access control systems, information about resources and attributes is stored in repositories called Access Control Lists (ACL). This is a problem since different proprietary systems have different ACL implementations, making it difficult to exchange and share information between them.

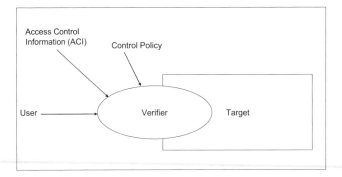

Figure 12-6. Access control

Authorization is the granting of rights, which includes the granting of access based on access rights. This typically takes place after authentication. Authorization is often confused with authentication, however it is a separate issue altogether. An access control implementation compares access control information such as the rights of the Requester with the policies or permissions needed to access the resource. If the rights of the Requester dominate the control policy, then access can be granted; otherwise access is denied. The two most common access control implementations are Access Control Lists (ACL), and RBAC. ISO 10181-3 specifies access control information used in making access control decisions.

3.1   ACL

ACL are often used in the Unix environment for file and directory security. Although ACL offer much more granularity than pervious *nix access control mechanisms, they can be cumbersome to implement and manage. There are difficult to manage because of the lack of relationships between the access control entities, i.e., resources, permissions, groups, and users. There is an obvious relationship between users and groups, users belong to groups and groups contain users. However, each shared resource must have an ACL file specified for it and the associated permissions are held within the file.

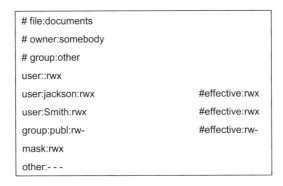

Figure 12-7. ACL example

Users within groups can easily be managed, but for resources that change frequently like those in Web services it is difficult to modify the ACL's for all these resources. Therefore management of a ubiquitous and dynamic resource environment is cumbersome at best. Furthermore, performance is affected each time ACL is accessed and inspected. A simple example ACL is given above in Figure 12-7.

3.2   RBAC

In 2004 the National Institute of Standards and Technology (NIST) published a standard (NIST, 2004) for defining the features of Role Based Access Control. The standard was largely based on the various features found in commercial implementations of RBAC. There are two parts to an RBAC system. The first is the Reference Model which consists of objects, operations, permissions, roles, and users. The second is the System and Administrative Functions which include system functionality, and administrative operations and reviews (NIST 2004). Our approach utilized the concepts of RBAC, so we will discuss it here. However, much has been written about RBAC over the past decade; in an effort not to be repetitive this is a summary-review.

RBAC contains Permissions sets. Generally speaking, Permissions express a privilege to access a resource. Permissions are a set of one or more objects and one or more operations. Objects refer to resources; for example a printer or a file. Operations are the invocation or execution of some function on a resource. An example of a Permission may be "create file in directory etc'. In this case, 'etc' is the Object and 'create file' is the operation.

Once Permissions are created, they may be assigned to Roles. A Role is a job function which is performed within an organization. A job function can be as concrete as a job title, 'Physician', or more general even abstract, 'internet user'. Once Roles are defined they may be assigned to Users who are actual people. Users may also include entire organizations, computers or networks (NIST 2004).

The HL7 committee has developed a simple and effective way for creating Permissions (Object, Operation set) and Roles. They call it a scenario driven approach. The concept is to first create scenarios for the 'organization'. These scenarios include resources, actions taken on the resources, and who is performing these actions, in terms of job function. Our Detailed Scenario is an example of this approach.

Figure 12-8 shows the relationships between the elements of the RBAC Reference Model. Permissions are an Object, Operation set. There is an assignment between Permissions and Roles, and Roles and Users. These relationships/assignments are many-to-many. There is another element present in the figure which has a one-to-many assignment with Users. That element is the Session Role (NIST 2004).

A Session is the activation of one or more Roles by a User. Simplistically and not entirely, a Session Role determines if a Users Role should be activated. This is determined by the constraints on the Roles assigned to the User and which Roles the User currently has active. The RBAC Reference Model provides fine granularity for authorization of resources. The RBAC Systems and Administrative Functions provide for distributed decision and enforcement points.

In our approach we conceptually map elements of RBAC to elements of Web services in order to an authorization function regarding the Web service and a prediction function regarding the Requester. In or approach, RBAC Operations are mapped to the action that an operation of a Web service performs. Keeping with our example, the Web service has an operation to review the medical history of a patient; this operation is mapped to the RBAC element 'read'. The RBAC element Object is mapped to the resource which the service accesses and the parameters of the operation; i.e. the medical history of the patient and the patient respectively.

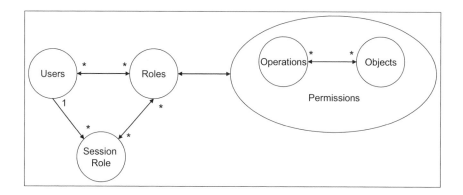

Figure 12-8. RBAC

We define an authorization function, and as mentioned in section 1.2, there is a variable of uncertainty between what a Web service provider is describing and what a Requester may assume the provider is describing. This variable is caused because our ontology is an upper level ontology; therefore each organization using the ontology must map Users, Roles, and possibly Groups to the ontology. This mapping is independent of any other organization; therefore there is uncertainty that a Requester and service provider have the same mapping. Our goal is to minimize the variable to achieve accurate results.

We define the authorization function as f:<UA, S, O, P_i,....,P_k) → {0,1} where S is the service, O is an operation, P is a parameter and UA is defined as UA $\subseteq$ U×R . UA is the many-to-many user-to-role mapping relationship within the RBAC ontology. However, to predict authorization we use UA′ which is a many-to-many mapping between UA and (U′×R′), the many-to-many user-to-role mapping within an organization. Therefore, UA′ is defined as UA′ $\subseteq$ UA × (U′×R′), the many-to-many mapping between the ontology and the organization structure. So our prediction function is defined as f:<UA′, S, O, P_i,....,P_k) → {0,1}

3.2.1 Structural role framework

Structural roles serve as access control decision information within the PMI (Privilege Management Infrastructure) by allowing authenticated users to establish a session or connect to a protected target.

To accomplish this function, the user asserts, in addition to authentication information, structural roles as a prerequisite authorization to "connect" to the task or workflow containing the requested session or target. An infrastructure access enforcement function grants or denies access to the session or target based on the structural role. Structural roles would be typically managed in identity certificates (per ASTM E2212) or directories. Structural roles are centrally managed, allowing any user to be granted access, suspended, or denied access (by means of the service-oriented Verifier) to any or all resources through this single point of control.

ASTM E1986 identifies healthcare persons for whom role based access control is warranted. These ASTM E1986 person types define basic healthcare role names as used within this standard.

3.2.2 Functional role framework

Functional role activation (session roles) cannot occur until the session is established, so structural role authorization/access is prerequisite to establishing a session or connection to the target. In the extended Control Model, what is desired is a decision on the user's authorizations to perform operations on the Target's protected objects. The result of the decision information is used as an input to the Verifier PEP (Policy Enforcement Point) for the purpose of access control.

Functional roles describe the permissions that a user has available once the session is established and his/her roles are activated. Functional roles are contained in applications, directories, attribute certificates, and XACML extensions. Functional roles specifically define, in terms of permissions, what authorizations are needed by an entity to access protected information technology or application resources. As a consequence, functional roles are much more healthcare specific than basic roles. Standard functional roles are applied across the enterprise and with business partners. Standard functional roles are aligned by mapping to underlying applications' enforcement mechanisms.

Functional roles should be expressed in a standards-compliant language for interoperability both inter and intra-enterprise. A standard language allows for leveraging policy and roles among applications, as well as consistent policy description and enforcement. The guideline standard language for this standard is OASIS XACML.

3.3   XACML

XACML is an OASIS standard for an XML representation of RBAC (XACML 2005). The Organization for the Advancement of Structured

Information Standards (OASIS) standards group developed the eXtensible Access Control Markup Language (XACML) as a language to express and evaluate access decisions.[i] The XACML technical specification includes a profile for RBAC using XACML that complies with the ANSI RBAC standard. Core RBAC, as defined above, is supported as shown in Table 12-2 below.

Table 12-2. RBAC core functionality mapping

Core Element	XACML Profile
Users	XACML Subjects
Roles	XACML Subject Attributes
Objects	XACML Resources
Operations	XACML Actions
Permissions	XACML Role <PolicySet and Permission <PolicySet>

The XACML RBAC profile also supports hierarchical RBAC, allowing inheritance between roles. Dynamic Separation of Duty is supported by the profile, and structural Separation of Duty can be supported via the user-role assignment mechanism. Additional XACML policies are provided to support system and review functions described in the ANSI RBAC standard. Specifically, the Role PolicySet (RPS) associates holders of a given role attribute with a Permission PolicySet. The Permission PolicySet (PPS) describes the permissions associated with a specific role. The RPS and PPS replace the role assignment and role specification ACs in the X.509 based role model.

The XACML role based PMI features a rich policy language integrated throughout the design. The concept of structural versus functional roles is supported using a two tiered system comprised of a role attributes. That is, users can have roles assigned to them in the request context. An entity separate from the policy decision point can use an XACML Role Assignment Policy or PolicySet to enable attributes within the user session.

Figure 12-9 illustrates a typical XACML usage scenario. A subject (e.g., human user, application) wants to take some action on a specific network resource, such a file system or Web service. The subject submits its request. The request for authorization goes to the entity protecting the resource, the PEP (Policy Enforcement Point). The PEP uses XACML request language to create a request based on attributes of the subject, action, resources and sends it to the Policy Decision Point (PDP), which evaluates the request. The PDP invoke the Policy Information Point (PIP) service to retrieve applicable policies written in XACML that are applicable to the request. The PDP compares the request against policies and determines whether access should be granted according to the XACML rules for evaluating policies. Policies contain information about the subject, the action, and other environmental properties. The result of the comparison can be either access granted or denied. The answer goes back to the PEP. If there is no match, the PEP denies user access; otherwise, it permits access by the user.

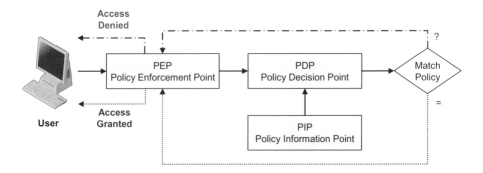

Figure 12-9. Typical XACML usage scenario

While there are many proprietary languages for controlling the access to resources, XACML has advantages. The use of a standard access control policy language can replace several proprietary languages making easier the interoperation of applications. Programmers and administrators can work more efficiently since they do not have to develop new policy languages and write code to support them and only need to understand one language. The use of a common language allows one policy to be used by many different applications, thus making policy management easier. Policies can also be distributed by referring to other policies stored in geographically disperse locations. For instance, a local-specific policy may refer to an organization-wide policy.

3.4   WS-Authorization

WS-Authorization is a proposed future specification regarding the description and management of authorization data and policies (IBM, Microsoft 2002). In particular, WS-Authorization will specify a standard on how to describe authorization claims within a security token and how the end-point should interpret these claims. It is widely thought that this specification will be a follow-on specification to WS-Privacy and WS-Security, as seen in Figure 12-10. WS-Privacy and WS-Security are implemented in WS-Policy, and it is believed that WS-Authorization will be implemented in WS-Policy as well. It is also believed that this specification will be similar in structure to the XACML standard (Rosenberg and Remy 2004).

IBM and Microsoft concur that the end-point policy files are the appropriate location for describing "execution capabilities" (IBM, Microsoft 2002) of an authenticated Requester. If the WS-Authorization specification ends up being similar to the XACML standard, this would offer many possibilities to an approach which uses RBAC and XACML concepts to annotate WS-Policy files with semantics to aid in the discovery of services which a Requester will be authorized to invoke or execute. By using ontological concepts, in this case RBAC and XACML concepts, to describe execution capabilities of an authenticated Requester, a potential Requester can automate the prediction of their authorization.

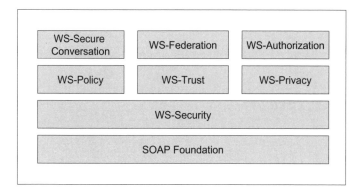

Figure 12-10. Web services stack

4. ADDING SEMANTICS FOR AUTHORIZATION

4.1 Why use semantics

The WS-Policy specification is a model and syntax for describing the policies of a Web services. It relies on its follow-on specifications, such as WS-Trust, WS-Agreement, WS-Security, and WS-Utility, which make within WS-Policy. The assertions are based on an XML based domain vocabulary. A Requester and service provider can make assertions in WS-Policy from any domain using the specifications which describe the vocabulary. When matching policies, if the policy matching mechanism is unaware of the domain context then it would be limited to using syntactical matching. Consider the following example where a Requester and a service provider have included authorization assertions from the Health Care domain.

•Service Provider:

Must be a physician working in *Emergency Service* of the *Health Services*

•Requester:

Is an *Emergency Room Physician* working at a *Hospital* in the *Emergency Room*

Figure 12-11. Roles in Web service example

These assertions are equivalent. The domain knowledge needed to determine that these assertions are equivalent are absent in a purely syntactic matching mechanism. Therefore, using a string matching algorithm would result in the denial of authorization for the Requester, which is a false negative result. These assertions can easily be determined to be equivalent by using domain information along with semantic reasoning. From the example, it can be determined that ∀*Physician WorkIn Emergency Room (Physician)* ⇒ *provides Emergency Services*; that is to say that a *Physician working in an Emergency Room* is an entity that *provides Emergency Services*.

There are several key "ingredients" that are needed for a semantic solution to the distributed authorization problem; which is after all what we are talking about. The first ingredient is Domain Knowledge and as we discussed, the domain is security, more precisely authorization. There will most likely be a second domain, such as the medical domain which we will use in our examples. The second ingredient is a means to express constraints. Also as we discussed, WS-Policy seems to be the appropriate place for to express constraints for the Web services arena. The third ingredient is how to express the constraints in the Policy file. The last ingredient is a means to compare the constraints with information about the Requester. Let's now look at each of these ingredients in more detail.

4.2　　Ontology

We will discuss a HL7 RBAC ontology which is represented in OWL-DL (OWL 2004), *Web* Ontology Language - Description Logics. It begins with two separate Upper Level domain ontologies, a RBAC ontology and a HL7 ontology, as seen in Figure 12-12. Then a HL7 RBAC ontology is created by expanding the RBAC Upper Level ontology through the use of the HL7 RBAC Permissions Catalog (HL7 Security Technical Committee 2005).

This catalog contains operations and objects which have been paired together to form permissions. For other domains in which an RBAC standard is not available, concepts from a domain may be imported into the RBAC ontology in order to create a domain specific Mid Level ontology.

A comprehensive list of medical departments (Hull and East 2006), and a list of the 31 broad industry categories provides the information for additional Domain Knowledge.

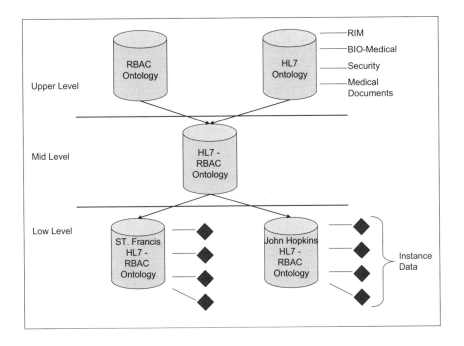

Figure 12-12. HL7 & RBAC Ontology Hierarchy

In the Figure there are two more specialized Lower Level ontologies, one for the requester and one for the service provider. These are created by extending the mid level ontology in an effort to more accurately model the real world. The requesters' ontology should be developed to reflect its organizational implementation. This can be done by adding users, assigning them to roles, using variations of the role names, and assigning appropriate permission to these roles. The service providers' ontology is extended in much the same way with the exception of not adding users, which is practical for security reasons. The fundamental difference between the ontologies is variation of role to permissions assignment, as well as role names. For the sake of a real world argument you will notice that we included some different role names between the ontologies, for the same job function. For example, 'Radiology Technician' and 'Radiology Tech', 'General Physician' and 'Family Practice Physician', and 'Pediatric Nurse' and 'Pediatric RN'. The above titles are all standard titles for positions in the Health Care domain. Since many organizations will implement systems using variants of position titles. We will discuss the use of these two Ontologies in a few moments.

Figure 12-13 below shows a portion of our HL7 RBAC Mid Level Ontology. The 'RBAC Reference Model Elements' is the parent to the actual elements, namely Objects, Operations, Permissions, Role, Session, and Users. There are relationships between these elements, more accurately ontological concepts. A Semantic Authorization technique, such as this, exploits these relationships. Let us now describe some of the relationships.

Figure 12-13. Classes in the RBAC ontology

As we stated earlier, permissions have a 'has object' relationship with Object and a 'has operation' with Operation. A Role has a 'assigned to' relationship with User, a 'department' relationship with Health Service (which is not visible in the figure), 'has permission' relationship with Permission, and so on. A User has a 'assigned to' relationship with Role, a 'employed by' relationship with Organization (which is not visible in the figure), a 'isA' relationship with Human, and so on.

As can be seen below, there are many instances of permissions. These are all from the HL7 Permissions specification. This is not an exhaustive list of the possible permissions; rather the committees' goal was to provide a general starting point which provides examples so that healthcare organizations could correctly create permissions tailored to their organization.

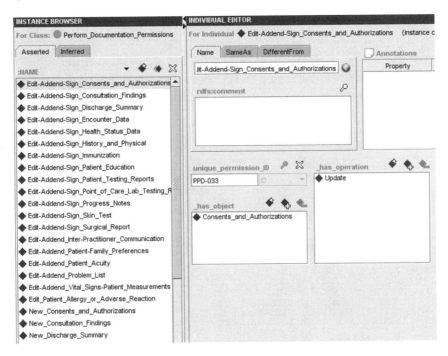

Figure 12-14. Instances example

4.3   Expressing constraints – extension elements

This section covers the second and third ingredients for a Semantic Authorization approach. There currently is no a WS-Authorization specification. After reviewing current specifications that are built onto WS-Policy (WS-Agreement, WS-Transaction, WS-Security) we assume that a future WS-Authorization specification would follow suite and therefore lack the semantics needed for an automated process. Therefore in our examples we have extended the WS-Policy to include a WS-Authorization specification which incorporates semantics. By automating the predication of authorization, a requester or consumer can save time and more efficiently allocate its resources.

The authorization annotations are extensibility elements similar to the extensibility elements provided in WSDL-S (Akkiraju et al. 2005), for example precondition and effect. The annotated WS-Policy file, called a SemPolicy in (Verma 2006), will provide extensibility elements for semantic representation of authorization. The extensibility elements are derived from the RBAC standard (NIST 2004) and XACML representation of RBAC.

RBAC was chosen because it is widely accepted, easily understood, and succinctly expresses authorization permissions. Here we will cover the extensibility elements, their descriptions, and give examples. Our first extension element is *permission*. *permission* is the operation an authenticated client is authorized to perform on a certain object, which is a resource.

The extension element *role* is a function within the context of an organization; some associated semantics regarding the authority and responsibility are conferred on the user assigned to the *role*. A role could be general, for example 'Employee', or more specific as in 'Radiologist'. As well, a *role* could be a group which confers authority and responsibility as in 'Hospital Executive'.

Since it is not feasible to name each user and the semantics of a subject can vary greatly we use an extension element *subjectCategory* to describe the type of a subject. Subjects can be users, which the National Institute of Standards and Technology define as a human, machine, network, or intelligent autonomous agent. In our context, this can also include an entire organization. Using *subjectCategory* as an extension element enables us to describe relationships. For example, the *subjectCategory* partner describes that the subject is in some kind of partnership agreement with the provider of the Web service.

Lastly, *modelReference* is used to handle the mapping of a schema element to an ontological concept. For example, this can be applicable when a Web service provider wants to demonstrate that authorization will be constrained to certain inputs for an operation. This might be done using an ontological concept like patient_identification_number.

An approach such as this provides the granularity needed for Web services. This is because a WS-Policy file may be attached to a message, a service binding, an operation, or a parameter such as an input. We assume that annotations are used to describe an explicit 'grant'; while we assume lack of the criteria or conditions is an implicit 'deny'.

The WSP-S is an annotated WSP. As seen in Figure 12-15, annotations can occur after the <All> tag in WSP. If there is one annotation for the entire WSP then it could be placed after the first <ExactlyOne> tag. The first annotation in Figure 12-15 describes authorization for a requestor whose *role* is "Emergency Room Physician". The second annotation is a *subjectCategory,* namely "Health Services". From the namespace it is seen that the concepts are from the HL7 RBAC ontology.

```
<wsp:Policy
xmlns:sp="http://schemas.xmlsoap.org/ws/2005/07/securitypolicy"
xmlns:wsp="http://schemas.xmlsoap.org/ws/2004/09/policy"
xmlns:base="http:/http://www.NationalEHR.com/policies"
xmlns:wsrm="http://schema.xmlsoap.org/ws/2004/03/rm"
xmlns:wsau="http://lsdis.cs.uga.edu/authorization/wsau"
xmlns:Ontology1="http://lsdis.cs.uga.edu/projects/meteor-s/wsdl-
s/ontologies/HL7_RBAC.owl">
    <wsp:ExactlyOne>
      <wsp:All>
      <wsau:role name="Emergency_Room_Physician" wsau:ModelReference=
       "Ontology1# Emergency_Room_Physician "/>
      <wsau:subjectCategory name="Health_Services"
       wsau:ModelReference="Ontology1#Health_Services"/>
      <wsse:SecurityToken>
        <wsse:TokenType>
          wsse:X509v3
        </wsse:TokenType>
      </wsse:SecurityToken>
      </wsp:All>
      <wsp:All>
      <wsau:permission name="read" wsau:ModelReference=
       "Ontology1#read"/>
      <wsau:role name="Executive_Administration" wsau:ModelReference=
       "Ontology1#Executive_Administration"/>
      <wsau:subjectCategory name="Health_Services"
        wsau:ModelReference="Ontology1#Health_Services"/>
      <wsse:SecurityToken>
      <wsse:TokenType>
          wsse:X509v3
       </wsse:TokenType>
      </wsse:SecurityToken>
      </wsp:All>
   </wsp:Policy>
```

Figure 12-15. Annotated WS-Policy file

This approach allows for multiple annotations within the policy file. This enables a provider to express multiple conditions regarding authorization. For instance, an 'Emergency Room Physician' who is also affiliated with an organization that is categorized as 'Health Services' may have authorization to a providers' resource, while all other Physicians do not. This is accomplished by placing both annotations within the <ALL> tag. This can be seen in the example below.

There is also the situation in which a requester can have authorization to access a resource if it meets one condition or one set of conditions described by the provider. In this case the annotations are placed within the <ExactlyOne> tags. Figure 12-15 shows two sets of conditions with in the <ExactlyOne> tags. The authorization information from this figure can be read as authorization may be granted to someone that is an Emergency Room Physician that is affiliated with an organization in Health Services or an Executive Administrator who has read privileges and is affiliated with an organization in Health Service.

Any domain specific ontology can be used for the annotations. However, a quality of RBAC is that it has a structural hierarchy with relationships which lends itself to the creation of an ontology schema. The concepts of RBAC include organizational and professional roles. This fits well with the extension elements derived from the XACML representation of RBAC.

The annotations begin with the namespace "wsau", as depicted in the previous figure, which is declared in XML declarations as follows: xmlns:wsau="http://lsdis.cs.uga.edu/authorization/wsau".

4.4   Constraint comparison

We assume here that a Semantic Web services framework has been implemented. This may be a stretch of the imagination for some since there are only a handful of these around, and mostly in academia. Never the less, let's assume that we have discovered a set of services using one of these implementations.

Once Semantic Discovery has returned a set of candidate services, the requestor can perform constraint analysis to determine which of the candidate services it most likely has authorization to invoke. This predication uses information given about the client, WSP-S, and ontologies to make the 'best choice'. One approach is to have authorization information for the requester contained in client WSDL's attached policy file.

During the constraint analysis process, if an authorization annotation is found then that information it should be passed to a 'manager' or 'engine' which can perform Semantic Comparison Analysis. Information contained within the annotation, regarding the service provider, and information within the client policy, regarding the client, is used for ontology based inferencing to predict if the client has authorization to use the resource.

Ontology inference engines, also called reasoners, are software applications that derive new facts or associations from existing information. Inference and inference rules allow for deriving new data from data that is already known. Thus, new pieces of knowledge can be added based on previous ones. By creating a model of the information and relationships, we enable reasoners to draw logical conclusions based on the model. For example, with OWL it is possible to make inferences based on the associations represented in the models, which primarily means inferring transitive relationships. Jena has a built in rule-base reasoner that provides OWL inferencing support. The RBAC standard requires the ontology have the ability to apply multiple restrictions and cardinalities to concepts in the hierarchy. The reasoner that is built into Jena is able to reason over these more complex ontologies.

If an authorization path is detected via dynamically generated queries then a relationship(s) exists between the concept(s) in the service policy file and the concept(s) in the client policy file. The RBAC standard provides a defined structure such a path exists only if the concepts are related in such a way that authorization should be granted. Therefore, we would predict that authorization will be granted. If a path is not detected then we move to a second phase.

In order to determine if two uniquely named concepts from different ontologies are equivalent, the relationships of those concepts to other concepts in their respective ontologies must be compared. Even in a highly standardized domain such as Health Care, two concepts may have different names. For instance, an "Emergency Room Physician" from one ontology may correspond to an "Emergency Physician" from another ontology, or "ER Doctor" or ER Physician".

One popular approach is to examine the relationships of the client and service concepts and those related concepts that are linked by these relationships. Because of the structure of the RBAC ontology, it is manually possible to quickly determine which relationships are most important. In most cases it will be necessary to place weights on the relationships in order to improve the accuracy of the results. This approach is based on (Dong et al. 2005) and (Aleman-Menza et al. 2006). However, applying weights requires a human to review the relationships within the ontology. An automated approach to the problem of weighting the relationships is as follows.

At each iteration of an algorithm, compare a concept related to the original service concept with one related to the original client concept. For example, in the first iteration compare the Physician concept related to ER Doctor from the client ontology to a concept related to Emergency Room Physician(ERP) in the service ontology. This continues and the concept

Physician related to ERP is found, Figure 12-16 (1). As shown in the figure, after the algorithm terminates, we have found three concepts related to ER Doctor that are similar, if not equivalent to, the concepts related to ERP. This is a simplistic example because the names of the relating concepts are the same. However, if names of the related concepts are not the same this approach can be expanded upon.

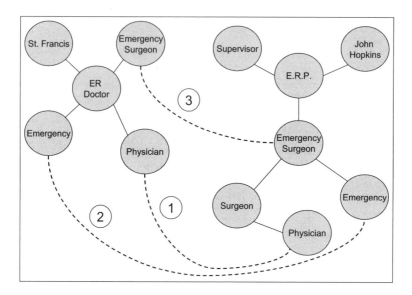

Figure 12-16. Concept comparison

Consider expanding the approach by comparing the names of the concepts as well as the relationship type through an advanced string comparison algorithm. We suggest the n-grams (Damashek 1995) algorithm to compare the labels of the related concepts and the relationships, i.e. Physician and instanceOf respectively. By using a string comparison that returns a decimal between 0 and 1, one could create a weighted score and a threshold for predicting authorization. This approach, although using syntactic comparison, uses semantics from the schema to exploit relationships to other concepts, concepts names, and relationship names; as well the number of relationships.

Another approach to consider is to create SWRL (Semantic Web Rule Language) rules that are specific enough to capture relationship information regarding a resource but general enough to be applicable to an entire class. For example, we could have created a rule that a technician, like 'Radiology Tech, belonging to the same department, 'Radiology.', as another technician, 'Radiology Technician, and are therefore equivalent concepts. However, this approach may result in an unacceptable amount of false positives and in a domain less structured than the HL7 domain, it would require many rules and a priori knowledge of the ontology.

5. OTHER APPROACHES

Authorization in Web services is currently a research area of great interest. WS-Authorization is one of a few Web service specifications remaining to be standardized (IBM, Microsoft 2002). In the Semantic realm, including both Semantic Web and Semantic Web services, research interests in Semantic Authorization are rapidly growing.

Some previous research regarding authorization in Semantic Web services has been focused on implementing an access control enforcement structure (Yague et al. 2003). (López et al. 2005) discusses an approach to access control in a distributed heterogeneous network in which XACML and SAML are used for access control. The novelty of their approach is to convert between these standards for the enforcement of policies.

Agarwal et al. (2004) uses attributes from credentials like SAML or Digital Certificates to make access control decisions in their implementation. While this can be done, these credentials were designed for authentication. A similar approach to the one discussed in this chapter is (Kagal et al. 2004), in which the authors use ontologies to add authorization annotations to OWL-S. OWL-S is used to add semantics to Web services. This is done through a mapping of concepts in OWL-S to WSDL types. Their approach adds extensibility elements to the OWL-S constructs for the purpose of supplying authorization information.

An idea that has gained momentum recently is that of a hybrid approach. This approach incorporates real world concepts in ontology with rule based ontology and is described in (Kagal et al. 2004). The strength of their approach is in describing access control policies with multiple ontologies. This provides for greater expressiveness since the semantics of rules may be incorporated.

When developing a system to perform a function that is currently in research, it is important not to reinvent the wheel. For example, extending the accepted standard WSP by adding semantic annotations. Instead of creating an entirely new standard it is better to build on an accepted standard. In addition, using the RBAC standard for an annotation scheme and for our ontologies. Other approaches have developed their own authorization ontologies, however RBAC is an accepted standard.

Policy matching in Semantic Web services is a complicated area of research. (Verma et al. 2005) details an implementation of Semantic Policy matching using the Semantic Web Rule Language (SWRL). (Wu et al. 2002) describes how to incorporate access control in a business process (workflow). It illustrates fundamental capabilities in a workflow and why authorization and access control need to be expressed semantically. This is particularly relevant to our research on the client side where we had to decide on the appropriate location for client information. Anyanwu et al (Anyanwu et al 2003) examines the issues of complex processes inherent in healthcare applications in a heterogeneous cross domain environment.

6.   QUESTIONS FOR DISCUSSION

Beginner:

1. Why are traditional Web services authorization techniques not adequate for Semantic discovery? (Traditional authorization techniques do not suggest what types of users may have access to the resource provided through the Web service.

2. Why is the concept of Roles important in Semantic Authorization? (They are the concepts built upon an existing standard which describe users. This information along with domain knowledge provides the basis for Semantic reasoning, or inferencing.)

Intermediate:

1. How could independent enterprises exchange their authorization ontologies with those enterprises that have discovered their Web services? *(through accounts, place them freely on the internet for download)*

2. What security risks are involved with placing the ontologies on the internet? *(Exposing too much information regarding user accounts).*

3. Can you think of a solution that would alleviate the security risk mentioned in the previous question? (This answer may differ depending on your previous answer. However, for exposing too much information, a generic ontology for an entire domain would allow enterprises to share this information across any domain. The ontology implementation details in regards to a specific enterprise would not be shared.)

Advanced:

1. Discuss some of the relationships between RBAC concepts and a real world enterprise. How could these relationships be exploited in Securing Semantic Web services? *(Discussion question, meant to be thought provoking. No right or wrong answer.)*

2. Can you think of any ways that semantics could benefit the security technologies currently in use; i.e. authentication, encryption, etc.? What kind of ontology would you design to do this? (*Discussion question, meant to be thought provoking. No right or wrong answer.*)

7.   SUGGESTED ADDITIONAL READING

- Rosenberg, J and Remy, D. *Securing Web Services with WS-Security: Demystifying WS-Security, WS-Policy, SAML, XML Signature, and XML Encryption.* Sams (May 12, 2004). 408 pp. This book explains the basics of securing Web services through traditional and current technologies.
- Alesso H. P. and Smith C. F. *Developing Semantic Web Services.* AK Peters; Bk&CD-Rom edition (October 2004). 445pp. This book provides further reading on creating semantic Web services and discusses there limitations.
- Ferraiolo D. F., Kuhn D. R., and Chandramouli R. *Role-Based Access Control.* Artech House Publishers (April 2003). 338pp. This book is an authoritative look at Role Base Access Control and discusses many of the complexities associated with a distributed implementation.

8.   ACKNOWLEDGMENTS

This work was partially funded by FCT, POCTI-219, and FEDER.

9.   REFERENCES

Akkiraju R, Farell J, Miller J, Nagarajan M, Sheth A and Verma K, "Web Service Semantics - WSDL-S" Proceedings of the W3C Workshop on Frameworks for Semantics in Web Service (W3CW'05), Innsbruck, Austria (June 2005) pages 5.

Boanerges Aleman-Meza, Meenakshi Nagarajan1, Cartic Ramakrishnan1, Li Ding, Pranam Kolari, Amit P. Sheth1, I. Budak Arpinar, Anupam Joshi, Tim Finin, International World Wide Web Conference, Proceedings of the 15th international conference on World Wide Web, Edinburgh, Scotland, SESSION: Social networks, 2006, pp 407 - 416

Kemafor Anyanwu, Amit P. Sheth, Jorge Cardoso, John A. Miller and Krys J. Kochut, "Healthcare Enterprise Process Development and Integration," Journal of Research and Practice in Information Technology (JRPIT), Special Issue on Health Knowledge Management, Vol. 35, No. 2 (May 2003) pp. 83-98. Australian Computer Society, Inc.

Kemafor Anyanwu and Amit P. Sheth, "The ρ Operator: Discovering and Ranking Associations on the Semantic Web" ACM SPECIAL ISSUE: Special section on semantic web and data management, Volume 31 , Issue 4   2002 pp 42 - 47

S. Agarwal, B. Sprick, S. Wortmann; "Credential Based Access Control for Semantic Web Services"; http://www.aifb.uni-karlsruhe.de/WBS/sag/papers/Agarwal_Sprick_Wortmann-CredentialBasedAccessControlForSemanticWebServices-AAAI_SS_SWS-04.pdf.

Census Bureau, 2000 Industry Categories for the Special EEO File, 2000.

Christensen E., Curbera F., Meredith G. and Weerawarana S., 2001, Web Services Description Language (WSDL) 1.1, W3C Note, http://www.w3.org/TR/wsdl.

M. Damashek. Gauging similarity with n-grams: language independent categorization of text, Science, 267(5199) pp 843--848, 1995

Dogac A., Cingil I., Laleci G., Kabak Y., Improving the Functionality of UDDI Registries through Web Service Semantics, 3rd VLDB Workshop on Technologies for Eservices (TES-02), Hong Kong, China, August 23-24, 2002

X.L. Dong, A. Halevy and J. Madhavan (2005) Reference reconciliation in complex information space, In Proceedings of the 2005 ACM SIGMOD International Conference on Management of Data, ACM Press: Baltimore, MD. Pp. 85-96

FaCT (2005) FaCT++, http://owl.man.ac.uk/factplusplus/.

Fensel D. and Bussler C., The Web Service Modeling Framework WSMF, http://informatik.uibk.ac.at/users/c70385/wese/wsmf.paper.pdf

S. Gavrila, D. Kuhn, R. Chandramouli; Proposed NIST Standard for Role-Based Access Control; http://csrc.nist.gov/rbac/rbacSTD-ACM.pdf

Gandon, F. L. and N. M. Sadeh, OWL inference engine using XSLT and JESS, http://www-2.cs.cmu.edu/~sadeh/MyCampusMirror/OWLEngine.html, 2003.

HL7 http://www.hl7.org

HL7 Security Technical Committee, Role Based Access Control (RBAC) Healthcare Scenarios Version 1.0, 2005.

HL7 Security Technical Committee, Role Based Access Control (RBAC) Healthcare Permissions Catalog Version 2.0, 2005

Hull and East Yorkshire Hospitals NHS Trust, 2006.

IBM Corporation and Microsoft Corporation, Security in a Web Services World: A Proposed Architecture and Roadmap Version 1.0, 2002.

Hewlett-Packard Development Company, LP., 2006. http://jena.sourceforge.net/

L. Kagal, M. Paolucci, N. Srinivasan, G. Denker, T. Finin, K. Sycara; Authorization and Privacy for Semantic Web Services; IEEE Intelligent Systems (Special Issue on Semantic Web Services), July 2004.

Leymann F, Roller D, Schmidt MT, Web services and business process management, IBM Systems Journal, 2002

G. López, Ó. Cánovas, A. Gómez-Skarmeta, S. Otenko, D. Chadwick; A Heterogeneous Network Access Service based on PERMIS and SAML; In Proceedings of 2nd EuroPKI Workshop, University of Kent, July 2005.

National Institute of Standards and Technology (NIST) FIPS Publication 180: Secure Hash Standard (SHS). May 1993.

National Institute of Standards and Technology (NIST) Role Based Access Control Standard (RBACS). April 2004.

Deborah L. McGuinness, Frank van Harmelen, W3C Recommendation 10 February 2004

Minswap, http://www.mindswap.org/2003/pellet/ , 2003

Cary Pennington, "Policy Based Optimal Composition of Web Services," Masters Thesis (M.S. in CS Degree) July 2006.

Jothy Rosenberg and David Remy, Securing Web Services Security with WS-Security, Sams, 2004.

SAML 2.0 profile of XACML v2.0 OASIS Standard, 1 February 2005, http://docs.oasis-open.org/xacml/2.0/access_control-xacml-2.0-saml-profile-spec-os.pdf

Joel Farrell, IBM Semantic Annotations for WSDL, Editors Copy

Holger   Lausen,   DERI   Innsbruck,   August   08,   2006. http://www.w3.org/2002/ws/sawsdl/spec/SAWSDL.html

Evren Sirin, Bijan Parsia, Bernardo Cuenca Grau, Aditya Kalyanpur, and Yarden Katz. Pellet: A practical owl-dl reasoner. Submitted for publication to Journal of Web Semantics.

Sivashanmugam, K., Verma, K., Sheth, A., Miller, J., Adding Semantics to Web Services Standards, Proceedings of the 1st International Conference on Web Services (ICWS'03), Las Vegas, Nevada (June 2003).

A. Toninelli, J. Bradshaw, L. Kagal, R. Montanari; Rule-based and Ontology-based Policies: Toward a Hybrid Approach to Control Agents in Pervasive Environments; Proceedings of the Semantic Web and Policy Workshop, International Semantic Web Conference, 7 November, 2005.

UDDI Spec Technical Committee Specification, 2002. http://uddi.org/pubs/uddiv3.00-published-20020719.htm

Verma K, Sivashanmugam K, Sheth A, Abhijit Patil, Oundhakar S and Miller J, METEOR-S WSDI: A Scalable Infrastructure of Registries for Semantic Publication and Discovery of Web Services, Journal of Information Technology and Management, Special Issue on Universal Global Integration, Vol. 6, No. 1 (2005) pp. 17-39. Kluwer Academic Publishers.

Kunal Verma, "Configuration and Adaptation of Semantic Web Processes" Doctoral Dissertation (Ph.D. in CS Degree) June 2006

K. Verma, R. Akkiraju, R Goodwin; Semantic Matching of Web Service Policies; Second International Workshop on Semantic and Dynamic Web Processes (SDWP 2005), Third International Conference on Web Services (ICWS'05), July, 2005.

Verma K, Aggarwal R, Miller J and Milnor W, "Constraint Driven Web Service Composition in METEOR-S" Proceedings of the 2004 IEEE International Conference on Services Computing (SCC'04), Shanghai, China (September 2004) pp. 23-32

Wielemaker,   J.,   SWI-Prolog   Semantic   Web   Library,   http://www.swi-prolog.org/packages/semweb.html, 2005.

D. Booth, H. Haas, F. McCabe, E. Newcomer, M. Champion, C. Ferris, D. Orchard, Web Services Architecture (WS Architecture), http://www.w3.org/TR/ws-arch/#security Feb. 2004

Siddharth Bajaj, Don Box; Web Services Policy Framework (WS-Policy), ftp://www6.software.ibm.com/software/developer/library/ws-policy.pdf

Web Services Security (WS-Security) Version 1.0 05, 2002 et al Bob Atkinson, Giovanni Della-Libera;   Specification: Web   Services   Security, ftp://www6.software.ibm.com/software/developer/library/ws-secure.pdf; April 2002

S. Wu, A. Sheth, J. Miller, Z Luo; Authorization and Access Control of Application Data in Workflow Systems; Journal of Intelligent Information Systems: Integrating Artificial Intelligence and Database Technologies (JIIS), Vol. 18, No. 1 (January 2002) pp. 71-94. Kluwer Academic Publishers.

eXtensible Access Control Markup Language, (XACML) Version 2.0 OASIS Standard, 1 Feb 2005, http://docs.oasis-open.org/xacml/2.0/access_control-xacml-2.0-core-spec-os.pdf

XML Signature Syntax and Processing (XML-Signature) W3C Recommendation 2002 http://www.w3.org/TR/xmldsig-core/

XML Encryption Syntax and Processing (XML-Encryption) W3C Recommendation 2002 http://www.w3.org/TR/xmlenc-core/

M. Yague, A. Mana, J. Lopez, J. Troya; <u>Applying the Semantic Web Layers to Access Control</u>; 14th International Workshop on Database and Expert Systems Applications (DEXA'03)

Index

matcher 216
mediation 226
message level protection 282
message privacy 280
message validity 283
metadata 247
municipal services 73

natural language processing 78

ontologiy 175
ontology 3, 42, 79, 101, 127, 214, 247
ontology design 108
ontology management system 8
ontology reuse 259
ontology-based search 46
ontology-based visualization 48
Oracle database 27
Oracle technology network 29
OWL 1, 60
OWL-S 303

production line 258

queries 106
query 203

RBAC 287
RDF 1, 26, 112, 276
RDF graph 115
RDQL 132
recruiting services 21
relationships 104
resource description framework 17
REST 132
re-usable ontologies 107
role based access control 287

rule language 203
rules 128, 179

scales for competencies 161
search engines 85
semantic annotation 83
semantic descriptions 83
semantic heterogeneity 174
semantic Web services 144, 276
service composition 211
Siderean's seamark navigator 29
software 19
SPARQL 19
steel industry 243
structural heterogeneity 174
subsumption 102
supply chain 251
syntactic interoperability 174
system heterogeneity 174

visonto 263

Web Ontology Language 18
Web service security 279
WS-Authorization 292
WSDL 278
WSDL-S 278
WSMO 213
WSMO framework 144
WS-Policy 293

XACML 290
XBRL 55
XML 276
XML encryption 281